Restorative Justice in Urban Schools

The school-to-prison pipeline is often the path for marginalized students, particularly Black males, who are three times as likely to be suspended as White students. This volume provides an ethnographic portrait of how educators can implement restorative justice to build positive school cultures and address disciplinary problems in a more corrective and less punitive manner. Looking at the school-to-prison pipeline in a historical context, it analyzes current issues facing schools and communities and ways that restorative justice can improve behavior and academic achievement. By practicing critical restorative justice, educators can reduce the domino effect between suspension and incarceration and foster a more inclusive school climate.

Anita Wadhwa is a graduate of the Harvard Graduate School of Education and is currently restorative justice coordinator at the Spring Branch Academy of Choice (AOC) in Houston, Texas.

Routledge Research in Educational Leadership Series

Restorative Justice in Urban Schools

Disrupting the School-to-Prison Pipeline

Anita Wadhwa

 Routledge

Taylor & Francis Group

LONDON AND NEW YORK

First published 2016 by Routledge

2 Park Square, Milton Park, Abingdon, Oxon OX14 4RN

711 Third Avenue, New York, NY 10017, USA

Routledge is an imprint of the Taylor & Francis Group, an informa business

First issued in paperback 2017

Library of Congress Cataloging-in-Publication Data
Names: Wadhwa, Anita, author.
Title: Restorative justice in urban schools : disrupting the school-to-prison pipeline / by Anita Wadhwa.
Description: New York : Routledge, [2016] | Series: Routledge research in educational leadership series ; 6 | Includes bibliographical references and index.
Identifiers: LCCN 2015024806
Subjects: LCSH: Urban schools—United States—Case studies. | Restorative justice—United States. | Juvenile delinquency—United States—Prevention. | School discipline—United States. | Educational sociology—United States. | Community and school—United States.
Classification: LCC LC5131 .W33 2016 | DDC 371.009173/2—dc23
LC record available at http://lccn.loc.gov/2015024806

ISBN: 978-1-138-91129-1 (hbk)
ISBN: 978-1-138-08607-4 (pbk)

Typeset in Sabon
by Apex CoVantage, LLC

Contents

Foreword

Justice has been argued by philosophers since the time of Plato as a central virtue of social institutions, the foundation of which is upholding fundamental human rights, along with distinctive children's rights. In the context of our primary developmental institution—schools—each and every student should feel valued, powerful and needed. The social and emotional echo of institutions should cradle each child; wherein, they deeply feel and understand that each child matters, their cultural and racial identity matter and, through this diversity, we are stronger. As many of us have learned through our traditional indigenous teachers, our human work is to hold each other up, individually and racially.

Yet, many students in many schools do not feel they belong; they do not feel valuable, powerful or needed. In fact, some students are disposable. As John Braithwaite has said, "[T]he lived experience of democracy is alienation, the feeling that elites run things, that we don't have a say in a meaningful sense." Anita Wadhwa argues this experience of alienation resonates strongly for African American males in the U.S. Study after study has shown that African American males are disproportionally pushed out of school and into the justice system, forming the school-to-prison pipeline. In the five decades since African Americans won their civil rights, their lifetime risk of incarceration has doubled. With less than 5 percent of the world's population, the U.S. has nearly 25 percent—2.3 million—of its prisoners, with Black men being particularly vulnerable to mass incarceration. Today, Black men are imprisoned at 6.5 times the rate of White men. This trend has been aptly named the *New Jim Crow: Mass Incarceration in the Age of Colorblindness* by Michelle Alexander.

The sentiment of a nation looking for a new way forward on race relations was powerfully captured by Common and Legend in their performance and acceptance speech at the 2015 Academy Awards for the song "Glory" from the film *Selma*.

> *First, I would like to thank God, who lives in us all. Recently, John and I got to go to Selma and perform "Glory" on the same bridge that Dr. King and the people of the civil rights movement marched on*

50 years ago. This bridge was once a landmark of a divided nation but now is a symbol for change. The spirit of this bridge transcends race, gender, religion, sexual orientation and social status. The spirit of this bridge connects the kid from the South Side of Chicago dreaming of a better life to those in France standing up for their freedom of expression, to the people in Hong Kong protesting for democracy. This bridge was built on hope, welded with compassion and elevated by love for all human beings. (Lonnie Lynn—Common)

Thank you. Nina Simone said it's an artist's duty to reflect the times in which we live. We wrote this song for a film that was based on events that were 50 years ago but we say that Selma is now because the struggle for justice is right now. We know that the Voting Rights Act that they fought for 50 years ago is being compromised right now in this country today. We know that right now the struggle for freedom and justice is real. We live in the most incarcerated country in the world. There are more black men under correctional control today than were under slavery in 1850. When people are marching with our song, we want to tell you we are with you, we see you, we love you, and march on. God bless you. (John Stephens—John Legend)

With courage and compassion, honesty and eloquence, Anita Wadhwa builds a bridge of hope for African American males and other marginalized groups, making a strong argument that our work for justice must begin in our schools, wherein suspension rates for Black students are two to three times those of White students.

This book adds an important critical lens to the importance of race in the context of justice, particularly restorative justice. In 1990, Howard Zehr wrote the book that ground much of the modern day thinking about restorative justice—*Changing Lenses*. Anita Wadhwa adds the lens of race to the growing social movement of restorative justice, inviting us to critically analyze and engage in thoughtful and vulnerable discussions and move beyond the age of colorblindness.

Anita Wadhwa and her students at the AOC have a dream, and they are inviting others to join their movement in finding a new way forward. By way of example, the Restorative Justice Club at Simon Fraser University has joined the movement through sponsoring students at the AOC to attend Harvard's Alumni of Color Conference at the School of Education, where they help teach conference participants what they have learned about the restorative justice process through role-play scenarios.

These young people, across borders and racial identities, are leading the next generation of restorative justice, through deeply recognizing that we need a new story of justice—a form of justice that bridges racial divides of structural inequalities inherent in social institutions, a form of justice that pluralizes our common humanity, a form of justice that is not colorblind but embraces cultural diversity as a way of dancing with new possibility while inviting ancient wisdom. Through embracing race we can move from being agents of cultural destruction to becoming agents of cultural survival. Culture that holds justice as a primary virtue of social institutions strengthens the ethical and moral fabric of our humanity, moving beyond cultures of bullying, violence and alienation.

Anita Wadhwa inspires us to embrace a critical restorative justice and, in so doing, to transform the structural inequities of institutions. With determination and commitment, Anita Wadhwa has walked with her students. Her journey and theirs are eloquently illuminated in this book, illustrating the hopes and hazards of a journey to belonging that embraces the power of race.

Brenda Morrison, PhD,
Associate Professor,
Director, Centre for Restorative Justice,
School of Criminology, Simon Fraser University

Preface

Founded in 2013, the slogan of the Restorative Justice Collaborative of Houston, an organization led by myself, fellow teachers, students, advocates, and community members, is "Let's start a movement." That year, I started a program at the AOC, a small nontraditional academic high school in Houston.[1] With the support of a principal who is a restorative justice advocate, I taught a leadership course in which students were trained in how to conduct peace circles—a restorative process that is explored in depth in this book. In the first cohort I selected 10 students. I saw extreme leadership potential in two particular young students, who I will call Miguel and José. As the in-school suspension teacher, I had spoken at length with the two young men when they were placed with me for behaving defiantly with teachers. Both are highly intelligent, strong willed and outspoken.

I was unaware that they belonged to rival gangs. They hated one another. They individually requested that I take them out of the class but would not explain why. I told them it was their choice, but they always decided to stay. Perhaps I was daft, but I did not detect any animosity between the two. They did not speak to each other that often, but it did not feel like they were avoiding one another. Toward the end of the semester each student was required to write a "story of self," an assignment I myself completed as a student in Marshall Ganz's course on community organizing at Harvard. The story of self is a narrative that is used to move an audience to action. In the case of our class, students were to share a story from their life and connect it to the principles of restorative justice. The goal was to move the audience to consider restorative justice as an alternative to traditional disciplinary and criminal justice measures.

Miguel read his first. He talked about being born with a clubfoot and contemplating suicide as he grew up, until he found a home with fellow gang members. He also talked about losing a good friend and finding a sense of connectedness through his work as a peacemaker in the restorative justice leadership program. A day later José read his narrative. He did not choose the gang life; those choices were made many years before by family members who were part of a long legacy of gang members. He desperately wanted out but told me that in the case of his group, the only solution would have been lethal: blood in, blood out. He wanted to finish high school and go to college but knew those decisions would be frowned upon. He was frustrated that his life had been constrained by those around him. After he read, Miguel walked up to him and shook his hand, proclaiming loudly, "You and I have been through the same things. We come from the same community. It doesn't make any sense. We have to stop this. Let's start a movement!"

Though both students remained in their respective gangs—one dropped out of high school, and the other eventually graduated despite many absences due to late, drug-induced adventures with his fellow clique members—their words remained inspiring. We bought T-shirts with the catchphrase, "Let's start a movement" and raised money so that they could go to Harvard that year and attend a conference on education, where Miguel shared his story of self to an audience of 50 people. All 10 students in the class trained attendees in the peace circle process. Our program was featured on National Public Radio, and after the Collaborative was formed, we began receiving requests from all over the city from people in the education and criminal justice systems who were seeking alternatives to exclusion and incarceration.

I share this not simply to boast about our achievements but to emphasize that all of our success has been due to the mentoring and generosity provided by the participants in the research I did for this book. All the lessons culled from my two sites, Bridge and Equity High School, as well as my mentor Janet Connors, culminated in the creation of a restorative justice program that is gaining traction and starting a movement in Houston. This book is based on the methodology of portraiture, which seeks to highlight the goodness at research sites. That does not mean it does not raise questions about the process that all practitioners and researchers must consider. Namely, I consider how power dynamics can be reified within restorative processes if we do not ground our work in a greater understanding of the structural inequalities inherent in the institutions in which we operate. Therefore I hope that this text offers a framing in which to understand why students of color are disproportionately suspended, expelled and criminalized—but that it also offers the kind of qualitative data that truly captures the challenge of transitioning away from a punitive paradigm to a restorative one.

NOTE

1. At the Academy of Choice (AOC), students arrive from schools all over the Spring Branch Independent School District. They come for the nontraditional education we provide through smaller classes, night school, blended learning, credit recovery opportunities, and an onsite nursery for students with young children. Many are returning to school after having dropped out or been expelled and desire ways of teaching and learning that diverge from the typical modes of schooling that alienate so many students in schools.

Acknowledgments

This book is dedicated to Janet Connors and Martin Garcia. I love you and thank you for your friendship and guidance. I have learned a tremendous amount from your narratives and hope that others feel likewise as they read about your lives in these pages.

I would like to thank those teachers who through their attention to relationships, incisive knowledge of content and often irreverent attitude toward established norms showed me the best of what schooling could look like: from Mrs. Washington, my kindergarten teacher in Ruston, Louisiana, to many other elementary, secondary, college and graduate school educators: Mr. Norton, Ms. Rooney, Mrs. Baerenstecher, Mrs. John, Coach Speer, Mrs. Tull, Mrs. Hemme, Mr. Garvin, Allen Gee, Valerie Martin, Mark Warren, John Diamond and finally, my doctoral committee, a trifecta of brilliance: Professors Sara Lawrence-Lightfoot, Brenda Morrison and Mica Pollock. Dr. Lawrence-Lightfoot held me to impeccable standards as a writer and made me work harder than anyone I have ever known; Dr. Morrison was a constant voice of optimism, encouraging me all the way from Canada with her belief that I had something vital to say; and Dr. Pollock was essential in helping hone my analysis of micro-moments in the classroom and in being more precise in my language around race.

Thank you to all the participants in this book from Equity and Bridge who were open to speaking with me even when it was difficult or inconvenient. I was honored to enter your classrooms, homes, and community establishments. In particular I thank those in Boston who were foundational to my understanding of restorative justice in theory and practice: Adina, Kati, Hilary, Schiller, Roy, Travis, Cindy, Rigo, Susan and Susan. Thanks to Janet, Kay Pranis and Carolyn Boyes-Watson for your mentorship; you have truly shaped how I view and practice circles.

I first heard of a youth movement for restorative justice through my work on a multiyear research project on community organizing, formed by Professors Karen Mapp and Mark Warren. They convened a group of doctoral students who were committed to studying community organizing for education and other issues. I am grateful to have been included in the project, and in particular want to thank Juan Evangelista of Padres y Jovenes Unidos, the organization I was fortunate to study, for walking me through all that you and your peers did to promote restorative justice in Denver Public Schools.

Many thanks to my doctoral writing group, intellectual juggernauts who bolstered me academically and, much more importantly, emotionally: Sherry Deckman, Chantal Francois and Shari Dickstein-Staub. Thanks to my roommates at Hancock Street for shared meals, tears, laughter and support: Meredith Mira, Alex Fuentes, Cynthia Gordon da Cruz and Anjali Adukia.

I'll always be grateful to Dr. Michele Hilberth for allowing me to pursue my dream of implementing restorative practices in Houston and to Nicole Harris and Udoro Gatewood for joining the movement. I am indebted as well to my students, who have taken on the charge of pushing themselves out of their comfort zones. They have inspired me (and hundreds of adults) in the community with their knowledge and advocacy of restorative justice. They have allowed me to restore justice for myself as my work with them has helped heal the pain I experienced during my own tender teenage years. I have tried to push them the way I so desired to be pushed at their age—especially as a young person grappling with depression, desperate for attention but so lacking in self-esteem that I didn't want to be acknowledged.

Thanks to Routledge for agreeing to publish my work and to the folks at Living Justice Press for their selfless service and support for restorative justice practitioners, scholars and advocates.

Big hugs to my long-distance Harvard buddies, who radicalized my thinking during my many years at the Education School and helped support me through the often tumultuous moments that accompany the world of academia: Moneek Bhanot, Keith Catone, Kenneth Russell, Jen Dorsey, David Knight, Paul Kuttner, Thomas Nikundiwe, Carla Shalaby and Nicole Simon to name only a few. Shout out to those who have organized and will continue to support the Alumni of Color Conference at that institution, including my fellow Texans and tri-chairs, Christina Dobbs and Rosario Martinez.

Thanks to friends who I met through writing, teaching and traveling: Amy Fenwick and Tre Johnson, for hours of laughter, camaraderie, continued friendship and writing group memories; Chris Shen, for befriending me at Choate and beyond; Erin Gerber for sustaining me through my difficult MFA days; Lee comrades Mary Kennedy and Yolanda Rodriguez; Beena and Sehba Sarwar for your artistry and activism and Rajesh Parameswaran, a true example of someone committed to the craft of writing.

Much gratitude to my family, extended and otherwise: my parents and most important teachers, Darshan and Pinky Wadhwa; my brother Dev, the hardest-working screenwriter in accounting; Alka, Satish and Ravi Wadhwa; my in-laws, including Chris, Poochie, Bomba-ji, Alex, Anton, Ben, Cynara, Sally and Tumaree; and my childhood friends and University of Houston clanswomen—Blanca Contreras, Amisha and the entire Dalwadi family, Shannon Garth-Rhodes, Krupa Parikh, Niti Patel, Selina Pishori, Erica Rodriguez and Mamta Swaroop.

Finally, all my love and admiration go to my partner Seth for showing me the right path when I falter, and to my beloved daughters Suhani and Naya.

1 Restorative Justice and the School-to-Prison Pipeline

I wake up and smile cuz [sic] I got all my close peoples
but it saddens me that most corrupted by pure evil
and most falsely incarcerated by crooked racist laws
where the only freedom comes from walking county halls
or doin' years in the pen hopin' to make that first parole
we live the daily life that people hope they'll never know
dis the life we live and was warned about
the life teachers and parents said don't go down that route . . .
    —from "Do you know" by Martin Garcia, former student

For four years, Martin Garcia was incarcerated. Teachers aren't supposed to have favorites, but he was one of mine. When I think of our relationship, one of my first memories is of him arguing with me more than a decade ago. I can transport myself to my old stomping grounds, my classroom on the third floor of Lee High School in Houston, Texas, and visualize it immediately. I sit on a stool by the chalkboard at the front of a first-period ninth-grade English class, clutching a thin, green, spiral-bound attendance book. It is October 2002, and I am a second-year teacher. The room is spacious. It is bound by three walls with chalkboards and one wall with windows that look out on a small, concrete courtyard. Books populate every corner, from the windowsills to the blonde wooden bookshelves that span the back of the classroom. The floors are slick from a dysfunctional air-conditioning system that spews fetid mist, and above this din I can barely detect the presence of students, some of whom pick at English muffins provided by the school breakfast program and some of whom write in their journals.

My eyes flit to each desk as I mark who is present. Martin Garcia has once again slipped out of his front-row seat to the back of the classroom. Like most of his peers, his head is down, eyes concentrated on a black composition book. Suddenly he gazes up at the journal topic written on the chalkboard behind me. He sees me, and I raise my eyebrows, tilting my head toward his empty seat. He sighs, folds his arms, and does not move. We have played this game for the past five days. I walk to the back of the classroom and kneel down next to him.

"I'm not going to tell you to move every day," I say.

I gaze at him sternly. Martin has failed ninth grade and is larger and taller than the other students. In the hallways, he strolls to class, occasionally tugging at pants that are oversized even by the standards of his peers. He has dark, narrow eyes and full cheeks. He looks defeated, eyes downcast while he speaks.

"Why won't you let me sit here?" he implores in a quiet and strained voice.

In a class of only 15 students, it makes no sense for him to sit four rows behind everyone else. I worry that he is trying to separate himself because he is either ashamed that he is repeating ninth grade or because he wants to project a tough image—or both.

"It's easier for me to keep track of your progress if you sit in the front."

"I'm failing this class anyway, so what does it matter?" He eyes the linoleum floor.

Martin makes this claim on a weekly basis. Every Friday I hand out weekly progress reports, yet he does not believe them. I consistently compliment him on the poetry he writes in his journal through long, scribbled responses. He completes his work with minimal effort, so I try to challenge him with modified assignments. He reads whatever I recommend from the classroom library—most recently, the complete works of Kafka.

"What are you talking about?" I say. "I just updated the grades. You have an 83!"

"I do?"

"Yes. Now why are you so bent on sitting all the way in the back?"

"I told the other teachers, but no one believes me," he says. "I don't have glasses, so I can't see. I'm farsighted or nearsighted—I can't remember which."

I throw up my hands. Journal time is up, and although students are still writing, we are wasting precious learning time.

"Why didn't you just tell me that? You could have saved us from all this arguing. Of course you can sit in the back."

He lifts up an eyebrow. "I can?"

"Yes, I trust you. Don't you already know that?"

He does not. Despite his looming stature, and no matter how much I have praised him, inside he is a small child in need of affirmation. I regret that I have not praised him more.

"Well, you kept yelling at me telling me to sit up there when I didn't want to . . ."

"If I yell at you, it's not because I don't like you Martin," I say. "It's because I love you." "Oh," says Martin. He is silent for several seconds.

I pat him on the back. "Keep writing, and stop complaining."

This conversation marked a turning point in my relationship with Martin. Though he continued to doubt his academic potential, he did well in my class. I incorrectly assumed that his experience in my class was a watershed moment and that he would continue to be successful for the rest of his high school career. Consumed by a new batch of students, I could not track him the following year as he disengaged from his classes, verbally battled teachers, skipped school, and failed 10th grade. He hid—or perhaps none of us teachers noticed—a severe bout of depression. He even tried to commit suicide, after which all seven of his high school teachers sat in student desks, huddled in a circle around him during our lunch period, bearing witness to the white gauze wrapped around his wrists. We begged him to come to us to work through any of his problems, and he solemnly agreed. He was referred for counseling, though he never took advantage of it, and we made a collective effort to check in with him more often throughout the year.

Regardless of this and other interventions, we could not control his life outside of school or protect him from the loss of his friends to street-related violence. Later he told me that his grief manifested into anger that erupted in fights in the hallways, leading to suspension after suspension.

At our school, we had a dictum for students like Martin: "Write them up until they go to CEP," or Community Education Partners, the local alternative school known on the street as Children Entering Prison—a school where students were clustered with peers who had committed violent acts, profited from selling drugs, or behaved unruly in school. In 2007, police arrested him for sticking someone up. In a letter he explained to me that he carried weapons because of "paranoia" that members of a certain gang were after him and described how he got arrested:

> The very night before I pulled the gun, I had been robbed at gunpoint and I had already decided to chill and not mess with [the other gang] anymore because one of my closest friends got pistol whipped and they broke his jaw and he begged me not to do anything and stop messing with them. So I agreed. After that night . . . I'm [driving] close to where I live and some guy cuts me off right in front of where I live. I spin to avoid hitting a light pole and I regain control. He stopped and [I] pulled right behind him and before he could do anything, I put the gun in his face.

After being put on probation, he returned to school and immersed himself in old patterns: boasting about his arrest, getting into fights, refusing to do work, and cycling through numerous suspensions. Years later he told me the he would attend my class first period then leave and take off with his friends to Galveston and hang out at the beach all day. The school began issuing him truancy tickets, and he failed to appear in court. He became further ensnared in gang life. The summer of 2008 at age 19, he was half a credit away from graduating and planned on taking summer school. Before the summer session began, he was sent to prison when he violated his parole by brandishing a knife during a fight—though he tells me he never had a weapon and that he was framed by five people from an opposing gang who jumped him.

The myriad pivot points that could have kept Martin engaged in school and out of jail are difficult to disentangle. Martin was not a pinball shuttled around by friends, siblings, teachers, administrators, police, judges and enemy gang members in a game whose final destinations was either school or prison. He made the choice to do or not do work, to ally himself with gang members, and to place himself in areas and around people who made him more vulnerable to attack from opposing gangs. But I can still conjecture that institutional policies, attitudes and "ordinary acts taken by educators on a daily basis" (Pollock, 2008, p. xvii) contributed to not only his successes along the way but also his ejection from school. Such factors included the practice of saddling teachers in small learning communities with multiple class preparations, such that several of us spent more time developing curriculum, grading, and fulfilling administrative tasks than developing relationships with students; the biases of some of those teachers, fed up with Martin's indifferent demeanor, who believed he would never graduate; and a lack of viable alternatives to suspension and expulsion, save a disciplinary alternative school described by the American Civil Liberties Union as a "warehouse for poor children of color" (Plocek, 2008). And I cannot help but feel that the confluence of these acts pushed him one step closer to an inevitable path to prison where he sat until 2012, at the age of 24.

THE SCHOOL-TO-PRISON PIPELINE

For students like Martin, disciplinary practices such as suspension and expulsion have the capability to reduce the chances of graduating, becoming employed and engaging with the broader community in positive ways. When I heard from a former colleague that Martin was in prison, I wrote him, unsure whether he would respond. Martin and I kept in touch through monthly letters. I sent him books that I thought he should read, and he sent me poems and asked that I provide feedback so that he could become a better writer. In one of his letters Martin wrote, *"I'd like to really believe in my heart that if you would have had more resources you would have done a lot more for us. You did your best though, even with the scraps you were given, and some of us loved you for it. I did and I do."* Martin wasn't just writing about himself but of a collective "us," others like him who were defiant in school, faced similar hardships, dropped out—and some who also went to prison.

I had not heard of the "school-to-prison pipeline" until I came to graduate school, but the phrase, which describes the phenomenon in which students who are repeatedly suspended and expelled have an increased likelihood of dropping out of school and ending up in the justice system (Fasching-Varner, Martin, Mitchell, & Bennett-Haron, 2014; Ladson-Billings, 2001; Sandler, Wong, Morales, & Patel, 2000; Wald & Losen, 2003), seemed an apt metaphor for Martin's situation. Nationwide, students with disabilities and Black[1] students are overwhelmingly affected by this pipeline and are disproportionately suspended when compared to their White peers (Gregory, Skiba, & Noguera, 2010; Jordan & Bulent, 2009). The data on disproportionality for Latino students is sometimes less consistent (Skiba, 2001, p. 166), although a study of 364 elementary and middle schools in 2005 and 2006 revealed that both Black and Latino students were overrepresented in school suspensions and expulsions for displaying the same behaviors as their White counterparts (Skiba et al., 2011). A data snapshot (OCR, 2014) of 49 million students from every public school in the U.S. found that Native American students are also disproportionately suspended and expelled. This occurrence that has been dubbed the "racial discipline gap" (Gregory et al., 2010, p. 59).

THE RACIAL DISCIPLINE GAP AND ZERO TOLERANCE

The racial discipline gap was first documented in 1975 when the Children's Defense Fund found that suspension rates for Black students were two to three times those of White students (Skiba, 2001, p. 177). More than 30 years later, the gap persists. In 2007, Black students comprised only 17 percent of the public school population, yet 49 percent of Black males in Grades 6 through 12 reported being suspended at least once in their lives (National Center for Education Statistics, 2008). By contrast, White students comprised 56 percent of the population that same year, yet only 21 percent of White males in Grades 6 through 12 reported being suspended. Gregory et al. (2010) suggest that the discipline gap and achievement gap are "two sides of the same coin"; students who are repeatedly suspended miss important instructional time, can become more disengaged in school and are more likely to participate in illegal activities and eventually drop out (p. 60).

The use of suspension and expulsion as the primary modes of discipline are rooted in zero tolerance, defined by the U.S. Department of Education as a policy that "mandates predetermined consequences or punishments for specific offenses" (as quoted in Boyd, 2009, p. 573). Zero tolerance can be traced to drug enforcement policies of the 1980s, when the approach was used preemptively to prevent the expansion of drug cartels by punishing "all offenses severely, no matter how minor" (Skiba & Peterson, 1999, p. 372). The U.S. customs agency first used zero tolerance during the Reagan era to penalize cocaine, heroin and marijuana traffickers (Giroux, 2001; Martinez, 2009).

Due to mounting pressure to end the punitive policies of seizing ships, passports and private property from individuals found with even minute amounts of drugs, the U.S. Customs agency officially ended its zero tolerance policy in 1990. However, the concept had taken hold in other arenas of society: zero tolerance policies emerged in schools in the early 1990s in response to high-profile school shootings and a general fear that drug use and violence were rampant in schools (Skiba & Peterson, 1999). The

Clinton administration passed the federal Gun-Free Schools Act in October 1994, which made it mandatory for administrators to expel a student who brought firearms on campus for a minimum of one year (Casella, 2003, p. 874). Schools that did not comply with the directive were denied federal funding. Following the Columbine[2] shootings in 1999, administrators broadened the federal mandate of zero tolerance by expelling students for drug and alcohol use and fighting (p. 875). After 1995, zero tolerance expanded when the Gun-Free Schools Act was amended so that the word "firearms" was replaced with "weapons," which allowed administrators to expel students who had "nail clippers, files, and pocket knives" (p. 874).

Zero tolerance has since become the de facto policy for dealing with school discipline nationwide (Blumenson & Nilsen, 2002; Gregory et al., 2010). For more than 15 years the policy has come under much scrutiny for its use in relatively minor incidents: under one school's drug policy, two fifth graders were suspended four days for using a nasal spray inhaler (Willis, 2012); under a weapons policy, a high schooler was suspended when he brought a knife to school for a demonstration on healthy school eating (WOIW, 2014); and a teenager who posed in a photo with the number three—his football jersey number—was indefinitely suspended for presumed gang involvement (Aronowitz, 2014).

Due to the excessive reliance on suspension, exclusionary practices have increased multifold across the country; since 1973, the number of students suspended annually has more than doubled to 3.3 million (Dignity in Schools, 2009). In Chicago, expulsion increased by 3,000 percent "from 21 in 1994–95 to 668 in 1997–98," while suspensions increased 51 percent during the same time (Michie, as quoted in Giroux, 2001).

School districts' reliance on zero tolerance might be more understandable if the policy curbed or improved behaviors such as truancy, fighting and verbal disrespect—behaviors that administrators have reported as the most prevalent and worrisome in their day-to-day school experiences (Heaviside, Rowand, Williams, & Farris, 1996). However, a substantial body of literature points to the failure of zero tolerance to create safer schools or improve student behavior (APA Zero Tolerance Task Force, 2006; Dignity in Schools, 2009; Gregory & Cornell, 2009; Martinez, 2009; Skiba & Peterson, 1999). As Martinez (2009) explains, "If zero-tolerance is truly an effective deterrent, then it would be expected that there should be a reduction in the use of suspension, but in reality there has been an increase in the use of suspension" (p. 155). These findings suggest that schools need to find alternatives to zero tolerance to create safer schools.

While the majority of teachers recognize that suspensions in themselves rarely remediate student misbehaviors, many still resort to the practice to provide immediate respite in their classrooms (Eaton & DeLauri, 2010, p. 37). In schools as well as in the policy world, the rationale behind zero tolerance is often that suspensions "interrupt the education of those students who do not want to learn so that learning and teaching for others are not interrupted" (Reyes, 2006, p. 48). However, there is now evidence that suggests suspension harms not only students who are excluded for their behaviors but those who remain in the classroom once they leave. Perry and Morris (2014) conducted a longitudinal study of 17,000 students in Kentucky over three years and discovered that higher rates of suspension in a school correlated to lower math and reading end-of-semester scores for *non-suspended* students—suggesting that punitive discipline practices negatively impact all students, not just those sent out of the school.

While it could be easy to blame teachers and administrators for excluding suspended and expelled students from the right to an education, Eaton and DeLauri (2010) rightly note:

> We must be cautious, however, not to demonize educators who employ ill-advised, ineffective zero-tolerance policies . . . In our most distressed, poorer communities, teachers, guidance counselors, and principals have quite often been left alone to respond to the host of social ills and inequities that undermine their daily efforts to educate children and teens. (p. 16)

The "host of social ills and inequities" students in low-income communities face include violence, concentrated poverty, lack of access to health care, exposure to lead poisoning and unhealthy food, and limited economic resources. Because professionals in schools of concentrated disadvantage cannot ameliorate these inequities alone, and because they often do not have the time to uncover the roots of student misbehaviors, suspension offers a quick—albeit short-term—solution to disciplinary issues. And while suspensions have an impact on students in all communities, zero tolerance is more punitively and subjectively applied when sanctioning students of color.

For example, in 1999 44,000 students in Maryland were suspended for "insubordination," "disruption," and "disobeying rules" (Advancement Project and Civil Rights Project, 2000). Skiba (2000) documents how African American students in a major urban school district in the Midwest received more referrals to the office at the classroom level for offenses such as "disrespect, excessive noise, threat and loitering," while White students were referred more often for more objective offenses such as "smoking, leaving the building without permission, vandalism, and unseemly language" (p. 181).

In addition, it has become increasingly common for students to be suspended, expelled and arrested on campus as early as preschool, where according to the Schott Foundation, students are expelled at a rate "more than three times that of their older peers in grades K–12" (Gilliam, 2005). One highly publicized story involved an African American five-year-old girl in 2005 who had a "temper tantrum" in school (Schoonover, 2009). Jaesha Scott, whose arrest was filmed by school authorities, can be seen being handcuffed by three police officers. Eventually she was charged with a felony and two misdemeanors for hitting a police officer. Similarly Michael Taylor, an African American five-year-old boy with documented attention deficit hyperactivity disorder (ADHD), was cited with battery on a police officer in Stockton, California (Hibbard, 2011). Unbeknownst to Michael's mother, the school had called the police officer to scare the boy so that he would improve his behavior. The data on suspension, expulsion and school arrests, then, paints a dismal portrait of school discipline and the encroachment of the criminal justice system on the education of our most academically vulnerable—students of color and, in particular, males of color like Martin.

WHY RESTORATIVE JUSTICE?

Once aware of the racial discipline gap and the history of zero tolerance, I was reminded once again of Martin, anchored throughout the research process by thoughts about what could have been done differently to keep him in school. Teachers and administrators can contribute to the school-to-prison pipeline through individual decisions about when and how to sanction students (Pollock, 2008). Yet I wanted to know how educators like my colleagues and I could also resist and actively disrupt the pipeline, despite the matrix of poverty, violence and school disciplinary practices and policies that sometimes overwhelmed us. What could school staff do to help students engage in constructive behaviors? What alternatives to out-of-school suspension were being used, and were they successful?

I discovered a range of alternatives, including in-school suspension, counseling, peer mediation, peer courts, bullying prevention, social and emotional curricula and national programs with memorable titles such as Stop and Think and Love and Logic (Martinez, 2009; NASP, 2010; Peterson, 2005). All of these alternatives stressed the need to create mutually respectful relationships among young people and adults in schools, but broadly speaking, they fell on a continuum. At one end were practices, such as in-school suspension and peer courts, often rooted in behaviorism, the "carrot and stick" model of discipline in which positive behaviors are rewarded and negative behaviors are punished. This model relies on extrinsic motivation to influence students to behave respectfully. On the other end of the continuum were interventions such as social and emotional curricula (e.g., Stop and Think), counseling and peer mediation that emphasized the need for students to build their internal capacity to address conflict in productive ways (Knoff, 2005). Somewhere in between were models (e.g., Love and Logic) that synthesized principles of behaviorism with psychology (Parnell, 2008, p. 38). Yet there were two models repeatedly mentioned as the most promising alternatives to zero tolerance in urban schools—alternatives that, though seemingly similar in intent, fell on opposing sides of the continuum: *Positive Behavioral Interventions and Supports* (PBIS) and a philosophy referred to as *restorative justice* (Advancement Project, 2009; Dignity in Schools, 2009; Edutopia, 2010).

PBIS

PBIS began with a mission to address the behaviors of students with special needs, in particular those with behavioral and emotional disorders (Sugai & Simonsen, 2012). This goal is vital given that students with special needs, and in particular behavioral disorders, have been historically excluded from schools (PBIS, n.d.). Because of this focus on students in special education, PBIS is the only behavioral intervention that is highlighted in the amended Individuals with Disabilities Education Act (IDEA)[3]—legislation that was passed, among other reasons, to grant students with special needs developmentally appropriate disciplinary responses. PBIS is now used in mainstream classes as well, and is defined as

> an application of a behaviorally-based systems approach to enhance the capacity of schools, families, and communities to design effective environments that improve the link between research-validated practices and the environments in which teaching and learning occurs.[4] (PBIS, n.d.)

PBIS promotes positive behaviors by sustaining three tiers of support: at the primary or school-wide level through common disciplinary procedures, at the secondary or classroom level for students needing specialized attention, and at the tertiary or individual level for the few students who may be highly disruptive.

At the primary level some schools provide students who abide by school "rules, routines, and physical arrangements that are developed and taught by school staff[5]"—such as showing up to class on time, completing homework, walking on the right side of the hallway, and respectfully asking a question—with tokens that can be cashed in for rewards (PBIS, n.d.). In one elementary school, students who earned five chips could get a free pencil from the office, take their shoes off in class for a day, or bring a stuffed animal to school for a day. Secondary schools that use PBIS also use a rewards-based system to reinforce positive behaviors: students who lowered their number of office referrals at one high school were provided a study hall period that "allowed for peer interaction and the use of technology," while another high school rewarded good behavior with "cool tickets" that could be redeemed for candy and entrance to school dances (Culos et al., 2006, p. 138).

Consequences for misbehavior, on the other hand, could include a time-out, detention, referral to the office or a positive call home. Schools that use PBIS are expected to systematically collect data about the outcomes of the program to analyze and improve disciplinary outcomes. As a result, there is a plethora of research that documents the positive outcomes of PBIS, including the reduction of student misbehaviors, school dropout and suspension rates, and the improvement of school climate and student achievement (Cregor, 2008; Eber, Lewis-Palmer, & Pacchiano, 2002; Green, 2009; Netzel & Eber, 2003).

In contrast to PBIS, there is far less research that addresses both the outcomes and processes associated with the implementation of another paradigm being used in urban schools—restorative justice. There are significant overlaps between PBIS and the practice of restorative justice in schools: both attempt to improve relationships among students and teachers, and strengthen school culture by creating common values and address infractions through positive interventions (Dignity in Schools, 2009). Yet, restorative justice is inherently different from PBIS in one compelling way: it is both a practice and a philosophy, not a program (Elliott, as quoted in Zellerer, 2011).

RESTORATIVE JUSTICE

The roots of restorative justice extend centuries back to indigenous peoples in every continent who felt collectively responsible for building and repairing community[6] (Boyes-Watson, 2008). If a member of a community committed an offense, he or was expected to face those he harmed and commit to an agreement to rectify the problem. Although indigenous peoples in North America—including the First Nations people of Canada and Native Americans within the U.S.—are not a monolithic people, they do share community-based notions of what constitutes justice. These values form the foundation for restorative justice as it is practiced in the U.S.:

> [Restorative justice] is a modern restatement of traditional values of balance between those in conflict . . . within their communities, and signifies an approach to crime and conflict that heals parties through embracing them and their place in the symbiosis while simultaneously rejecting the destructive act that sundered them. (Dickson-Gilmore & La Prairie, 2005, p. vii)

Individuals who commit harm are not conflated with the "destructive act that sundered" their relationship with others, and after being reprimanded, they may ultimately be embraced and reintegrated into the community.

What attracted me to restorative justice was this focus on relationships— creating them, sustaining them and repairing them when harm occurred. Martin did not behave or succeed in my class because I rewarded him materially. Rather, he thrived academically because we built a personal relationship. That is, we talked about what he was reading and about how his need for material objects—clothes, jewelry or shoes—partially dictated his involvement in illegal activities. In other words, we trusted each other. Our written correspondence provided an opportunity to heal a relationship that may have been severed his junior year, when he alienated himself from teachers and, without explaining why, stopped talking to me. Indeed, we were practicing restorative justice through our letters without even realizing it, and I wondered what the philosophy looked like when carried out intentionally.

I was particularly intrigued by restorative justice because those who spoke of the philosophy described it as a *movement*—not only in schools, but in prisons, hospitals, board rooms and community centers where people are looking for meaningful ways to address and repair conflicts (Pranis, 2005).

THE HISTORY OF THE RESTORATIVE JUSTICE MOVEMENT

The term "restorative justice" was first popularized in the U.S. in the criminal justice system, when the framework was offered as a way for victims to participate in the punishment of individuals by verbalizing how they were impacted by a crime and what they needed to feel like justice would be served (Zehr, 1990). Since then restorative justice has been broadly conceived as a philosophy and practice[7] in which a variety of harms—interpersonal harm, harm against communities and violation of state laws—are reframed not as a traditional breach between individual parties, or between the state and its offenders, but as harms among relationships that impact an entire community.

The philosophy behind restorative justice contrasts with traditional notions of justice or what Zehr (1990) calls "retributive" justice, in which the focus is often on punishing the offender rather than healing the victim. Yet the reintegration of the offender to the broader community through atonement and redemption is also recognized. Restorative justice additionally acknowledges that the offender has needs as well, possibly including the need to be held accountable, to develop social and emotional skills, and to contribute to society (p. 200). In fact, restorative practitioners often eschew traditional labels such as "victim" and "offender," recognizing that such polarizing terms fail to acknowledge that offenders have often been victims and victims sometimes offenders.[8] Restoration occurs not only in relationships: restorative justice can also restore human dignity, property loss, injury, communities and the environment, among other things (Braithwaite, 2002).

Today restorative justice manifests itself in a variety of practices, such as:

- Victim Offender Mediation (VOM)[9], which first emerged in the 1970s as a process in which a victim engages in a mediated dialogue with an offender to express how he/she was impacted by a crime, and what—if anything—can be done to remediate the harm (Umbreit, Coates, & Vos, 2007).
- Family Group Conferencing, a variation on VMA first developed by the Maori community for youth offenders in New Zealand; this process includes not only the victim and offender but their respective family and friends (Wachtel, 1997, p. 60).

- Community Reparative Boards, in which a group of trained citizens from the community address and create sanctions for offenders who are diverted by the traditional court system (Bazemore & Umbreit, 1998).
- Circles, a ritual descended from indigenous communities around the world that is becoming one of the most common restorative practices in schools (Pranis, 2005).

It is this last ritual that I explore in this book—a practice being implemented in schools transitioning away from exclusionary disciplinary practices.

CIRCLES

It is common practice to see students in elementary school seated in circles as teachers read to them or direct conversations. Increasingly, circles[10] are being used at the secondary level as well for a multitude of purposes: *talking* circles for having formal and informal conversations and building community and *healing* circles for addressing conflict (Pranis, 2005). In healing circles, the responsible parties, the harmed parties and other members of the community engage in a conversation by sitting in a circle. The dialogue is embedded with rituals based on Native American practices, such as having a keeper and a talking piece. A *keeper* acts as a facilitator. Rather than impose rules, the keeper reminds everyone to "keep" to the agreements they have jointly made, such as promising to be truthful or only speaking when they have the talking piece. The talking piece—which can be any small object, such as a stone or a shell—is passed in one direction. The circle employs three core principles of restorative justice: identify the harm, ask community members to say how they were impacted by the harm, and then come up with concrete ways for the responsible party to repair the harm (Zehr, 2002, p. 21). In Native American communities, circles have "profound cultural significance":

> Symbolizing the interconnectedness of all things and directing consideration of the impact on all partners in that symbiosis when decisions are taken, the concept of the circle is synonymous with balance, openness, and a holistic approach to life. It is not surprising, then, that this concept, and the cultures which define it, have been closely linked with the restorative justice movement, which shares the values of the circle both philosophically and in much of its architecture. (Dickson-Gilmore & La Prairie, 2007, p. viii)

GAPS IN THE RESEARCH

Restorative practices such as circles have been found to help educators and students uncover the root of conflicts, create space for individuals to be accountable for their actions, teach social and emotional literacy, foster a sense of community and improve academic outcomes, relationships, and school climate overall (Adams, 2008; Cameron & Thorsborne, 2000; Karp & Breslin, 2001; Lewis, 2009; Macready, 2009; Morrison & Thorsborne, 2006; Shaw, 2007). The International Institute for Restorative Practices researched six American schools—two rural schools, one urban school, and two suburban schools—and documented how the implementation of restorative justice was correlated with a decrease in referrals to the office, student detentions, out-of-school suspensions and incidents of disruptive behavior (Lewis, 2009). In West Philadelphia High School, an urban school in which 90 percent of the population is African American, 84 percent receive free or reduced lunch and 27 percent have special needs, "violent acts in serious incidents were down 52%" in the first year of implementing restorative justice (Lewis, 2009). Restorative practices provide an ecological approach to addressing misconduct and improving school culture. As Russell Gallagher, assistant principal at the school, notes:

> Before implementing restorative practices, we had a lot of issues of violence, fires, kids misbehaving in class, disrespect. [Restorative practices] change the emotional atmosphere of the school. You can stop guns, but you can't stop them from bringing fists or a poor attitude. A metal detector won't detect that. (Adams, 2008)

While the literature on restorative justice in schools provided compelling descriptive statistics and interview data about positive outcomes in schools that used circles, I was skeptical. Restorative justice was correlated with a reduction in suspensions, but teachers could have merely been suspending students less because administrators expected that they do so—were conflicts truly resolved? Were students and teachers transformed? And what actually occurred in the circles, a ritual that sounded, admittedly, mystical and touchy-feely in its premise? The research seemed to lack in-depth examinations of the process itself through long-term immersion in a school attempting to make a paradigm shift toward restorative justice. All of my research interests were grounded in my experiences with students like Martin at Lee High School in Houston. How could one take a school like Lee, centrally located in a poor neighborhood swirling with gang activity, and convince teachers and administrators that circles were worth the time and energy?

Moreover, while the majority of researchers who study restorative justice in schools focus on positive outcomes, they are largely mute on the broader context of racialized disciplinary practices—that is, the disproportionately high rates of suspension and expulsion of non-White students (Amstutz & Mullet, 2005; Braithwaite, 2001; Cameron & Thorsborne, 2000). In a review of 13 publications[11] that explore the use of restorative practices in schools in Canada, Europe, Australia, New Zealand and the U.S., not one included a critical examination of racial disparities in school disciplinary practices. Nor do they mention that in urban schools where the majority of teachers are White and female (Edutopia, 2006), and the majority of students suspended are of color, male and from working-class backgrounds, the implementation of restorative justice may necessitate an examination of race, class and gender. This is especially true because schools with larger populations of Black students—arguably the sites where alternatives to zero tolerance are most needed—are less likely than other schools to implement restorative justice (Payne & Welch, 2013).

This oversight is glaring given that leaders in urban high schools and districts across the country[12] (and around the world) are responding to the disproportionate rates of suspension of students of color through restorative justice (Advancement Project, 2009; Drewery, 2004). For example, the revised Denver discipline code, amended to include restorative justice in 2008, explicitly states that "the policy and accompanying procedures are intended to help the District eliminate racial and ethnic disparities, and any other protected class disparities, in school discipline, while improving behavior, school climate, and academic achievement for all students" (Denver Public Schools, 2008). In New Zealand disciplinary practices also are used to address the racial disparities in suspension rates between Maori and White youth. Maori students in New Zealand are more than three times as likely to be suspended as non-Maori students (Wearmouth, Glynn, & Berryman, 2009, p. 58), and schools have responded by incorporating indigenous practices of restorative justice in discipline (Wearmouth, McKinney, & Glynn, 2007).

From within these gaps I formulated my research questions. I wanted to understand how restorative justice was conceptualized and implemented at two urban high schools composed largely of students of color. What roles did students, educators and community members play in the implementation and practice of restorative justice? How did participants make meaning of the purposes and outcomes of circles? What strides were made in replacing punitive disciplinary practices with restorative ones? Finally, how was race explicitly addressed or not addressed in discussions about the utility of restorative justice in an education system where students of color are disproportionately punished?

My research questions weren't formulated to fill a conceptual hole in the literature. As I write this, Martin stares at me from a photo of his graduation from painting class. He wears a white prison shirt, and the dark gray outline of a tattoo seems to have surreptitiously made itself known from beneath his half sleeve. His thick arms are folded. His serious, dark eyes are softened by a mouth that seems on the verge of smiling. His full, black eyebrows seem cocked, and although this is their natural arc, I imagine they demand, "What are you writing about? Why does it matter?"

The narratives in these pages—of Janet Connors, who decided to keep circles in schools after her teenage son was murdered, and of Bridge and Equity, two high schools where educators are acutely aware of how restorative justice can disrupt pathways between schools and prisons—matter to the broader discourse around the dropout crisis, school discipline policies and alternatives to zero tolerance. They offer insights for teachers working to build relationships with students, their families and the communities in which they work. They speak to people in neighborhoods working to improve schools and keep their children safe and to young people who have become inured to the phenomenon of their brothers, sisters, cousins and parents ending up in prison. It is my hope that the portraits in this study will add to the small but growing body of literature that explores alternatives to exclusionary discipline practices so that students like Martin—who consumed self-help books, graphic novels, autobiographies and literary fiction daily when behind bars—can nourish their love of learning in schools rather than prisons.

NOTES

1. While racial categories are social constructions (Pollock, 2008), in this book I recognize groups in the same manner by capitalizing the names of all racial signifiers (White, Black, Latino, Asian and Native American). I do this because it feels incongruent to capitalize the word "Latino" when speaking of one people and the lowercase "black" when describing another group. In addition, I use the word "Black" as opposed to "African American" to signify that students who are overrepresented in the school-to-prison pipeline are of African descent and not necessarily from the United States.
2. The fourth deadliest school massacre in U.S. history, in which two high school seniors shot 12 students and one teacher before committing suicide (Kass, 2009).
3. See http://idahoresultscenter.org/Behavior-Support-PBIS-Idaho/PBIS-and-the-Law.
4. See http://www.pbis.org/school/default.aspx.
5. See http://www.pbis.org/school/primary_level/default.aspx.
6. It should be noted that the term "restorative justice" is highly contested (Gavrielides, 2008; Vaandering, 2011) and that I am not claiming to provide a universally agreed-upon definition. However, this book seeks to highlight restorative justice from the perspective of practitioners in schools. As such, it does not aim to contribute to the theoretical debate about what constitutes restorative justice. The definition used relies on the "lived experiences" of people who are highlighted in several empirical, qualitative studies, including this one.
7. For the purposes of this book, I use the terms *restorative justice, restorative discipline,* and *restorative practices* interchangeably, although the literature on restorative practices differs on the use of these terms (McCluskey et al., 2008, p. 209). According to the International Institute for Restorative Practices, *restorative practices* is an umbrella term that can include both *restorative justice* and *restorative discipline* (Schenk, 2008). This distinction is made because *restorative justice* or *discipline* is thought of as reactive, whereas *restorative practices* include proactive community building use of peacemaking circles *before* a conflict ever occurs.
8. Whereas this may be the case, I continue to use these terms in my definitions to stay true to the wording used in my sources.

9. Also referred to as Victim Offender Dialogue, this practice is discussed in more depth in the portrait of Janet Connors.
10. Referred to sometimes as "conferences" by other practitioners and theorists.
11. Amstutz & Mullet, 2005; Braithwaite, 2001; Cameron & Thorsborne, 2000; Hansen, 2005; Karp & Breslin, 2001; Lewis, 2009; McCluskey et al., 2008; Morrison, 2005; Morrison, Blood, & Thorsborne, 2006; O'Brien & Bazemore, 2006; Palazzo & Hosea, 2004; Shaw, 2007; Varnham, 2005.
12. These cities include, among others, New York, Chicago (http://www.chica goareaproject.org/programs/restorative-justice), Oakland, Jacksonville, San Francisco, Los Angeles, Denver, Philadelphia and Detroit.

2 The Intersection of Race and Punishment in Schools

"More African American men are in prison or jail, on probation or parole than were enslaved in 1850, before the Civil War began."
—Michelle Alexander (2010)

It is impossible to ignore the U.S.'s long history of criminalizing African American males when examining how and why students of color are disproportionately punished in schools and overrepresented in the criminal justice system. Several scholars (Alexander, 2010; Blackmon, 2008; Wacquant, 2000) argue that slavery is the prelude to a longer narrative marked by multiple attempts by Whites to maintain the second-class status of African Americans. These authors contend that as one system of racial control ends, another one ultimately crops up in its place: "Since the nation's founding, African-Americans repeatedly have been controlled through institutions such as slavery and Jim Crow, which appear to die, but then are reborn in new form, tailored to the needs and constraints of the time" (Alexander, 2010, p. 21). Wacquant (2000) refers to these systems of control as "peculiar institutions"[1] that have "operated to define, confine, and control African-Americans in the history of the United States" (p. 378). He names four peculiar institutions: chattel slavery, Jim Crow, hyperghettos and prisons. Along with Alexander (2010), he argues that the racial caste system borne from slavery, and perpetuated in Jim Crow laws, persists today in the U.S. penal system, where African American males are incarcerated at a rate six times that of White males (Human Rights Watch, 2009).

Given that schools consistently punish Black students at rates disproportionate to their population, the history of the racialized punishment of Black Americans provides a broader context in which to analyze the racial discipline gap. This context is therefore also important when framing and analyzing solutions to the gap such as restorative justice, which is being used in many schools to end racial disproportionality in school discipline. Researcher and practitioner Tom Cavanagh (2009) notes, "Those of us working in the field of restorative practices in education are ethically obligated to acknowledge that our work is directly linked to the statistics of disparity that disproportionately affect students from these minority groups."

Restorative practitioners aiming to reduce racial disparities in school discipline must be familiar with the institutions in which they are operating to create lasting, system-wide change. In understanding the historic antecedents to the racial discipline gap, they may be better able to craft a new paradigm of addressing harm that can disrupt racialized disciplinary practices in schools. In this chapter, I outline the development of our peculiar institutions and ponder the role of urban schools on this historical continuum, interrogating whether and how schools have become our fifth "peculiar institution" and situating my analysis of restorative justice in this historic, racial and institutional context.

PECULIAR INSTITUTIONS: CHATTEL SLAVERY, JIM CROW, GHETTOS AND PRISONS

The first three peculiar institutions, chattel slavery, Jim Crow and ghettos, fulfilled two purposes: they were used to ostracize Blacks both socially and materially and extract their labor through forced servitude or by limiting economic opportunities (Wacquant, 2000). These systems of control were dismantled by what I will refer to shorthand as "progressive institutions"— organized social movements (such as the Civil Rights Movement) and government mandates that expanded Black civil rights (such as Emancipation and Reconstruction). However, following the demise of each peculiar institution,[2] and the rise of each progressive institution, Whites in power inevitably renewed efforts to contain and forcibly work former slaves and their descendants (Alexander, 2010). In this way new peculiar institutions sprung up when old ones died, a pattern that began with chattel slavery (see Figure 2.1).

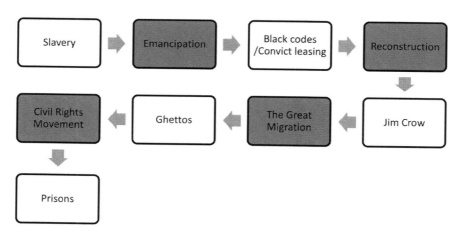

Figure 2.1   The Evolution of Racialized Practices of Punishment and Isolation in the United States

Chattel slavery. Though the 13th Amendment of the Constitution banned the first peculiar institution of chattel slavery in 1865, its authors included an exception for those who have been incarcerated: "Neither slavery nor involuntary servitude, *except as a punishment for crime whereof the party shall have been duly convicted*, shall exist within the United States, or any place subject to their jurisdiction" (U.S. Const. Amend. XIII, emphasis added). The phrasing "except as a punishment for crime" left open the possibility for slavery to continue as long as freedmen were convicted of breaking laws. After all, Emancipation created two dilemmas for Southern Whites: how to retain the labor of 4 million former slaves and at the same time "sustain the cardinal status distinction" between Whites and freed slaves (Wacquant, 2000, p. 380). To accomplish both aims, they needed a new system that would both preserve this distinction and perpetuate slave labor. Both aims were accomplished through the second peculiar institution defined by Wacquant (2000)—Jim Crow—as well as its precursor, a series of laws dubbed the Black codes.

Following Emancipation, the Black codes were regulations institutionalized throughout ex-Confederate states,[3] and their implementation led to the imprisonment of thousands of freedmen[4] who were selectively targeted and convicted for the most arbitrary of infractions, including "changing employers without permission, vagrancy, riding freight cars without a ticket, [and] engaging in sexual activity—or loud talk—with white women" (Blackmon, 2008, p. 7). Those convicted through the Black codes were sent to county jails and leased out to companies and plantation owners, working for little or no pay. Though de jure slavery ended in 1865, W. E. B. DuBois concluded that these newly drafted laws created a de facto form of slavery: "The Codes spoke for themselves . . . No open-minded student can read them without being convinced they meant nothing more nor less than slavery in daily toil" (as quoted in Alexander, 2010, p. 28).

In fact, these prisoners were subjected to conditions that were often worse than slavery—so much so that Blackmon (2008) refers to this period as *neo-slavery.* Prisoners who worked for one mining company were shackled at night, and their waste was filled in gunpowder cans that occasionally spilled out onto the beds. They left for work at three in the morning in chains, forced to move at a quick pace and work excruciatingly long hours: "the grueling task of boring rock for dynamite, exploding sections of a seam of coal, and shoveling tons of the remains into cars lasted until 8 PM" (Blackmon, 2008, p. 70). In contrast to antebellum times when owners valued their slaves as a commodity, private contractors had little investment in treating leased prisoners well; even if men died, convicts were plentiful. The current phenomenon of mass incarceration was foreshadowed during the convict leasing era, when the country experienced what Alexander (2010) calls our "first prison boom." The sentences doled out during that era gave rise to a prison population that grew exponentially, "10 times faster than the general population" (p. 32). Convict leasing was finally banished by

1945, mainly because, according to Blackmon, the government needed to recruit as many soldiers as possible during World War II. Moreover, in the midst of German and Japanese publicity about the hypocrisy of a country that enslaved its own citizens, the country was facing international scrutiny and needed to repair its image on the world stage.

Jim Crow. Though the Black codes were largely dismantled in 1867, they were resurrected once again in the form of Jim Crow, an institutional response to the gains made by African Americans during Reconstruction when, protected by the Freedmen's Bureau, African Americans began voting in large numbers, opened their own schools and businesses and took political office. In fact in 1870, Blacks comprised 15 percent or more of all elected officials in the South—whereas, ironically, by 1980 less than 8 percent of all southern elected officials were Black (Alexander, 2010, p. 29). In light of this progress, Southern[5] Whites in power attempted to reassert political and institutional control through the passage of Jim Crow laws, a caste system that stipulated that, among myriad other restrictions, Blacks use their own restrooms, learn in separate schools, travel in separate trains, and be buried in segregated cemeteries. As Alexander puts it, "After a brief period of progress during Reconstruction, African-Americans found themselves, once again, virtually defenseless" (p. 32). This caste system was enforced through lynchings and mob killings, and in response, millions of African Americans fled north during the Great Migration. Wacquant (2008) asserts that Whites, resistant to the influx of the descendants of slaves, excluded and extracted labor from Blacks through the third peculiar institution—ghettos.

Hyperghettos. African Americans provided an abundant source of cheap labor in the industrial economy of the North, but Whites maintained the racial order through the convergence of "racist attitudes, private behaviors, and institutional practices that disenfranchised blacks from urban housing markets" (Massey & Denton, 1993, p. 83). For example, a study from the 1950s revealed that 80 percent of realtors in Chicago refused to sell Blacks homes in White neighborhoods, and 68 percent would not rent them such property either (p. 50). Thus African Americans were marginalized in urban ghettos, segregated areas in which they continued to experience social, spatial and economic isolation due to a job ceiling that limited them to dangerous and menial professions: "Continued caste hostility from without and renewed ethnic affinity from within converged to create the ghetto as the third vehicle to extract black labor while keeping black bodies at a safe distance, to the material and symbolic benefit of white society" (Wacquant, 2000, p. 381).

To protest their economic, spatial, social and political isolation, Blacks began organizing in record numbers. As the Civil Rights Movement gained momentum, these early ghettos began to crumble. Blacks were "at long last full citizens who would no longer brook being shunted off into the separate and inferior world of the ghetto" (Wacquant, 2000, p. 382). While the earliest ghettos were mixed-income communities, over time middle- and upper-class African Americans migrated out of these isolated spaces, leaving behind families living in concentrated poverty. Wacquant (2000) refers to these spaces as *hyperghettos* because they served not only to contain African Americans but destitute African Americans in particular. One-third of all African Americans now live in hyper segregated areas where they are

> not only unlikely to come into contact with whites within the particular neighborhood where they live; even if they travel to the adjacent neighborhood they would still be unlikely to see white faces; and if they went to the next neighborhood beyond that, no whites would be there either. (p. 77)

The isolation of poor African Americans was further compounded by rising unemployment in the late 1960s, partially the result of a switch from an industrial economy, reliant on goods producing work, to a service economy— and partially the result of globalization and rising competition from immigrant laborers (Wilson, 1987). Deindustrialization particularly hurt African American men, who comprised a large part of the industrial workforce in the automobile, rubber and steel industries. A rising population of unemployed Black men emerged in these hyperghettos. While 70 percent of African American men living in urban areas engaged in blue-collar work in 1970, only 28 percent had such jobs in 1987 (Alexander, 2010, p. 50). Now considered "deviant, destitute, and dangerous," these men were marginalized in the deindustrialized economy, which made them "redundant and undercut the role of the ghetto as a reservoir of unskilled labor" (Wacquant, 2008, pp. 64–65).

The economic deprivation and frustration suffered in these hyperghettos found expression in an outbreak of urban riots from 1964 to 1968. Politicians began equating the unrest surrounding the Civil Rights Movement— which included riots, acts of civil disobedience and violent clashes during integration efforts—as a violation of the social order. And the inner city was depicted as the epicenter from which crime was rampantly spreading. As Representative John Bell Williams stated at the time, "This exodus of Negroes from the South, and their influx into the great metropolitan centers of other areas of the nation, has been accompanied by a wave of crime" (as quoted in Alexander, 2010, p. 41). Capitalizing on White fears about competing and sharing resources with Blacks following the Civil Rights Movement, politicians crafted a legislative agenda that increased the state's ability to target and imprison men of color who were deemed dangerous. They did so not with the explicitly racist language of Jim Crow but through coded language around "law and order," the "War on Crime," and its corollary, the "War on Drugs." This war most visibly punished people of color, who went from comprising one-third of the prison population in the 1960s to comprising two-thirds of the population now (Wacquant, 2008). Prisons, then, currently operate as the fourth peculiar institution used to contain, isolate and punish lower-class Black and Brown people (Wacquant, 2000).

Prisons. Over the last 25 years, the confluence of zero tolerance drug policies and "tough on crime" rhetoric has resulted in unprecedented numbers of people being arrested, convicted and jailed, despite the fact that crime rates have fallen sharply since 1992 (Alexander, 2010). Though the U.S. comprises 5 percent of the world population, we have the highest incarceration rate in the world and imprison 2.2 million people annually, or approximately 25 percent of the world's inmates (Loury, 2008). We incarcerate more people than China (1.5 million) and Russia (870,000) combined (Vicini, 2006). And if you include those who are in prison, on parole and on probation, the number of people in our justice system totals 7 million (Alexander, 2010).

The burgeoning prison population can be attributed to more punitive laws as well as longer sentences. Antidrug legislation passed by Reagan preceded a crack cocaine epidemic that devastated inner-city communities in the 1980s. In 1986 the government responded by mandating "far more severe punishment for distribution of crack—associated with blacks—than powder cocaine, associated with whites" (Alexander, 2010, p. 52). Two-thirds of the current prison population have been convicted of nonviolent offenses, namely drug use, and since the 1980s African Americans and Latinos have been disproportionately punished for such crimes: "Although African-Americans only represent 13% of all monthly drug users (consistent with their proportion of the population), they account for . . . 74% of those sentenced to prison for drug possession" (Allard, 2002, p. 26).

Though all four peculiar institutions share similarities, they differ in the manner and degree to which they have isolated and punished African Americans. Alexander (2010) describes slavery as a racial caste system based on *exploitation*, Jim Crow as a system based on *subordination*, and mass incarceration as a system defined by *marginalization*. Each new system of racial control, says Wacquant (2000), "is less total, less capable of encompassing and controlling the entire race" (p. 380). Indeed, the systems of control seem increasingly less punitive over time, with subordination more preferable to exploitation and marginalization more preferable to subordination. However, marginalization may be more pernicious than exploitation because it pushes people into prison, especially poor Black men, out of the public's gaze altogether. Because prisons specifically contain thousands of African American men from hyperghettos, Wacquant (2000) refers to the phenomenon of the exploding prison population as *hyper incarceration*, not mass incarceration:

> *Mass* incarceration suggests that confinement concerns large swaths of the citizenry (as with the mass media, mass culture, mass unemployment, etc.). But the expansion and intensification of the activities of the police, courts, and prison over the past quarter-century have been finely

targeted by class, ethnicity, and race, leading to what is better referred to as the hyper incarceration of one particular category: lower-class black men in the crumbling ghetto. (p. 59)

The justice system continues to disenfranchise millions of poor Blacks and Latinos upon their release, leaving them with few opportunities to join the workforce or even receive social services. In alignment with Temporary Aid to Needy Families (TANF), passed in 1996 by Clinton, former felons convicted of using or selling drugs are banned from social assistance benefits *for life* in approximately 20 states (Meiners, 2007, p. 101). As of 2006, 5.3 million former prisoners could not vote because of felony disenfranchisement (Holding, 2006). Prisons, then, segregate and isolate those convicted of drug-related offenses even after they leave, resulting in what Meiners (2007) calls their "civil death" (p. 100).

Wacquant asserts that prisons are unlike the first peculiar institutions of slavery, Jim Crow, and ghettos because they do not extract labor from incarcerated individuals: "The monstrous penal state that now clutches the black sub proletariat is not 'neo-slavery' and penitentiaries are not latter-day plantations (if only because inmates produce no economic value and constitute a colossal fiscal drain on the nation)" (2008, pp. 65–66). Instead, posits Wacquant, the penal system has not expanded because of the exploitation of Black labor but to house bodies that are seen as no longer relevant to the new economy. However, this may be changing. Whereas only a small percentage (3 percent) of prisoners work for private industries, those who do earn anywhere from pennies to $.22 per hour for companies like IBM, Motorola, Microsoft, Revlon, Victoria's Secret and Starbucks (Meiners,

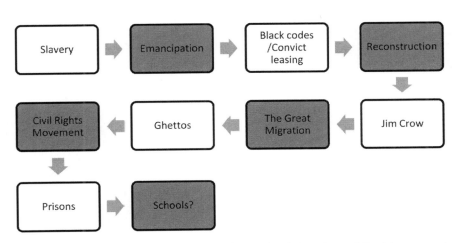

Figure 2.2 The Continued Evolution of Racialized Practices of Punishment and Isolation in the United States

2007, p. 73). Moreover, the prison system employs more than 400,000 people (Regoli & Hewitt, 2007, p. 16). Rural towns are increasingly reliant upon prison construction to boost their economies. And state governments are increasingly allowing privatized companies to use prison labor to offset the costs of prisons (Brown & Severson, 2011), as we have spent "$200 billion annually on law enforcement and corrections at all levels of government, a fourfold increase (in constant dollars) over the past quarter-century" (Loury, 2008, p. 5). In this way prisons may have begun to resemble the first peculiar institutions after all: they place poor Black Americans (and other groups of color) outside of the public gaze while still relying on them for economic growth and manual unskilled labor (see Figure 2.2).

SCHOOLS AS PECULIAR INSTITUTIONS

With specific regard to school discipline, the outcomes of the four peculiar institutions outlined by Wacquant—isolation, exclusion and ostracism from mainstream culture—parallel many outcomes of the racial discipline gap in schools. Just as people who are not valued in the service economy have been socially excluded and contained in prisons, young people who are unable to perform on grade level or adhere to behavioral norms are often excluded through suspension and expulsion and contained in alternative schools or juvenile detention centers.

On the other hand, schools do not directly extract labor from students, a prerequisite of a "peculiar institution." However, schools have operated to isolate and exclude minority students from mainstream culture through curriculum and physical segregation. In the late 1800s Christian boarding schools sprung up to "civilize" Native Americans by teaching them to devalue their own culture (Smith, 2007). Today, Black and Brown students geographically isolated in the peculiar institution of hyperghettos are now often also isolated in ghetto schools (Orfield & Lee, 2007). Schools do not become peculiar in isolation but are impacted by local, state and federal policy. Federal measures such as No Child Left Behind and Race to the Top sometimes prompt teachers who are held accountable through standardized test scores to exclude low-performing students by suspending them on testing days (Keen, 2006). As a result, many scholars and educators describe students who drop out as students who have actually been *pushed* out (Dignity in Schools, 2009) because they do not pass academic muster—those who are suspended are often the least literate, and these educational deficits are reflected in the prison system. Nearly 70 percent of prisoners in 1997 never graduated high school, and approximately 70 percent of juvenile offenders have learning disabilities, while a third of juvenile offenders read below the fourth grade level (Wald & Losen, 2003, p. 11).

In addition, schools punish and exclude students through physical structures such as metal detectors and through organizational structures such as the sorting of students into special education. The education system alone cannot be scapegoated for the morass of the prison industrial complex. But the system fails to serve certain populations of students who are at an increased risk of ending up in prisons, where their labor may end up being extracted after all—and this makes schools, if not peculiar institutions themselves, conjoined with and complicit to our current peculiar institution:

> As the interlocking relationships between schools and the judicial system increased the 1990s, select schools in the United States not only resemble prisons and apply the same disciplinarian surveillance technologies, but they also use the same language, 'pedagogies,' and philosophies espoused by prisons and jails (Saltzman & Gabbard, 2003). (as cited in Meiners, 2007, p. 3)

RESTORATIVE JUSTICE AND PECULIAR INSTITUTIONS

While schools have certainly resembled peculiar institutions, they have also historically been progressive, liberatory spaces, as exemplified by the movement to build freedom schools during the Civil Rights Movement. Today, there are schools across the country partaking in a larger social justice movement and are aiming to overhaul both the prison system and zero tolerance discipline policies. If history follows, our current peculiar institution of prisons likely will be followed by a new progressive institution. I contend that the restorative justice movement is part of a larger social justice movement working to fight the expansion of prisons. Collectively teachers, community members and students in many urban schools are responding to the punitive, rarely rehabilitative nature of prisons and school disciplinary practices with organic, context-specific restorative practices. This book frames restorative justice as one component of schools that, though not always successful, are *aiming* to be progressive—schools like those included in this study.

At their most effective, restorative practices not only keep students accountable for their behaviors but also create space for young people to critically analyze the political and economic structures that contribute to their behaviors as well as the very phenomenon the practice is being used to counter—the school-to-prison pipeline. For example, at Boston Green Academy, an alternative school for students who have traditionally been unsuccessful academically, humanities teacher Aparna Lakshmi crafted lessons around student-generated interest in the pipeline:

> Studying the prison industrial complex was valuable for students on a personal, political, and academic level. The class offered students the

opportunity to move beyond pathologizing their own lives, families, and communities by helping them put their experiences in a broader social context—an experience that was deeply strengthening for both the students and myself. (Lakshmi, 2011)

As Lakshmi notes, teaching students about the structural conditions that affect them allows them to "move beyond pathologizing" their own individual circumstances by understanding how the "broader social context" impacts them and everyone around them. In doing so, students may be inspired to act on this knowledge and to change the very institutions that are negatively impacting the community.

Throughout the study I was conscious of our history of racialized practices of isolation and punishment, but I did not want to highlight the same, tired pathology of schools that feed into prisons. On the contrary I wanted to illuminate the work of educators trying to change the punitive paradigm of discipline I have dissected thus far. Given that restorative justice is being used both in the criminal justice and education systems, it has the potential to reshape the current paradigm of how we run schools, honor our students and address them when problems arise. Challenging the school-to-prison pipeline and ensuring schools do not act as peculiar institutions involves more than discipline reform—it necessitates new decisions around a constellation of factors such as curriculum, pedagogy and the very foundation of restorative justice, building relationships. Schools do not have to bear the entire brunt of the problem, but they are a powerful space in which to effect change:

> The school-to-prison pipeline doesn't just begin with cops in the hallways and zero tolerance discipline policies. It begins when we fail to create a curriculum and a pedagogy that connects with students, that takes them seriously as intellectuals, that lets students know we care about them, that gives them the chance to channel their pain and defiance in productive ways. Making sure that we opt out of the classroom-to-prison pipeline will look and feel different in every subject and with every group of students. But the classroom will share certain features: It will take the time to build relationships, and it will say, "You matter. Your culture matters. You belong." (Christensen, 2011)

NOTES

1. "Our peculiar institution" was actually a euphemism for slavery, commonly used by slave owners in the antebellum period (Stampp, 1989). In this instance "peculiar" was not used to describe something strange but instead connoted a sense of ownership—that is, the institution of slavery is *peculiar* to the South.
2. The white boxes in the figure indicate peculiar institutions; the gray boxes indicate progressive ones.

3. They also had been in existence in northern states such as Illinois and Indiana as early as the 1830s (Berg, 2008).
4. African Americans were not the only people targeted for such violations. For example, in California Whites also devised similarly arbitrary laws to indenture indigenous peoples for loitering, being intoxicated or being orphaned (Ogden, 2005, p 63).
5. It must be noted once again that such laws already had existed in the North.

3 Research Design and Methodology

THE METHODOLOGY OF PORTRAITURE

This study called for a methodology that could capture the complex process of transitioning to restorative justice, one that would highlight the goodness of teachers and students engaged in restorative practices *as well as* address the frailties, shortcomings and limitations associated with the implementation of circles. I wanted to meet teachers who aimed to make their schools progressive institutions, who told their students, "You belong." And I wanted to explore the multifaceted process of relationship building—and mending—that is central to restorative justice. To accurately understand the meanings that community members, parents, administrators, teachers and students attached to restorative practices, I also wanted to embed myself within the school culture in a meaningful way, not only to engage in rigorous data collection but, equally as important, to engage in ethical data collection by fostering trusting, reciprocal relationships.

Portraiture, an ethnographic methodology pioneered by sociologist Sara Lawrence-Lightfoot, fulfilled all of these desires. The history of portraiture is helpful in illuminating why this method complements the study of restorative practices in schools. Participating in a seminar in 1980 in which academics and teachers gathered regularly to discuss educational issues, Lawrence-Lightfoot (1983) noted a tendency in discussions to "focus on what is wrong rather than search for what is right" in schools—to focus on "malignancies and the search for their cures" (p. 10):

> It seemed easy for us to recite all of the problems teachers and students confront and create in secondary schools—the truancy and drop-out rates, the vandalism, the alcohol and drug addiction, the illiteracy of graduates, the teacher "burnout," the undisciplined curriculum, the rigid tracking, the racial warfare, on and on—but it seemed difficult, even awkward, to find the goodness and talk about the successes.

Portraitists counter this tendency toward negativity by searching for "goodness" in their research settings (Lawrence-Lightfoot & Davis, 1997,

p. 9). When documenting social phenomena, they ask, "What is good here?" and in so doing approach and observe the actors in their study with "empathetic regard" (p. 148). Those unfamiliar with portraiture might presume that such a methodology requires a researcher ignore all the flaws or inconsistencies at a research site. However the concept of goodness is complex, and portraitists do not aim to create documents of "idealization or celebration." Rather, in examining goodness,

> [t]here will, of course, be ample evidence of vulnerability and weakness. In fact, the counterpoint and contradictions of strength and vulnerability, virtue and evil (and how people, cultures and organizations negotiate those extremes in an effort to establish the precarious balance between them) are central to the expression of goodness. (Lawrence-Lightfoot & Davis, p. 9)

This emphasis on goodness was important for my study for three reasons. First, given the massive body of literature on disciplinary policies and practices devoted to pathology and deviance in schools, I wanted a methodology that would allow me instead to focus on initiatives seeking to dismantle inequity. Second, portraiture's epistemological stance on goodness aligned with the ontological stance of restorative justice: one that identifies the essential goodness of the majority of individuals and is deeply aware of how context shapes human behavior. Third, portraiture also encouraged me to think of my work as a potential force for social change; Lawrence-Lightfoot (1997) defines the research process as one in which portraitists "engage in acts (implicit and explicit) of social transformation" (p. 11). Indeed I wanted my research to be an act of "social transformation"—an intervention, even—not only a study that would fill a gap in the literature on restorative justice. For example, I wanted my research to help stakeholders at both sites reflect on their transition to restorative practices. Moreover, I wanted to reach an audience "beyond the walls of the academy" (p. 9), including parents, teachers, students and researchers who have the power to impact policy and practice changes that can lead to more equitable schooling outcomes for students. I hoped I would be able to publicize an intervention and philosophy, with all its potential and imperfections, which might inspire other practitioners to examine disciplinary practices at their own schools.

Yet if portraits reach a broad audience outside of academia, it is as much due to their form as their content or ethical stance. Portraits do not read like traditional educational research, nor do they follow a prescriptive outline that lists research questions, literature review, theoretical framework, validity, findings and implications. Instead they employ metaphors, narrative arcs, and often lyrical, engaging language to convey the analysis—blending, as Lawrence-Lightfoot and Davis (1997) puts it, art and science.

Thus in all of its components, portraiture provided guideposts for each stage of the research process, including site selection, relationship building, data collection and analysis, and finally the write-up. Of course, these are not discrete stages: relationships continue to evolve throughout the research project and beyond, and analysis and data collection occur throughout the entire process. Nonetheless in what follows I trace the chronology that shaped my research design—from the beginning of the process to what is now written on the page—in an attempt to illuminate the methodological decisions I made in this study.

ARTICULATING MY RESEARCH QUESTIONS AND LOCATING MY SITES

While the literature on restorative justice in schools calls for a paradigm shift away from suspensions, few studies examine how schools make such a shift or what the practice looks like on site in schools transitioning to restorative discipline. Daly (2002) notes that "in contrast to the voluminous critical and advocacy literatures, there is a thin empirical record of schools in transition" (p. 55). Moreover, research on restorative justice in schools has offered thin descriptions of how disciplinary incidents are referred to circles (Cameron & Thorsborne, 2000), what circles look and feel like (Karp & Breslin, 2001) and how stakeholders respond to and evaluate the restorative process (McCluskey et al., 2008; Shaw, 2007). Thus I wanted to know, *How do urban high schools transition from zero tolerance policies to restorative practices? What roles do students, educators, parents and community members play in such a transition?* Finally, given the paucity of literature addressing how race intersects with the practice of restorative justice in urban schools, *What strides were made in replacing punitive disciplinary practices with restorative ones? How was race explicitly addressed or not addressed during the implementation of and practices of restorative justice?*

Focusing on this transition in *one* high school in a meaningful way could yield fruitful, nuanced answers to this question. However, I was curious about what was happening at multiple schools simultaneously engaged in interpreting, reinterpreting, and enacting the principles of restorative justice—schools early on in the process, in their first five years of implementation,[1] that had experienced some self-defined measure of success. Examining restorative justice in multiple contexts could provide more robust results than focusing on a single school (Yin, 2009). But I was concerned, as Creswell (1996) states, that the inclusion of too many research sites might "dilute the overall analysis" (p. 76). To balance my interest in breadth with the kind of depth my questions demanded, I decided to search for two schools in the local area. Given the constraints of time, I could visit each site one to two times a week—regularly enough, I hoped, to draw conclusions about the implementation of restorative justice based on "thick description" (Geertz, 1973).

I began my search for sites in the Boston Public Schools (BPS), the largest urban school district in my vicinity.[2] Similar to nationwide trends, expulsion and suspension rates in Massachusetts, which are collectively referred to as "student exclusions," show that Latino and Black students are overrepresented when it comes to disciplinary referrals. Though Black and Latino students respectively comprised only 8 and 15% of all public school students in Massachusetts in the 2009-to-2010 school year, they represented 15 and 28 percent of the excluded population (Massachusetts Appleseed Center for Law and Justice, 2012). White students made up the majority of the student population at 69 percent but only 52 percent of excluded students. At the time of the study, BPS had the second-highest exclusion rate in Massachusetts, making it prime ground to study school disciplinary practices.

Initially I had no contacts in the school district and no access to teachers who would willingly invite me into their classrooms several times a week. My professor, Dr. Mark Warren, suggested I speak to his colleague, a fellow sociologist named Carolyn Boyes-Watson. As head of the Center for Restorative Justice at Suffolk University, Carolyn was able to provide me with an overview of the work that was happening in schools. She and Shari Dickstein, a colleague and friend from my doctoral writers group, suggested that I speak to Angela Temple,[3] who was implementing restorative justice at Bridge High School in BPS. Once I e-mailed Angela she willingly obliged to talk about my project, and we met on the green in Boston Commons, the sun ablaze one afternoon in June of 2007.

A second-year teacher, Angela engaged me not only through her intimate knowledge of restorative practices in schools but through her warmth and pensive nature. During a one-year hiatus from teaching, she learned about restorative justice and familiarized herself with peacemaking circles. Having witnessed the failure of suspensions to curb conflicts among students the prior year, she was now was ready to practice the restorative philosophy in her classroom. She was a researcher's dream—open to my presence in her classroom "at any time," in her words—and hoped that my observations would allow her to reflect on the progress of peacemaking circles.

Angela worked in SLC A, one of five small learning communities[4] at Bridge High. There were approximately 200 students Grades 9 through 12 in SLC A; Angela and four others taught freshmen and sophomores in what was termed the "lower school," while five teachers taught juniors and seniors in the upper school. As an advocate for restorative justice, she worked with SLC A administrative leader Rebecca Stern and members of the Center for Restorative Justice at Suffolk University to lead professional development sessions on circles. During that time, I piloted my research by participating in circles, interviewing students and teachers who participated in circles, sitting in on classes, and observing professional development trainings around restorative justice. All lower school teachers used talking circles in their classrooms and participated in healing circles when conflicts arose.

I attempted to understand the "institutional culture and history" of the school—"the origins and evolution of the organization and the values that shape its structure and purpose"—so that I could more accurately interpret social interactions in context (Lawrence-Lightfoot, 1997, p. 52). I began by learning the typical demographic statistics: Bridge was an urban school of 1,226 students. Thirty-eight percent of the school was African American, 18 percent Asian, 36.6 percent Latino, and 6 percent White. Sixty-five percent of students classified as low income. Beyond these numbers, I learned that the school is known citywide as a site where police clashed with anti-integration crowds in the 1960s; as a school that over time has failed to retain a sizable population from the town, which is 54 percent White; as a school that some local residents associated with a shooting that took place in a housing project next to the building in 1986; and although racially diverse, a school where one-fifth of the student body, Asian students in a bilingual program, are cloistered in their own classrooms and rarely interact with students of other races. The often tumultuous racial and historical backdrop of the school—which I delve into in further detail in the portrait of Bridge—and the evolving racial dynamics within Bridge and among community members were an important context within which to answer my final research question: *How was race explicitly addressed or not addressed during the implementation of restorative justice?*

That year, I was unexpectedly inspired to write a portrait in addition to those I would write about my two sites—that of Janet Connors, a community activist from the Dorchester neighborhood of Boston. A fellow at the Center for Restorative Justice, Janet facilitated healing circles on a weekly basis. Having grown up within the city limits of Boston herself and raised three children in BPS, I observed that Janet related to the students in an authentic and immediate way. When facilitating circles Janet is open about her intimate connection to the philosophy of restorative justice and its use as a response to crime: her son Joel was murdered at the age of 19, and she has met with two of the four men involved in his death. She teaches students that restorative justice is a philosophy that not only addresses schoolyard fights but brutal crimes. Along with Angela, she is integral to maintaining the momentum and consistent implementation of restorative justice at Bridge. She was also instrumental in facilitating circles at Equity High, which ultimately became my second research site. Her life story and experience seemed to warrant its own portrait for she speaks to the powerful, often untapped role community members can play in the implementation of educational initiatives. She helped me understand the necessity of multiple stakeholders in the restorative process to answer, *What roles do students, educators, parents and community members play in a school's transition to restorative justice?*

When I officially embarked on my research in the fall of 2009—my pilot study of SLC A the prior year had provided vital context and helped me hone my research questions—I continued observing Angela and Janet. This was despite the fact that SLC A was dissolved due to school restructuring. Angela planned to implement circles in Project Graduation, a new program at Bridge targeted at helping traditionally unsuccessful students recover their credits and graduate. Janet continued to train teachers and facilitate circles along the way.

PROJECT GRADUATION

Project Graduation serves approximately 60 students at Bridge, the majority of whom have failed at least one grade, been suspended or expelled from prior schools, and dropped out or have considered dropping out. The student population is in flux, but the majority of students are Black, followed by a small group of Latino students, the even smaller group of Asian students and approximately three White students. The staff is small, and racially diverse, consisting of; Angela, Program Coordinator Carol Warren, a biracial[5] woman from New York with a background in art therapy; Assistant Unit Leader Nancy Lincoln, an African American woman who started at Bridge as a paraprofessional, has a background in social work, and grew up in Boston; Lucy Reed, originally from California, a White woman who taught English alongside Angela in SLC A; William Johnston, an African American male math teacher of Caribbean descent who also grew up in Boston and Mary Spellman, a White woman who went from being the school secretary to a study skills teacher in the program. The classes and circles in this tightly knit program offered an authentic glimpse into the social dynamics at play during the implementation of restorative justice. But I still needed another site, one where I could forge an equally meaningful relationship with a key informant such as Angela, and where I could gain access to classrooms and embed myself in the culture.

SITE 2: EQUITY HIGH SCHOOL

I met Mark Cooper nearly a year after I met Angela, although I cannot remember how—the restorative justice community in Boston is small, and he could have been referred to me by Angela, Janet, or even Carolyn. A former lawyer, Mark worked at Equity High School, teaching students about the criminal justice system and restorative justice in an elective called Law and Justice. Equity was founded in 2004 in Boston through the advocacy and organizing of parents, students and educators who wanted to create an environment that would foster student activism and critical thinking. Funded by the Bill and Melinda Gates Foundation, administrators of the small school of 300 students and 25 teachers worked with community organizations and student researchers and volunteers at Northeastern University to implement restorative justice as an alternative to harsh discipline policies. Sixty percent of the students are Black, 34 percent are Hispanic, 4 percent are White, and 1 percent are Asian (Massachusetts Department of Education).

When I walked into Equity for the first time, I felt I was part of a community; the social justice orientation of the school, although not always implemented effectively across the curriculum, permeated throughout discussions I had with various educators, most notably with Principal Stephen Dobbs. Dobbs immediately affirmed my research by stating that there would be a reciprocal benefit between my work and the school—that my work would shed light on the progression of restorative justice at the school or at least provide some data for teachers and administrators to reflect on how they practice discipline. I felt deeply honored, and fortunate, to find a site that not only welcomed me but saw some benefits my presence. Posters of Martin Luther King, Jr., Malcolm X, Rosa Parks, Gandhi and other notable social activists adorned the walls of the main office. The school was formulated with an explicit vision of offering an innovative curriculum that included internships in the local community, a senior-year portfolio project, and student involvement in a peer justice system rooted in restorative practices. Because the bulk of the restorative justice work at the school occurs in the two law and justice classrooms, where students are trained in how to keep talking and healing circles, I approached both teachers of this course, Donna Flaherty and Roger Françoise. They ultimately became key informants and invited me to sit in on their classes. I observed them model circles for students and followed students as they kept circles with their peers when incidents arose.

I anticipated that exploring this apprenticeship model of restorative justice at Equity, and comparing and contrasting it with the community-wide implementation of talking circles in Project Graduation, would yield robust findings around the variety of restorative practices being used across the country. Project Graduation is a self-contained program working within the constraints of a larger school-wide reliance on zero tolerance, whereas Equity is attempting to implement restorative justice school wide—yet concentrates its efforts in an elective course. Project Graduation consists of students who have traditionally been disengaged and disenfranchised from schools, whereas Equity consists of a student body whose academic success varies widely. Looking at

Table 1 Descriptive Statistics of Schools, 2008–2009[6]

	African American students	Latino students	Asian students	White students	Dropout rate	Teachers of color
Bridge HS	42.5%	29.6%	21.2%	5.9%	25.6%	34%
Equity HS	57.2%	36.4%	0.9%	4.4%	31.9%	42%

these schools simultaneously would allow me to appreciate the strengths and challenges associated with multiple models of restorative justice.

RESEARCH DESIGN

From the fall of 2009 to the spring of 2010, I visited Equity and Bridge for more than 100 hours, spending two full days from September to May at each site: Mondays and Fridays at Equity and Wednesdays and Fridays at Bridge. Umbreit, Coates, and Vos (2007) note that due to the communitarian nature of restorative justice, "observers of circle processes also have to be participants," (p. 31) so I sat in on every circle where I was present, sans notebook, in an effort to respect the sacredness of the space and not intrude on the process by taking notes. I hoped also that this would help minimize reactivity, or "the influence of the researcher on the setting or individuals studied" (Maxwell, p. 108). To gain a holistic view of how restorative justice was utilized at both schools, I sat in on various classrooms—observing daily lessons and participating in circles (a total of 35 at Equity and 29 at Bridge)—as well as professional development sessions around restorative justice, jotting down various impressions: dialogue, descriptions of the physical setting, gestures, surprising moments, facial expressions and anything that seemed significant during social interactions. I also noted spontaneous conversations that occurred after school with teachers and students and interactions that occurred when I walked around to other parts of the building, whether spending free time in the library, introducing myself to people whose faces I began to recognize, standing around with students at their lockers after school, sitting in circles at an afterschool restorative justice club or giving students rides home.

Within hours of each visit I fleshed out these jottings into more coherent field notes and wrote what Lawrence-Lightfoot (1997) terms an "Impressionistic Record," a document in which the portraitist "gathers, scrutinizes, and organizes the data, and tries to make sense of what she has witnessed" (p. 187). The Impressionistic Record is similar to what other researchers have called "memos" (Charmaz, 2006; Maxwell, 2005; Strauss & Corbin, 1998) and "describes shifts in perspective, points to puzzles and dilemmas (methodological, conceptual, ethical) that need attention, and develops a plan of action for the next visit" (Lawrence-Lightfoot & Davis, 1997, p. 188). Before each visit, I read through and coded the prior visit's Impressionistic Record to see if new themes emerged as I read with fresher eyes. I used the constant comparison method (Charmaz, 2006; Glaser & Strauss, 1998) by engaging in an ongoing and iterative process of coding; specifically, I coded for etic themes such as *Conceptualization of RJ, Introduction of RJ, Training around RJ and PD (professional development) around RJ* that corresponded to my research questions and for emic themes as they arose from interviews and observations.

I did not approach anyone to be interviewed until a few months into the project and got the lay of the land at each site—both because I was not clear who I would need to speak to right away and so that I could build a sense of mutual trust before approaching potential participants. I began with the snowball method of sampling (Maykut & Morehouse, 1994), asking for referrals from key informants like Angela and Mark and then subsequently from each person I interviewed. I approached all teachers who used circles in their classrooms, casting a wide net, open to speaking to anyone who approached me and vocal about my willingness to hear a multitude of voices. I employed the strategy of "maximum variation sampling" (Maykut & Morehouse, 1994, p. 57), wherein people are chosen who "represent the range of experience on the phenomenon" of interest. This meant variety in both *who* I interviewed—including students, teachers, administrators,[7] and community members who participated in restorative practices—as well as *how* those participants viewed restorative justice. After all, I came to both schools by way of individuals who clearly supported restorative justice and was aware that I needed to search for "deviant voices" (Lawrence Lightfoot, 1997), or those that deviated from common scripts heard in the field—in this case, the narrative that consistently praised restorative justice. Deviant voices offer "an important version of the truth" that allowed me to shape a more holistic and authentic portrait of restorative practices at each school" (Lawrence-Lightfoot & Davis, 1997, p. 187).

Through interviews I deepened relationships with participants and heard them articulate their own understandings of restorative justice. I conducted interviews wherever participants were comfortable, including local eateries, the Museum of Fine Arts, and their homes. I interviewed teachers at local cafés or in classrooms during their off periods and scheduled formal appointments with school principals and interviewed them in their offices. I met Janet at school, a restaurant, and several times at her home so that we had more privacy in which to discuss the relationship between her life story and work in schools. In all I interviewed 38 participants—Janet; five teachers, four administrators, one school resource officer and eight students at Bridge; and five teachers, three administrators, and eleven students at Equity. I conducted at least one hour-long interview with each participant over the course of the year and sometimes followed up with one or two more structured or unstructured interviews. In addition to general questions about the school climate around discipline, I asked participants in depth about particular circles I sat in on with them, such as what expectations they had going in to the circle and how they felt about the process and outcomes. During interviews I began to understand the meaning participants were making of circles and how, if at all, circles were seen as shifting disciplinary paradigms at each school.

I also collected disciplinary reports, which include the number and nature of referrals for circles, suspensions and expulsions. In addition, I reviewed the district discipline code, each school's mission statement, and any materials disseminated about restorative justice (such as training documents or circle referral forms) to gain a fuller picture of the context in which restorative justice was being implemented at both sites.

CRAFTING AUTHENTIC PORTRAITS

Portraitists use the term *authenticity*, rather than validity, to define the measure of how accurately a portraitist interprets a phenomenon. Authenticity is the standard for portraitists who seek not only to engage in rigorous research but to do so within a narrative—or an "aesthetic whole"—that is convincing and creative and relies on the "principles of composition and form, rhythm, sequence, and metaphor" (Lawrence-Lightfoot, 1997, p. 12). A portrait that is authentic, then, should then achieve *resonance* as the reader, researcher and participant read the piece; they should feel a click of recognition and say to themselves, "Yes, of course," (p. 260).

Authenticity is achieved not only through building reciprocal research relationships or triangulating interviews, documents and observations: portraitists engage in constant rumination about how one's autobiography shapes her biases and interpretations of the data: "In portraiture, the voice of the researcher is everywhere: in the assumptions, preoccupations, and framework she brings to the inquiry; in the questions she asked; in the data she gathers; in the choice of stories she tells; in the language, cadence, and rhythm of her narrative" (Lawrence-Lightfoot, 1997, p. 85).

I wrote frequently about my identity as a South Asian woman, former teacher, and researcher from an Ivy League school. I worked with Black and Latino youth, and several racialized me as White, as when one student told me, "When I first met you, I thought you were just another White girl from Harvard." I tried judiciously to include such examples in the final portraits only to the extent that they were necessary to better understand the vantage point from which I was interpreting the data. At the same time, I tried to avoid navel-gazing and to ground my work in the data while making sure not to "overshadow the actors' voices" (p. 85).

Once I completed my fieldwork, I looked for patterns in my data consistent with portraiture's recommended modes of analysis. I documented repetitive phrases my participants used—such as *community* and *repairing harm*—that would help me answer how the participants interpreted the philosophy of restorative justice. I also mined the data for metaphors, institutional rituals and "dissonant themes" identified by actors in the field (Lawrence-Lightfoot & Davis, 1997, p. 193). The holistic portraits of each site would include "measurable indices" such as test scores and disciplinary records but would also pay close attention to the "people, structures, relationships, ideology, goals, intellectual substance, motivation, and will" associated with the transition toward restorative justice (Lawrence-Lightfoot, 1983, p. 23).

I hand coded all of my interview transcripts and Impressionistic Records twice, sometimes three times, over the course of a year. Then I created a coding matrix in which I listed and defined etic and emic codes in one column and matched them with corresponding excerpts from all my transcripts in the other column. In this way I was able to identify emergent themes—those with multiple pieces of evidence and those representative of deviant voices— at each individual site and across both sites. I then distilled the most salient themes into a codebook, where I solidified the definition for each code and included subcodes which seemed to address multiple dimensions of each theme.

I first wrote my portrait of Janet. Without her, restorative justice may not have been implemented as deeply as it was at both sites; she was not always paid for her time, but she was committed to working with teachers and young people from the community, and the way circles are implemented has been shaped largely by her biography and training. I then wrote the other portraits, of Bridge and Equity, providing participants with drafts to solicit feedback and confirm the authenticity of the piece—with the understanding that the ultimate product was mine and that their suggestions, while valued, would not dictate the final version. I also shared my coding, Impressionistic Records, identity memos, and multiple drafts of the portraits with a group of colleagues well versed in qualitative research. The feedback from the group and my participants allowed me to view the data from other perspectives, to strengthen my arguments and ultimately, I believe, craft more authentic portraits. Feedback from restorative justice expert Dr. Brenda Morrison, race expert Dr. Mica Pollock and Dr. Lawrence Lightfoot, in particular, helped me bring more coherence and aesthetic shape to the work.

A PERSONAL NOTE: RECLAIMING MY VOICE THROUGH PORTRAITURE

One need not be an artist to engage in portraiture. But as someone with an MFA in creative writing who is also trained in scholarly writing, I have struggled over the years to maintain a love of the written word or rather a love of *my* written words, and to ignore the critical voice I gained in graduate school, the noise in my head that doubted every sentence and paragraph I wrote. The methodology of portraiture encouraged me to merge all the training I have received in various types of writing, both academic and creative, and demanded that I bridge art with science.

My process was clumsy. Sometimes I veered too far in the direction of art, writing an initial portrait of Janet that read more like oral history than empirical science. Other times I reverted to the dry, formulaic structure of traditional research, expunging my positionality and autobiography almost entirely and losing my own voice. As much as this book is primarily focused on the voices of the young people and educators I came to know over the course of two years. portraiture allowed me to realize that I could not do them justice, or engage in authentic and systematic data collection, without claiming my voice, both as a participant and observer in the field and on the page.

I am grateful, then, that portraiture has provided me the unique opportunity to once again play with language, savor words, and slowly build a cohesive narrative as I add my voice to the voices of the actors in this study. It is through this "cacophony of voices" (Lawrence-Lightfoot, 1997) that the reader can determine his or her own interpretation of how restorative justice is enacted in urban schools. I may have looked at only two schools and one restorative justice trainer, but their stories will feel familiar to anyone who has taught in urban schools or worked with young people. As Lawrence-Lightfoot (1997) proclaims not only in her writing, but in her teachings, "In the particular resides the general" (p. 14). Through the deliberate, thick descriptions of Bridge, Janet and Equity, the particular truths that emerge reveal lessons—if not generalizable, singular truths, then conclusions that may resonate with actors in other settings. Through physical descriptors, verbs, metaphors and sensory details, I am beginning to reclaim my voice and, in concert with the voices of participants, have aimed to write a book that "may play a critical role in shaping educational practice and inspiring organizational change," (Lawrence-Lightfoot, 1984) not only at my research sites but at other urban schools in the country.

NOTES

1. Morrison, Blood, & Thorsborne (2006) posit that it takes three to five years for school to make a shift toward a more restorative school culture.
2. In 2009, this project received permission from BPS' Office of Research, Assessment and Evaluation.
3. With the exception of Janet Connors (introduced later in the chapter), Martin Garcia, Susan Maze-Rothstein, her daughter Shana, and Carolyn Boyes-Watson, all names of people and sites in this study are pseudonyms.
4. A small learning community (SLC) is a school within a school in which students have a more personalized learning environment and share the same teachers (Cotton, 2001).
5. As much as possible, racial signifiers were provided by participants.
6. Boston Public Schools, 2009.
7. While I wanted to interview parents, they were largely not present in circles. I rarely saw them except for the times they were called in for healing circles that involved their children, an occurrence I witnessed only twice.

4 "Evolution, not Revolution"
Restorative Justice from the Ground Up

"Every revolution was first a thought in one man's mind."
—*Ralph Waldo Emerson*

"You can never have a revolution in order to establish a democracy. You must have a democracy in order to have a revolution."
—*G. K. Chesterton*

Rebecca Stern, administrative leader of one of five small learning communities (SLCs) at Bridge High School (BHS), looks up and smiles, admitting, "I almost forgot about you . . ." She is a thin, middle-aged White woman with an oblong face framed by wispy bangs and auburn hair. When I enter her rectangular, spacious office, she seems strangely distant, seated at a desk by the back wall, her fingers perched on a keyboard, eyes fixed on a computer screen. Casually dressed in gray pants, a maroon turtleneck, barely conspicuous earrings and a conservative jade necklace, she could easily blend in as a teacher. Only the weighty walkie-talkie she constantly carries in her delicate hands reveals her administrative status. The room resembles a prison cell in several ways: the painted cement block walls, fluorescent lights glaring onto a linoleum floor and, to the right of Rebecca's desk, a long rectangular window grated with thin, black lines. But in the midst of the oppressive space, Rebecca's personal and intellectual investments in her students intersect in a variety of artifacts. Lime-green, metal shelves drilled to the wall are filled with books and periodicals on pedagogy, such as *Rethinking Schools* and *Skillful Teacher*, as well as photos of her husband and daughters. I turn and glimpse a bulletin board filled with images of Rebecca's *other* children—pocket-sized prom and graduation pictures of her students. Teenagers trail in and out of Rebecca's office, saying hello, using her printer, or partaking of snacks.

Rebecca does not typify the stereotype of a revolutionary who leads the masses with a fist pumped in the air; she speaks in measured tones and facilitates discussions in staff meetings in a reasoned, sometimes even tentative manner. Yet she ignited the movement toward restorative justice at BHS in

2003 after witnessing something she had never seen in her 20-plus years in education: a suspension rate of epic proportions. Though she had taught, counseled, and consulted in numerous elementary, middle and high schools in Boston, she says, "Truthfully, I don't think I was ever in a suspension hearing. I don't think I had ever been in one."

Teachers at BHS were bringing students to her office on a regular basis, pressing her to send them home. She frequently saw clumps of hair on the hallway floors after fights between female students. "My first year here as administrator, I was really in shock when I saw how many kids were getting suspended. It was pretty much all I ever did." Through a friend, she met Carolyn Boyes-Watson, director of the Center for Restorative Justice at Suffolk University. Carolyn told Rebecca about a promising new practice being used in place of suspension—restorative justice. "Then I thought," says Rebecca, "wait a second, I've got to bring this over here. I just have to because the suspension stuff—we're going crazy here."

Initially, Rebecca did not feel there was enough critical mass to try an alternative to suspensions because she had difficulty relating to the teachers in her SLC. "The teachers were always bringing me kids to be suspended, and all the teachers in that [SLC] were very, very close. They could look at one another, and they knew exactly what they were thinking, and I felt very much out of it. I was not in sync with them at all." It was not until 2006, when Rebecca was moved to another SLC after a school restructuring, that she found an ally and catalyst for the work: second-year teacher Angela Temple, who was just as disturbed by the remarkably frequent use of suspensions and eager to try something new. A White woman in her late 20s, Angela exudes an electric energy when talking about restorative justice. Approximately five foot four, she is an attractive woman with wavy, shoulder-length brown hair that she often places behind her ears. Her chestnut colored eyes sparkle when she grins, and the apples of her full, flushed cheeks round out her smile. A graduate of an intensive and competitive teacher training program called the Boston Teacher Residency (BTR), Angela remembers that during her first year teaching at BHS, several students were habitually suspended; she was particularly concerned because so many of the students were Black boys and because suspensions seemed to spiral into actions that ultimately push students out of school:

> If you're suspended enough times, you get expelled. If you're expelled enough times you can't even go to school anymore. There's this ladder of discipline and it just keeps intensifying and the idea is you got to stop cold turkey what you're doing—even though [suspension hasn't] really resolved anything—or you're going to have this punishment. Restorative [justice] is just the opposite of that.

After a challenging first year teaching during which she says she was "burning out quickly and needed some space," she took a year off and worked at an organization called the Urban Teacher Residencies United. The hiatus allowed Angela to research alternatives to zero tolerance, and she read about how restorative justice was improving school climates across the country.

The following school year Angela introduced circles in her classroom as a first step to trying restorative practices. English teacher Lucy Reed, also a graduate and member of the same cohort of BTR, worked in the classroom adjacent to Angela's. Collaborating with Angela on this new endeavor came naturally to Lucy, who had worked with and befriended Angela early on in their experiences at the BTR. Lucy explicitly chose BTR because of its focus on urban education. She tutored young people at a juvenile hall in San Diego and says her experience with incarcerated teens shaped her desire to teach in city schools. "[I worked with] adolescents and especially males of color . . . I loved working with them." When Rebecca invited Carolyn to SLC A to train teachers in restorative justice, the concept was not entirely new to her. "When I worked at the juvenile hall we had a lot of training. It was in some ways to engage teenagers, but they talked a lot about [students'] mistrust of adults, especially white adults, and they talked a lot about how to help them repair trust with adults they don't know and trust with society and that's when the first ideas came through." Lucy's acceptance of restorative practices was likely linked to a number of factors: her already strong relationships with Rebecca and Angela and faith in their ideas, her preexisting exposure to practices to help students repair relationships, and perhaps the inherently intuitive nature of the practice as an alternative to, as Lucy puts it, "punitive punishments that weren't working."

Lucy and Angela used circles to check in about how students were feeling about school or to talk about topics such as love and loss, and the experience allowed students to deepen relationships among one another and with their teachers. Both women modeled how to be in circle by sharing parts of their lives that were not necessarily linked to their identities as teachers; in response, many students began to share their experiences outside of the classroom. For example, during one circle, Angela broke down crying and revealed that her grandfather had died over the weekend:

> We had check-in rounds and I just started talking about it, and all of a sudden I just got so upset, and I was like, "It's so hard to transition from Sunday. I'm with my family and we're all in this grieving process, and then all of the sudden I have to be back at school." One of the students came over and gave me a hug, and everyone went around and talked about how they were feeling about things, and everybody was sort of having a bad week, and things came up. One girl's mother had died when she was young and it was her birthday, and people had a lot of weight on their chests that came up.

Having this context helped Angela to understand her students' lives outside of school, which allowed her to better understand their behaviors within the walls of her classroom. Rebecca used circles with two groups of girls who had formerly been friends yet seemed perpetually locked in conflict with one another.

Through the use of circles, says Angela, SLC A achieved the highest attendance rate and the lowest suspension rate in the school. Moreover, there was not a single physical fight among girls for the rest of the year. "We can't prove a causal relationship between circles and these outcomes," she admits, "but we definitely think there's a huge correlation there." Rebecca says although ninth grade is usually a big year for fights, "I don't think we had one [fight], so it was kind of amazing. I'm not saying it was just because of the circles . . . But the circle piece was in the mix. That really convinced me; we have got to continue doing this." Rebecca's continued commitment to piloting restorative justice was spurred on by Angela's dedication to using circles in her own classroom: "I felt like her energy and her positive way of thinking about it, and her feeling that this was such a good thing for the kids—it energized me to keep pushing." She acknowledges that the support of Angela and Lucy was essential in getting the buy-in of other teachers. "If teachers weren't really into it, there wouldn't be much I could do. I could still push a little, but not with the enthusiasm that I wanted to, and not with the success, because you can't force people to do something that they really don't want." Rebecca's assertion that you can't "force people to do something that they really don't want" speaks to the importance of bottom-up, teacher-led initiatives. But her support of the implementation of restorative justice also speaks to the strength of symbiotic relationships between school leaders and teachers: Angela relied on Rebecca's leadership to promote and organize circles to resolve conflicts, and Rebecca relied on Angela's expertise as a practitioner to help sway other teachers in the SLC to try circles in their classes.

CREATING A RESTORATIVE SCHOOL CULTURE

Thus the models teachers and administrators can use to shift paradigms of discipline depend on how they view culture change. Is it the case, as Ralph Waldo Emerson states, that only one person like Angela Temple is necessary to spark revolutionary change? Does one, as Chesterton and Rebecca Stern imply, need some consensus among people to ignite a revolution? The situation at BHS seems to indicate that the reality is a little bit of both.

In this portrait I focus on the challenges of creating whole-school culture change around restorative justice. On the one hand, bottom-up implementation of the philosophy in one part of the school—in this case, one SLC— offered a small group of teachers freedom to cater restorative practices and responses to the individual needs of their students. On the other hand, in a school already strapped for resources, demanding that teachers take on the onus of spearheading such a reform meant that the *restorative discipline feedback loop*[1]—comprised of the necessary pairing of *talking* and *healing* circles to maximize the success of restorative practices—could not be closed. When working against the backdrop of a larger. punitive school-wide culture, the enactment of restorative justice was undermined when matters that could have been handled restoratively were handled in a punitive way. Nonetheless, even the partial implementation of restorative justice through talking circles had the capability to transform relationships between teachers and students.

Before engaging in the details of the multiyear efforts to implement restorative justice at the school, I begin by delineating the history of BHS, one fraught with racial tension since the era of forced busing. I then trace the evolution of restorative practices as practiced by a small group of practitioners. Finally, I discuss the strengths and challenges of transitioning an entire school toward a restorative discipline model from the ground up, in one small pocket of a school steeped in a traditional, punitive model of discipline.

THE EVOLUTION OF BRIDGE HIGH SCHOOL

Founded in 1845, BHS is located in Bridgeport, a part of Boston with a legacy of contentious race relations famously on display during school busing orders in the 1970s. Busing was introduced in response to the federal mandate to desegregate schools, and students of color from other parts of Boston were forced to ride the bus to Bridgeport, which was then a largely working-class Irish American community with a notable mob presence. Surrounded by hundreds of police officers, residents protested desegregation in large, sometimes violent crowds around BHS. The small number of Black students bussed to the school were hassled by students who wrote slurs such as "white power" and "buses for Zulu" on walls, lockers and desks. Individuals were bullied and beaten up in stairwells. In one especially notorious incident, a Black student was beaten up by a group of White boys. Clusters of young men of both races joined the melee, which surged down a lengthy hallway. Though four Whites were arrested for assault and battery, the school's discipline policy mandated that participants from both sides of any fight be punished, so several of the Black students were suspended as well. Research is now beginning to highlight how Black students receive more severe punishments than their White counterparts, but reading about this famed fight brought home the fact that such a pattern has existed in schools for decades.

I soon discovered that the BHS I would visit was not the same site where these historic events occurred. BHS has occupied three different buildings, and busing took place at the second one. Nonetheless, I anticipated that the legacy of that era might well permeate the racial climate in the school and the surrounding neighborhood. Indeed, Angela tells me that the prior year, she met with a White parent from the neighborhood who told her that the majority of students in the school acted like animals. However, this is the only example of any overt racism I have been told about.

Opened in 1978, the current school is a towering, five-story, red brick building bordered on four sides by a cemetery, small homes, boxy brown housing projects, and an expansive football field and track. Because of its proximity to downtown Boston, Bridgeport has experienced two waves of gentrification: first in the early 1980s and again in the late 1990s as commuters moved into renovated row houses. Currently, Bridgeport consists of a large number of working-class Irish Americans, middle- and upper-class professionals, and families of many races who reside in government housing. More than three quarters of the town is White, 12 percent is Latino, 5 percent is Asian, and 4 percent is African American. Due to busing, students commute from all over the city, sometimes traveling more than an hour to and from school. But the disconnect between the school and the surrounding community is clear: only 8 percent of students at BHS reside in Bridgeport. The director of an after-school program at the school says that students in the area "don't even think about going" to BHS. One parent attempting to recruit more local residents to attend says that people feel there is a "sense of chaos" there, especially after two students were involved in a shooting outside of the school in 2006.

BHS Principal Patricia Beatty arrived at the school that very year and acknowledges the school was "in chaotic shape." According to a school police officer, it was common for students to feel threatened en route to campus. He says, "It was horrible. There was always larceny, fights, people getting beat up on the way to school." Once, a 357 magnum was discovered in the school gym. After the shooting in 2006, the school installed cameras and metal detectors. School police officers worked with the Boston Police Department to arrest gang members in the nearby housing project. As a result safety at BHS and surrounding areas has increased dramatically, although the detectors are not foolproof; students who come in after the morning hours can enter without going through metal detectors, which are unmanned in the middle of the day.

Walking around the school and observing interactions among students and among students and teachers, I never feel any such sense of chaos or any palpable racial tension. But that does not necessarily mean that there are not hints of potential strains under the surface. Fifty-one percent of the population at BHS is Black, 23 percent is Latino, and 8 percent is White (BPS). Chinese immigrant students, who comprise 18 percent of the student body, primarily interact with one another in the same part of the building to receive Sheltered English Instruction.[2] In 2006 when Angela and Rebecca first piloted restorative justice, the rest of the student body was randomly assigned to one of four SLCs (A, B, C and D). The SLCs were not explicitly built on any particular themes, and each had its own administrative leader. I have heard that a few Black and Latino students, some of whom Angela has taught, have bullied or robbed students from the Chinese bilingual SLC. BHS Principal Patricia Beatty says she is uncertain whether these incidents are racially motivated: "It may be that [robbery] happens with other kids, and they just don't report it, whereas the Chinese students have reported it. Overall, it's not as though there's seething [racial] tension at all, and I think there's a lot of collaboration and goodwill and interest." Nonetheless, it seems clear to Angela that there is much work to be done around cross-racial communication. She would like to use restorative justice to "maybe have a circle with the Chinese bilingual unit to think about what they're feeling how stereotypes are perpetuated."

BHS's academic achievements are far from stellar. According to the Massachusetts Department of Education, 43.3 percent of students at BHS graduated in 2009, as opposed to the statewide average of 61.4 percent.[3] Although SLC A had the highest attendance rate in the school in 2006, BHS as a whole suffers from absenteeism. In 2008 and 2009, 83 percent of students were present on average, as opposed to the statewide average of 91.2 percent. The Massachusetts Department of Education states that 3.8 percent of BHS students received out-of-school suspension that year, which falls below the statewide average of 6 percent. Only a year earlier, however, the school reported having an 11.6 percent out-of-school suspension rate. Because of the stark variance between the figures for these two years, I am skeptical about the accuracy of these numbers, especially because data collection around school suspension rates often underestimates the amount of students who are sent out of school for disciplinary reasons (National Economic & Social Rights Initiative, 2012). In fact, the one time that Rebecca signed me into the computer system where suspension data at BHS is documented, the previous month's log showed that only one student had been suspended in the whole school—a figure that seemed unlikely given that I knew of two students in SLC A alone who had been suspended that very week. Rebecca says that when she logged into the system, she would often see a full page of suspension hearings from an SLC that mandated a one-day suspension for every student who skipped class. "But then they were not counted as suspensions. Actually [we were told] . . . if you suspend a student for one day, don't bother doing the paperwork," unless the suspension is "two or more days." And even though third-year BHS Principal Patricia Beatty believes suspensions such as these are largely ineffective, she has struggled with how best to implement disciplinary reform in a top-down manner while still providing what she calls a "restorative approach" to leading the school.

Top-Down Support: The Restorative Leadership of Principal Patricia Beatty

Acts of blatant violence at BHS have not occurred since the shooting in 2006, mainly because of an increased school security presence. Yet Principal Patricia Beatty is acutely aware of the impact of community violence on the behavior of her students as well as the need to address misbehaviors through options other than suspension. Patricia intuitively supported restorative justice upon learning about the philosophy and practice from Rebecca and Angela: "I really believe in it. I really think that schools are full of conflicts and I don't see conflict as bad. . . . I think restorative justice is a really constructive structure for working out conflicts." In fact, Patricia tells me she has used circles to mediate conflicts when students are sent to her office. "Things that end up in my office tend to be serious student issues . . . [Circle has] been very effective in terms of when we have a student, teacher or parent. Everybody's got a different point of view, a different take on the situation, and everybody goes around, and I'm glad I have a circular table because I use it."

Despite her interest in cultivating a restorative school environment, she did not automatically mandate that the school substitute suspensions with circles. Given the failure of past required professional development sessions— she says that teachers who were not interested in a session on cultural competency ultimately did not use the curriculum—Patricia feels top-down directives are ineffective. Teachers are not moved to act on reforms that "they didn't invent, they didn't construct, they didn't buy into, [and that] they didn't have a voice in." Rather, if teachers in the building want restorative justice, she hopes to see the work spread organically throughout the building, much in the same way it gained traction in SLC A—slowly, with buy-in from one administrator and one teacher and eventually other teachers. Moreover, she believes that by the very definition of restorative justice, she is not in a position to impose any kind of radical disciplinary change:

> I'm an evolution not revolution person . . . I'm trying to take a restorative approach to changing the building and that means giving teachers voice and giving teachers opportunities to be reflective and to work with each other and to trust that. That's what restorative justice says. Restorative justice says if you give students a safe, well-structured opportunity to be reflective about what they did, they'll do the right thing in almost all cases. In a way I'm trying to take that approach to the building. What I know is that telling teachers they have to do things, even if I think they're the right things, isn't going to result in constructive change.

Her disagreement with a top-down approach emphasizes her respect for both the philosophy of restorative justice and the autonomy of teachers to decide what discipline should look like in their classrooms. She says she would strongly support a top-down movement through school-wide professional development around restorative justice only if it can "unfold out of work and practice in the teaching and learning community. It can't just come out of my office: 'You will do circles.'"

And so, the work of restorative justice at BHS unfolded from the ground up in SLC A, over three years of implementation, when practitioners attempted to follow a model of restorative discipline that was ultimately constrained by a limited infrastructure.

THE FIRST YEARS: INFRASTRUCTURE AND THE RESTORATIVE DISCIPLINE FEEDBACK LOOP

One benefit of the small-scale evolution of restorative justice at BHS was that practitioners in SLC A could cater their model of discipline to their specific needs and resources. It was their collaboration that led to a model of discipline where *talking* circles laid the necessary groundwork for *healing* circles in what I call the restorative discipline feedback loop (see Figure 4.1), a heuristic that represents the necessary pairing of both circles to fully implement the principles of restorative justice. Carolyn Boyes-Watson of the Center for Restorative Justice tells me that talking circles must work in tandem with healing circles to achieve the greatest possible impact on school culture:

> You have to do both [talking and healing circles]. You can't do one or the other. So if you're just doing it for discipline, then you're not really building the kind of bonds and connections that you need to, including having [talking] circles that talk at the underlying level of what—how do we live together? . . . And then you need to use the same process for when things go wrong. You can't have one without the other, and you just need both. And schools that only choose one or the other don't get anywhere; they don't make significant change. You have to do both; otherwise, you're really just tinkering at the margins.

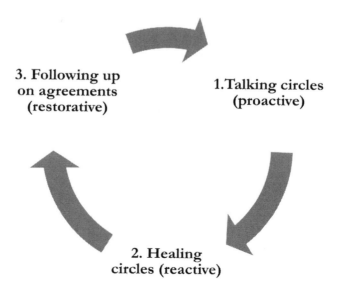

Figure 4.1   The Restorative Discipline Feedback Loop

As Carolyn notes, talking circles provide the foundation for restorative justice because they help "build the kind of bonds and connections" necessary for students and teachers to coexist peacefully. Intentionally building such community is an essential, *proactive* step of restorative practices that helps participants understand their commonalities: "The perspectives, facts and stories shared in the circle cultivate empathy and influence behavior" (Costello, Wachtel, & Wachtel, 2010, p. 23). Talking circles are also considered preventative because they reduce the likelihood of conflicts among participants. Says Lucy, "I feel I see a lot more of thinking before acting, and I think it's because [students] know each other better. Because when you don't really know someone, what are you going to stop and think about?" Moreover, talking circles are foundational because one cannot be restored back to a community that was never cultivated in the first place.

When harm occurred in SLC A, the parties involved in the conflict participated in the second part of the restorative discipline feedback loop, a *healing circle,*[4] or what Costello et al. (2010) define as a *responsive* circle, which forces students to reflect on a problem in a class or a relationship and make a commitment to repairing the harm. Such problems can include physical or verbal fights, skipping, tardiness, bullying and theft. Healing circles can involve an entire class or be confined to a few students. To ensure the success of the discipline feedback loop and create buy-in for restorative justice, the staff used a variety of approaches to professionally develop students and teachers around the philosophy, including curriculum, teaching circles, role plays and documentation. How they used these myriad tools provides lessons for educators seeking to implement restorative discipline—especially those working in isolation in schools steeped in punitive practices.

Laying the foundation: Curriculum. Before implementing the restorative discipline feedback loop, Angela and Lucy worked to make the philosophy explicit to their students and colleagues. Prior to introducing circles, Angela and Lucy taught an entire unit on the school-to-prison pipeline and restorative justice at the beginning of the school year to acclimate students to the disciplinary philosophy of SLC A. During this unit, Angela posted a small whiteboard with the definition of restorative justice: "a process through which a community heals and makes things right after someone has been harmed." She fleshed out the multiple dimensions of the philosophy through written assignments. For example, during a Do Now—the first activity that students in Angela's class complete upon sitting down—students were expected to define the restorative vocabulary underlined in the following passage:

> In order to uphold our classroom's *principles*, students need to follow certain *guidelines* such as to not interrupt each other and stay on topic. If a student chooses not to honor the classroom's *guidelines*, we will have a *circle*, where we will bring various members of the community to

discuss the *consequence* for his or her behavior. It is important that we hold each other *accountable* when we make mistakes. Our goal is not to *suspend* students but to figure out a way to resolve the conflict with *compassion* and understanding.

Such exercises not only strengthened students' vocabularies but also offered an efficient way to expose them to both the norms of her classroom and the principles of restorative justice.

Teaching circles. After introducing students to restorative terminology, Lucy and Angela used circles to reinforce the curriculum around restorative justice. Restorative practitioners Costello et al. (2010) describe such *teaching circles* as a "versatile technique" that can be used for "not only increasing student ownership in the classroom, but also to effectively administer curriculum" (p. 25). Lucy and Angela used teaching circles to facilitate discussions around why restorative justice was being practiced in SLC A. Students prepared for one such circle by answering the following during a Do Now:

1. What kinds of behaviors earn you a suspension in school?
2. Why do you think schools give suspensions as a consequence?
3. Does using suspension help students understand and learn from their behavior?
4. What else could the school do to resolve a conflict or address the behaviors that result in suspension?
5. How important do you think forgiveness is in resolving conflicts among students?

Angela used these questions to help students understand why their teachers were trying to rely less on punitive punishments like suspension and followed up by discussing how students of color were disproportionately punished when compared to White students. Through these teaching circles and curricular activities, students received at minimum a rudimentary knowledge of restorative justice and the context in which it is being practiced in urban schools across the country.

Professional development for teachers through role play. Restorative justice continued to evolve from the bottom up as Angela and Rebecca invited outside practitioners to professionally develop teachers in SLC A. Carolyn and a fellow from the Center for Restorative Justice, Janet Connors,[5] used role plays to model how to facilitate healing circles. In one of the first such professional development sessions, Carolyn apprentices teachers during their common planning time through a role play before an actual healing circle:

Six teachers, Carolyn, Janet, and I meet in Lucy's classroom and place our chairs in a circle. Carolyn takes on the role of the keeper. She begins by saying that we are sitting in a circle to identify a harm, discuss what can be done to repair it and then try to understand "how can we involve everyone to prevent" such a harm from happening again. She models the need to identify how people may be feeling in the moment in such a format and clarifies the expectations of circle. "I know this is difficult . . . I think it takes a lot of courage to be here . . . I want to emphasize that the purpose of the circle is not to decide whether someone is a good or bad person." She expects everyone to "speak respectfully and listen respectfully" and says that you may only say something if you have the talking piece in your hand.

After introductions Angela recounts the disciplinary incident. "I know that someone was yelling in the room. Timothy had been arguing with some boys, and I saw Jerome teasing him. Timothy was really upset . . . So I called on students to find out what happened. But it was the end of class."

Carolyn asks, "Can you talk about what happened after?" Before leaving class Jerome handed Angela an empty bottle of hand sanitizer with no explanation. She walked up to Timothy and found him yelling that someone had poured the substance inside his backpack.

Carolyn passes the talking piece and asks each participant to discuss what happened from their point of view. The teachers acting as Timothy and Jerome inhabit their roles with humor and an uncanny familiarity with their pupils, anticipating the challenges of conducting circle with students who may not want to participate or own up to their behaviors. Algebra teacher Simone Forrester plays Timothy. When she gets the piece, she crosses her arms. "I don't want to have to come to these stupid circles. Someone took my backpack and dumped that hand stuff in it. I just don't want people to touch my stuff."

History teacher Jack Jones plays Jerome. He slumps down in his chair and says, "I don't wanna snitch."

Carolyn follows up by asking participants, "So from your perspective, what is the hardest thing about this?"

Jerome passes the piece, shrugging and saying nothing. Rebecca, who plays Joseph's mother, says, "I want to be assured that this won't happen again. I work hard to buy things for my son, and no one should be touching anything that doesn't belong to them."

After the role play, teachers debrief about their concerns on the process. Jayna Phillips, an administrator from the upper school,[6] says she is concerned parents may feel circles are not responsive enough to their concerns. "We have some crazy parents," she says. "They may be expecting us to suspend to make things right. They don't know what we're trying to do."

Rebecca says, "I don't know that suspending someone would make things right."

Jack Johnson, who played Jerome, nods. "A lot of kids will flat out deny things." He's unsure whether students will follow up on agreements. "What if they say they're going to do something and they don't do anything?"

Rebecca emphasizes that there is value in the process regardless of the outcome. "It's important for the boys—whether they admit it or not—to hear that it [their behavior] had all kinds of consequences."

The role play involves stakeholders in the circle process and communicates key restorative principles: how to separate individuals from their acts and how to use an entire community to keep one another accountable for harm. The debrief allows teachers to openly discuss the shortcomings of, and any skepticism about, the process. Jayna points out parents "don't know" what SLC A is "trying to do," bringing to light how their professional development efforts have left out an important constituency: families. Even though she believes parents may be "expecting us to suspend," Rebecca hints at her vision for discipline in the community by saying suspension does not necessarily make a situation right. The conversation opens up many important questions for the continued implementation of restorative justice and provides a good starting point for future discussions the staff needs to have about having a common vision around discipline, including whether and how to include parents in circle implementation and whether and when suspension is appropriate. In the end the role play leaves a fair amount of room for teachers to question the process, learn from restorative practitioners, and buy in to the practice over time as they become exposed to sitting in actual healing circles the rest of the year.

Sustainability. Given the overwhelming amount of work teachers dealt with on a daily basis—and given that these teachers were working on their own without administrative support from the top—there needed to be a system to handle disciplinary incidents in the most time-efficient way. Angela addressed Jack's concerns about student accountability by creating formal documents to be completed before and after each healing circle. Prior to a healing circle, participants were expected to complete a Preparation Document created by Angela by answering the following questions:

1. Describe the incident from your perspective.
2. Describe what you were thinking or feeling during the incident.
3. Why do you think this incident happened? What is the root cause?
4. What might be the other person's understanding of why the incident happened?
5. What could you have done differently to resolve the conflict in a better way?
6. What are three possible ways you can make the situation better now?

The questions were intended to prompt students to reflect on the deeper roots of their own behaviors and engage in perspective taking to understand how other participants may have perceived the conflict. After the circle, students were also expected to fill out a Follow-Up Document, also written by Angela, in which they proposed solutions and answered the following:

1. What are each participant's next steps and responsibilities?
2. How will we hold each other accountable for each of these steps?
3. Date/s that Rebecca followed up with all people involved in the conflict: __/__/__

In step three of the restorative discipline feedback loop, Rebecca was responsible for checking in with students to ensure they had completed their agreements. Once a student repaired the harm, she was considered officially restored back to the community as the third and final part of the restorative discipline feedback loop. She continued to participate in talking circles, strengthening relationships with peers and teachers, thus perpetuating the cycle of restorative justice.

Challenges with infrastructure. One of the major challenges of implementing restorative justice from the ground up was a lack of infrastructure needed to follow through on step three of the feedback loop: checking in with students to ensure that they were keeping to their agreements. This was a labor- and time-intensive step that demanded that someone schedule each individual healing circle, contact all parties in the conflict to ensure they would be present, and maintain a paper trail that included the Preparation and Follow-Up Documents. In addition to handling healing circles and suspensions, Rebecca spent many hours on in-school suspension (ISS). When students were referred to ISS, she had to work with their content teachers to collect assignments, hand them to students, and turn them back in at the end of each day. "Literally ISS has driven us crazy," she tells me. During a staff meeting with SLC A in the fall of 2008, Rebecca expressed frustration with planning and maintaining healing circles on her own: "We always start things and let them go. It's been really hard to be consistent." For example, though some students did fill out the Preparation Document, I rarely saw students fill out a Follow-Up Document and never saw a circle in which Rebecca met with students to confirm whether students had kept to their agreements. This was not necessarily problematic; sometimes she checked in with students informally, conflicts resolved themselves naturally or an agreement involved nothing more than a simple apology. But the fact that staff relied so heavily on Janet to come in once a week to help resolve conflicts signaled a lack of internal capacity to plan and follow up on healing circles.

Says Angela, "Until you have the infrastructure to do [healing circles], it's really hard."

For Rebecca an ideal infrastructure would include hiring outside practitioners such as Janet to plan healing circles and follow up on agreements on a full-time basis. Janet concurs that schools must have a full-time person to carry out the work and complete the restorative discipline feedback loop. "It doesn't work for me as someone who's there one day a week or two days a week to be the person who keeps the agreements." But Rebecca feels that having Janet come even just once a week has played a vital role in sustaining healing circles, however imperfect they sometimes are:

I think having someone from the outside with a schedule made it a lot easier for us to actually implement, on a regular basis, the [healing circles]. Before that I think, in previous years, we had been relying on ourselves and everyone had so many other responsibilities that it was easy for us just to say oh, we can't do it today . . . But when you have someone who takes that on as their role, their responsibility, the day, even unknowingly, they really push that effort forward and this was really important for us.

Carolyn's view of sustainability contrasts with those of the staff in SLC A—she believes that once restorative practices are introduced and supported from the outside, teachers need to take ownership of the process themselves. "I mean Janet could hold [the process] for a little while, but then schools need to take it over themselves." Janet is concerned that if students are not held to their agreements, it can make a "sham" of the healing circle process and further perpetuate the misperception that restorative justice simply allows those who commit harm to express remorse without following through with concrete actions to right a situation. Moreover, she believes administrators who handle disciplinary matters should be the very people to hold students accountable. "If they have people who are doing discipline in schools, it makes sense for those people to be doing restorative discipline . . . really if you have managed to avoid a suspension by having some agreements to keep, then those should be kept."

Angela acknowledges it is difficult to sustain restorative practices when depending so much on outside staff. "It's so hard to rely on Janet because if she's not there, we can't do [healing circles]." Yet as committed as Angela is to a restorative school culture, she says that building a movement from the ground up necessitates *some* outside support—if not from the principal, then from additional staff. "I can't be a teacher and run a restorative justice program. My job is so much time as it is, and I think I've been a little protective of my time because I'm trying to make it through myself."

Another challenge to the continued implementation of restorative justice was the reorganization, once again, of the entire school in the spring of 2009. SLC A was dissolved to create learning academies for ninth and tenth graders, and the work around restorative justice was exported to a small new program of 60 students. Project Graduation, a program that has been implemented in schools across the country, was piloted at BHS to address the needs of students who have failed at least one grade level and have consistently been unsuccessful in school or are on the verge of dropping out. Principal Beatty approached Angela and Lucy, whom she considered exemplary teachers, to teach in and help shape the program. The women agreed to work in the program because of its orientation toward serving youth who wanted, and needed, an alternative form of education. Through the use of online credit recovery, smaller classes, and more personalized curricula, students progress from grade to grade at an accelerated rate.

For Principal Patricia Beatty, the program created a pathway in the school for students who she calls "overage" and "under credited" given their grade level. "Most of the students have been very unsuccessful for a range of reasons: social and emotional. I think more social and emotional than academic both because they're academically behind and because they have other issues that are keeping them from being successful." Angela and Lucy spoke to Patricia at length about their desire to implement restorative practices in the program to address these social and emotional needs. Once again, they would have the autonomy and freedom to implement restorative justice however they wanted in this specific context.

When I ask Rebecca how she plans to move the entire building toward a more restorative culture, she says simply, "I think supporting Project Graduation is a seed towards [that]." She sees the program as an ideal space in which to continue piloting restorative justice, particularly because Project Graduation is a "complete work of progress" crafted by teachers. Yet in reseeding restorative justice, Angela and Lucy struggled with readapting circles to a program that they themselves had yet to create from the ground up—a task that required them to reenvision how to implement, at least partially, the restorative discipline feedback loop.

NOTES

1. This is discussed later in this chapter.
2. According to BPS, students in language-specific Sheltered English Instruction (SEI) programs all speak the same language and study in content courses together. In addition, "Bilingual/bicultural staff are available to students and their families." See http://www.bostonpublicschools.org/ELL.
3. See http://profiles.doe.mass.edu/state_report/gradrates.aspx.
4. The process of the healing circle is described in detail in the portrait of Janet Connors.
5. Janet's pivotal role in the implementation of restorative justice—as a community member who participated in the first Victim Offender Dialogue in Massachusetts after her son was murdered—is discussed in her portrait.
6. SLC A was divided into the lower school, which consisted of ninth- and tenth-grade teachers and students, and the upper school, the eleventh- and twelfth-grade teachers and students. Both schools met during a common planning time to discuss discipline and pedagogy.

5   The Evolution Continues
Reseeding Restorative Justice through Talking Circles

Project Graduation is tucked at the end of a short hallway on the third floor. This program is a last-ditch effort for many of its 60 students, who have opted to be here. It is a place where their lack of credits, failures in schooling and even past criminal behaviors are put to the side and where four dedicated teachers and two administrators have reached out to students to create personal bonds and flexible scheduling to help them recover credit and get on a fast track to graduating. Beyond the door labeled "Project Graduation," one enters a large common area, which is surrounded by three classrooms and an administrative office. Against the back walls are bookshelves with signs detailing genres—*Adventure, Science Fiction, Autobiography*. In the corner of the room by the books are two armchairs and an old wooden table with hook legs.

Several students are seated along a row of computers against the wall on the left, laughing, checking e-mail or listening to music videos. Project Graduation Administrative Leader Carol Warren emerges from an office adjacent to the computers. Petite with a round face, caramel skin and sparkly eyes, Carol comes from what she describes as a mixed-race family, with an African American mother and White father. Carol's responsibilities include running the academic portion of the program and dealing with the most egregious disciplinary problems, such as fighting or theft, work that contrasts with her background in counseling and art therapy. With a master's in expressive therapy, she has used dance as a way to help students "release emotions or express themselves in a way where sometimes words aren't appropriate or safe or are uncomfortable." Both of her parents worked as teachers and counselors in alternative high school programs for students who were not successful in traditional classroom settings. She has continued that legacy by taking on a leadership position in Project Graduation, where she was excited to be able to apply her skills as a counselor to "be part of a movement to really shape and define what we want this program to look like . . . The thought of having this blank canvas to build what you want to build was really exciting."

Once Carol was hired, Angela and Lucy spoke with her at length about restorative justice, providing her with the documents that Angela had created the year before. Carol did not have difficulty buying into the philosophy; it felt intuitive because it was a perfect complement to her background in fostering social and emotional well-being in her students. "It seemed like something that I should have been in sync with all along . . . It is so similar to some of the stuff that I was doing already [in group therapy]; it was just called something else." Carol says that restorative justice was initially conceived *both* as a social and emotional literacy tool and a model for doing discipline in the program:

> They talked to me about the structure of the circle, how it allows for equal voice and listening time. We talked about how we wanted to use it [circles] in Project Graduation as an alternative to a suspension, as community building . . . and I think at the time really thinking about how can we have this structure be this core element that is one thing that makes our program different.

The implementation of restorative justice in Project Graduation versus SLC A differed in one key way: the *practice* of circle became ritualized in the program, but the tenets of the *philosophy* of restorative justice were less emphasized. As Carol states, *circles*, as opposed to restorative justice, differentiated Project Graduation from the rest of the school. All staff and students were able to describe a circle, but only Angela, Lucy, and Carol were familiar with the term "restorative justice." When I asked study skills teacher Mary Spellman about the philosophy, she said, "I haven't had it explained to me. Or if I did, it wasn't enough for me."

William responded similarly: "The restorative justice piece I haven't been a part of at all."

Having a common understanding of the philosophy can help create a common restorative environment because "the use of restorative language becomes an indicator of organizational movement towards a restorative culture" (Drewery, 2004, p. 349). As well, without the philosophical understanding of restorative justice, Angela says some students misunderstand why discipline looks different within the program versus the rest of the school—for example, why staff try to suspend as little as possible:

> I think [students] need to have a more explicit kind of understanding of [restorative justice] . . . Some students think we're not tough enough, we don't call home enough, we don't punish enough. If they understood the rationale for this or if we spent more time talking with them about what we think really helps students move forward and grow, then it would help them. I think [it] would help to talk about that phrase [restorative justice] for sure.

Angela shows how it can be difficult to be restorative and "tough," especially if the same structure used in many restorative places—healing circles—is not used to complement talking circles by keeping students accountable even when it seems that teachers do not "punish enough."

Healing circles were not introduced to students as a formal alternative to suspension—although as I will show, they were occasionally used—and once again, the bottom-up implementation of restorative justice was limited by a lack of infrastructure. Because the program was built in a matter of weeks over the summer without much support from the national Project Graduation network, the staff was also taxed with having to recruit and select students, create curriculum and become familiar with the online credit system. Janet scheduled sessions to introduce staff to restorative justice through role plays as she had done the prior year in SLA A, but they were consistently canceled due to last-minute circumstances—sometimes because she was unable to get to the school that day and sometimes because staff needed to address student concerns or conflicts. Although this portrait reveals that the lack of explicit knowledge of restorative justice did not impede the success of circles, it did lead to basic misunderstandings about how they work. This is exemplified by a meeting between Assistant Principal Nancy Lincoln and Leslie Roberts, an intern from the Center for Restorative Justice, who came to Project Graduation in March to provide more support to develop restorative practices:

> Leslie and Janet have scheduled a meeting with Nancy Lincoln, the primary point person for discipline in the program. They hope to brainstorm how to implement a formal structure for [a] healing circles model in the program. After the meeting they will help Nancy facilitate a healing circle with four boys who have not been doing work in class. The meeting is running late. Nancy is working on her computer in her office as we wait outside in the common area. Twenty minutes later she calls us into her office and says, "I'm really sorry I was unable to meet earlier. I've been filling in discharge forms for students who have been suspended for behavior in other parts of the building."
>
> Leslie produces a packet of papers from another local Boston school that has implemented a restorative discipline model. She says, "These are some of the plans that have been put in motion at another school."
>
> Nancy nods and occasionally her eyes rove back to the computer screen, where she types a few words every now and then as Leslie explains different parts of the packet. Finally Nancy says, "Unfortunately, if you explain something to me in person then I will be able to understand this. If you hand me a pile of papers," she says, signaling to the other stacks of paperwork on her desk, "Will I read this later on? Probably not." Janet and Leslie nod sympathetically. The meeting, which has lasted 15 minutes, ends on this note as it is now time for the next class period.
>
> As we gather our things, Nancy steps out into the common area where two of the four boys from the scheduled healing circle sit in front

of computers right outside her office. One of them tells her he does not want to participate. We overhear her tell them, "You have to partici-pate, or you're going to fail."

Janet shakes her head and slumps her face in her hand before laugh-ing along with Leslie. "Circle is supposed to be optional," says Janet, as though repeating a mantra.

Says Leslie, "This is why we need professional development around restorative justice."

It is ironic that during the very time allotted for development around restorative discipline, Nancy's attention is split as she focuses on filling out suspension discharge forms. As I discuss later in the portrait, none of Project Graduation staff supported the reliance on suspensions in the rest of the building and wanted to handle disciplinary matters differently within the program. Yet in a sense staff were building the ship as it sailed, supporting the notion of restorative discipline but dealing with the daily realities of not having the time to develop and flesh out that vision. Carol says the next step in implementing restorative justice would be to carve out weekly profes-sional development time and institutionalize healing circles, although it has been difficult to imagine what exactly that would look like given all of her varied responsibilities. She envisions having a "structure in place [so] that when something happens we have a clear process and protocol for what the response would be and how you'd be able to use circles in that way."

How, then, do a small group of practitioners build an entire program from the ground up *and* simultaneously implement restorative practices, despite a lack of infrastructure? Even without institutionalized healing circles or an explicit, shared understanding of restorative justice, teachers in Project Graduation partially implemented the restorative discipline feedback loop through talking circles, which had the capability to build and repair rela-tionships. Angela states that teachers did not have a shared understanding, or "common vocabulary," around restorative justice, but "in terms of the practices, I think that, in a way, every teacher in [the program] has their own way of doing it [restorative justice] in their own classroom," particularly in terms of how each develops one-on-one relationships with students.

Though she no longer works with Angela, Rebecca has observed that Project Graduation works hard to build a strong school culture rooted in such relationships. She describes such a culture as "the real alternative to suspension": "that means students feeling cared about, supported, timely interventions when issues come up, trust between students and teachers, really good communication between students and teachers." Thus the implicit restoration of relationships took place in program-wide circles, small talking circles, and staff circles—suggesting that for practitioners lack-ing an infrastructure necessary to support the entire restorative discipline loop, building relationships with students and implementing talking circles can still provide a potent first step in transforming a school culture.

TALKING CIRCLES: SPACES OF HEALING

While Project Graduation did not have regularly scheduled healing circles to address conflicts, program-wide talking circles, by their inherent nature, sometimes acted as spaces of healing. At least twice a month, sometimes every Friday, all 40 to 50 Project Graduation students gathered for a program-wide community building circle in which they checked in, discussed their academic progress and became better acquainted. The circles were initially facilitated by the most experienced circle keepers—Janet, Angela and Lucy—who modeled the process for students and staff. Study skills teacher Mary Spellman remembers learning about how to facilitate circles by simply observing these women in circles at the beginning of the year. "I think the thing that I'll not forget about them is Lucy's way of waiting till the talking piece came back to her and then addressing the things that had happened. She modeled it very intensely and very strongly, about the talking piece and what it's all about, what we're trying to. That impressed me a lot." Over time, Carol, Nancy, William, Mary and even students began keeping these circles as well. Says Carol,

> We use [circle] consistently and it really stands out as something that's going on in this program that's not happening in the rest of the school . . . They put chairs in a circle; they know the importance of that, that they understand that it's a time for listening, it's a time for being heard, it's a time for sharing, it's a vehicle to discuss something difficult that's happened or challenges that have come up and to really build together as a community.

In fact, the first program-wide talking circle was actually a healing circle convened to address the use of cell phones, tardiness and students not completing work. Teachers thought the initial circle could serve multiple purposes: it would allow them to build community, model the process and keep students accountable for the harmful behaviors. "There was a high lack of discipline as far as students cutting and just not being respectful of community norms," says Carol. "And the first thing we thought about was maybe we need to have an assembly, and we can talk about the rules and let them know that this is serious business. And then we were, like, that's already talked out. How where they gonna respond to that? Where is their voice?"

After staff discussed their frustrations about student behaviors one Thursday afternoon, Lucy took the lead in planning a program-wide circle the very next day. Lucy acknowledged that it was "scary" to think about doing a circle with more than 50 people but that she thought it would be "more meaningful, sacred, and organic than a top-down assembly." That Friday Lucy agreed to keep the circle to model and apprentice those new to the process, namely Math Teacher William Johnston, Administrative Leader

Carol Warren, Study Skills Teacher Mary Spellman and Assistant Program Leader Nancy Lincoln:

We're in the common area of the program. The book stands, reading chairs and rows of tables with computers have been shoved to corners of the room. Students trickle in, staring at the vast space in the middle of 60 empty chairs that have been squeezed together. Lucy provides teachers and students with a script in which she has listed an opening quote, purposes of the circle, a question prompt for each round of the circle and a closing quote. The seating is tight, and the chairs form not so much a circle as much as a jelly bean; I have to crane my neck to see the people to my left. As the spaces fill up, Lucy asks students to put their backpacks away and make sure nothing is in their lap so that they can really participate. I overhear a student say, "I'm not comfortable doing stuff like this."

"Just try it on," says Angela. "Have faith and trust us that we know what we're doing here." Because of student absences there are a few empty chairs that are pulled out—40 students are present in total, and including the staff, there are around 50 total participants.

Lucy has posted a butcher paper that states: "Behaviors that are HARMFUL to our community: fighting, physically and verbally, skipping/cutting class, not caring/being tardy, not being focused in class, not being of sober mind, and not following school rules for things like cell phones." Once everyone is seated, she asks everyone to rise so that she can read the opening quote. I sense resistance as a few people grumble and stay seated—but within a minute or so, everyone is on their feet. Lucy reads, "Be careful of your thoughts, for your thoughts become your words. Be careful of your words, for your words become your actions. Be careful of your actions, for your actions become your habits. Be careful of your habits, for your habits become your character. Be careful of your character, for your character becomes your destiny."

She begins by reading out the list of behaviors and asks how everyone has contributed positively or negatively to the environment. Some students say how they have been coming to school entirely focused on their work and how they help their peers in class. Other students are frank about what they have done that has promoted harm. Sophomore Janice Nichols counts off with each finger on her right hand as she rattles off each infraction. "I've been coming late, sometimes I don't come at all, I don't focus in class, and sometimes I talk too much."

In the next round, Lucy asks students to make agreements to improve their behaviors. Lucy says that she would like to make the choice to start each day fresh, and to treat each student as though each day is a new beginning. "That doesn't mean I won't remember what happened in the past, just that I want to have a clean slate with students each new day." Several students nod.

Angela says, "Sometimes I get mad at one class and take it out on the next class, so I'm going to work on checking my emotions."

Math Teacher William Johnston says, "I know that I can be quick to make judgments about students."

"At least you know," says Sophia Joseph, an African American girl with small, nutmeg-shaped eyes and a toothy, mischievous smile. Her comment, muttered quietly under her breath with an edge of sarcasm, evokes laughter throughout the circle.

William smiles and continues. "I usually decide early on who is really working hard, and I tend to focus on those students. I want to make an effort to not give up on the students who seem not to be fulfilling their potential or succeeding academically."

As if in response, senior Jaylen Robinson looks up at William and says, "I need support from the teacher . . . Remember how you act towards us is how we act. If a student is not acting right and you want to send them out do that, but don't put them on blast."

Students, too, state what they want to commit to doing in order to improve, and several thank those who have helped them. Many also provide unsolicited advice for their peers:

"I will keep reminding my friends to do what you need to do to succeed."

"I'm going to try to keep the class from being distracted. Laughter is good, a little chuckle chuckle, but that's it."

"Thank you to the teachers who go the extra mile for us."

"Walk away from your friends when you need to."

In the last "shout-out" round, we are asked to praise one person in the community who supported us. The tone of the conversation shifts from that of a healing, reactive circle to a proactive talking circle. "I want to start with Sophia," says William, referring to the young woman who teased him for his tendency to judge students. Throughout the circle, she has made jokes or talked to the people around her from time to time. "Everybody knows you are loud!" he says, emphasizing the last word. The group burst into laughter. "But you bring a certain energy to the room that all of the other students appreciate, and I think it makes all of us in the class better." Sophia smiles coyly, her face deepening in color the longer he speaks.

Jaylen Robertson turns to Liam, one of two Asian students in the program. Both Jaylen and Liam were Angela's students the prior year in SLC A. Liam's hair is black and spiky, and for much of the circle he has passed or said one word—indeed I have never heard him speak. "I want to give a shout-out to Liam," says Jaylen. "I mean, you're a nice guy. I know I don't know you well. But last year [you] always had your head down every day. And this year, you don't talk to anybody, but your head is up, and you are getting your work done every day." Liam smiles as the circle starts clapping for him. Every time a student is acknowledged thereafter, students began applauding.

Lucy ends the circle by asking everyone to rise. This time there is no grumbling. She asks everyone to repeat the following sentence, written on our half sheets of paper, out loud: "TODAY I MAKE THE CHOICE TO COMMIT TO DIPLOMA PLUS." A male student spontaneously calls for a team huddle, and the students converge, heaping their hands on top of one another and yelling, "Project Graduation!"

Even without explicit professional development around restorative justice, students and teachers in this circle implicitly promoted the principles of community, egalitarianism and responsibility: "Circles, by their very structure, convey certain important ideas and values without the need for discussion" (Costello, Wachtel, & Wachtel, 2010, p. 22). Students were asked to make themselves accountable for their actions, but teachers also kept themselves accountable for student success, creating an egalitarian space in circle. Students not only acknowledged their own negative behaviors but committed to engaging in behaviors to support their peers. Students like Liam—who usually fly under the radar—are identified, praised and supported by the community. And according to Angela, any resistance to the process seemed dispelled by the end of the circle:

> I think it got more powerful as it went on. At the beginning it just seemed like some students were resisting, and even one student said, "Do you sense the hostility?"
>
> One student said, "I don't want to be here" because he thought we were going to call him out for his behavior, but I had to explain to him that we were talking about community and how to support each other. I saw this total lack of connection and the connection seemed to grow by the end.

Study Skills Teacher Mary Spellman was surprised that students genuinely seemed invested in the process, as witnessed by their enthusiasm during the shout-outs and their cheer at the end. "I was amazed that it worked, quite honestly. I was not totally a believer in all that."

Like Mary, several students I interviewed also expressed some initial ambivalence about the process but echoed that they felt comfortable by the end of circle. Senior Jacob Stillman says that when he first walked into the common area and saw the circle, "I thought it was lame. Why are we sitting in a circle to talk?" He grew to appreciate the process when he realized that he had things he wanted to share, feelings that he was not able to express during regular class time. "While it was happening, I thought it was getting better as it goes. Usually I feel like my voice is unheard sometimes." Now he says, during the weekly circles, "When they pass me the talking piece, I felt the attention's on me, and I get heard."

Darius Riker is a junior with braids and a hearty, unbridled laugh. I first met him when he sat next to me during that first circle and continued to get to know him when he sat next to me during subsequent ones. He is friendly, always greeting me with a smile, a raise of his thick eyebrows, and a "Hey, circle buddy!" He says that when he walked into the first community circle and saw all the chairs spread out in the room, he thought, "Oh cool, that's what's up." Circle was intuitive for him because he used to have something similar during advisory at his old school, and he remembered sharing experiences in an intimate way there:

> I've been automatically judged my whole life, like as soon as I was seeing on the spot I was judged, you know, and it actually feels good that someone's trying to look inside the box instead of looking outside and seeing what they see inside of me . . . I think circle is about [teachers] them actually trying to get to know and understand us.

Talking circles did not only implicitly address obvious harms such as interpersonal disagreements or rule infractions. Particularly in this program, there was a deeper, more pervasive need to heal students' relationships with the institution of schooling. Expelled from his prior high school for possession of a knife that he carried for safety, Darius was out of school for three months and not provided an alternative placement. When he entered Bridge, Principal Beatty recommended that he enroll in Project Graduation, where he says he finally feels engaged in school. "I don't know if they know this but [all the teachers] are like a role model to me. They actually help a lot . . . The work that they give me, the way that they challenge me, I haven't really been challenged like this before." The week that I speak to him, his is one of eight names on a posted list of students who are "in good standing," which means he is completing all of his assignments and on track for graduation. He ascribes his academic success to the culture created by the teachers, and circle is one piece that has cultivated relationships:

> When I first started the program, there were a lot of separate groups. We weren't as one, as a family, and there was a lot of animosity . . . Now it seems like after all the circles and after all the hell that Ms. Reed and all of [the teachers] have been going through . . . It just feels like we've come closer together. Circle now is like one big unit, a bunch of kids who can actually express themselves.

Like Darius, Jacob Stillman's academic career has been marred by failing grades and school exclusion. Tall and somewhat heavyset, Jacob has a round face, cherubic cheeks, and a wide smile with perfectly straight teeth. It is hard for me to imagine him getting in trouble with any of his teachers. Yet in middle school his teachers repeatedly suspended him; he spent more time out of school than in class but was still promoted to BHS. A few eighth-grade teachers placed a chair permanently outside of the classroom, where he could sit once he returned from a suspension—quite a contrast to his experience sitting in a chair as part of a large, supportive circle in Project Graduation. "Sometimes [my middle school teachers] wouldn't even let me in the classroom." He doesn't remember exactly why he was suspended so much, though he says he was sent home for "little things" like talking back or chewing gum. He was not close with any of his teachers and did not feel comfortable telling them how he had witnessed domestic abuse at home and was homeless at the time—circumstances he has shared with some of his teachers in Project Graduation. A therapist also recently discovered an undiagnosed learning disability that he thinks explains his past struggles with schoolwork. But this year he attributes his academic motivation to the relationships he has with one of his teachers, who consistently show how much they care: "At the end of class every day, when I'm doing my work, [Lucy] Reed will tell me she's very proud of me for how I've been acting in class."

The first program-wide talking circle did not produce a complete cessation of all of the harmful behaviors listed on Lucy's poster. At the second circle, students were asked whether or not they had followed through on their commitments, and several admitted that they had not. Positive changes in behavior might come to fruition over time, one student at a time—and even then, not all students necessarily improve their negative behaviors. However, talking circles composed one feature of a larger school-wide culture rooted in developing relationships. Says Jacob, "Without circles I don't think I'd know half of the kids in Project Graduation."

Nearly every student I spoke to described doing better academically in the program because of relationships. "I'm doing well because of the program. It's not like the fifth floor," says Junior Marisol Dominguez, pointing upward to another SLC. "There it's like the ocean, and they let you down. This one teacher stopped giving me the paper each day with our work. I wasn't going to do it anyway," she admits with a laugh, "but still, that's what made me give up." A petite Latina girl with sideswept bangs, curly, shoulder-length black hair and clear braces, Marisol did not begin the year feeling so positive about the program.

As a friend of hers states, "When Marisol first came, she just sat in the back of class and talked, and she wouldn't do her work. Now she's real serious, and she even helps the rest of us out." Marisol's poor relationship with schooling at BHS, where she felt like she was in an ocean where she might drown, began to heal through such relationships with Project Graduation teachers—and she became a consistently vocal participant in classes and circles. She even tried to make amends for past behavior during one talking circle:

Marisol says, "Finally, I have a shocking shout-out." She waits for silence somewhat dramatically. "I want to shout out Natasha. I know we are not friends and have not gotten along in the past, but in class you do what you have to do so that we can get our work done, and I really respect that, so I want you to know that."

A few students gasped and several started clapping. Natasha, a Latina girl with a round face, sharp jutting chin and straightened hair has a look on her face that is hard to read—is she rolling her eyes? Is she perturbed?

"Take it, Natasha!" a few students say.

"No, I'm happy she said that," clarified Natasha, before smiling and looking down.

It is only after talking to the teachers that I understand the significance of this brief exchange. Although hardly arch-nemeses, Natasha had violated her parole the previous year because of a fight with Marisol. In a sense, Marisol's actions are restorative: despite not expressing her culpability in the conflict, she worked to repair the relationship by acknowledging Natasha's academic improvement. Doing so in a public forum amplifies the restorative aspect of what feels like an implicit apology—and sometimes the only concrete action necessary to repair harm *is* an apology. Like Darius and James, the longer she was exposed to circle, the more comfortable she became participating and the more academically engaged she became in school; "At first I didn't want to do circle, but I'm glad we do them."

Small talking circles. Though not set up to address harms, proactive talking circles with targeted groups of students led to closer bonds and, sometimes, improved student behaviors. Study Skills Teacher Mary Spellman is a middle-aged White woman of medium height with shoulder-length gray hair cut in feathery layers. In her class she teaches students how to use the online credit recovery system so that they can recoup courses they have failed. She dresses casually, donning Hawaiian shirts, khaki slacks and sneakers, a black purse perpetually slung over her left shoulder and glasses hanging around her neck from an eyeglass rope. She is devoted and attentive to each of her students, approaching them in between classes to check in, chide them, or lecture them when they haven't shown up to class. Mary has years of experience as a middle school math teacher and principal.

A two-time cancer survivor, Mary chose to work at the school as the registrar the prior year to have a low-stress job. "My main concern is I just want to be OK. Then they cut that position, so here I am in Project Graduation." She speaks in a no-nonsense way, declaring that she initially "didn't have any faith at all" that a weekly talking circle with more than 50 students in the program would work. She now describes them as "invaluable," going so far as to say that the tradition has helped sustain her through the difficult transition from doing administrative work the previous year to teaching in the program: "They put me back together at the end [of the week] when we're doing them on Friday. I wouldn't have been able to make it this far at all, if we didn't have a bunch of those . . . It helped me remember what it is we're trying to do and give chances to connect with everybody in a meaningful way. I like them a lot for myself." The formative experience that revealed the value of circles occurred a few months into the year when conflicts arose among a small group of female students in one of her classes:

> The staff has decided to organize a series of small talking circles composed entirely of the girls from Mary's class. Before one of these circles in January, she says, "I don't look forward to teaching the class." The girls quibble with each other, sometimes putting each other down. Girls who were friends have been arguing loudly with one another during class, though it is unclear to her why. "I like every student individually but not the class. I raised three boys. I don't know how to deal with difficult girls."
>
> Fourteen of us—Janet, Mary, Angela, Lucy, Carol and nine students—gather in Mary's room, a sparsely decorated space with a whiteboard, chalkboard, old wooden teacher's desk and a smattering of student desks. We push the desks aside and pull the chairs in to form a small, intimate circle. There is a plant on one side of the room, and a glass case of dictionaries in the back as well as a black-and-white poster of Martin Luther King with the quote, "Darkness cannot drive out darkness; only light can do that." The students quietly take their seats, settle in and get comfortable.
>
> Layla, a junior in jeans, form-fitting T-shirt and hair pulled back in a sloppy ponytail says, "I hate being sick!"
>
> "Take this," says her friend Melissa, handing over a travel-size bottle of antibacterial gel.
>
> "You always have gel," remarks Layla, turning to the rest of us. "She even hands it out to strangers on the subway!"
>
> For much of the circle Janet asks us to talk about what we like and don't like about being female. We say we like how we trust one another, but we don't like how we become jealous. As the minutes pass we begin talking about boys and dating. The students become so verbal that they decide to "popcorn" by handing the talking piece to whoever wants to talk, rather than passing it sequentially. Sophomore Natasha Lawrence asks Junior Charlotte Adams, whose arms are folded across her chest, "How does it feel to be pregnant?"
>
> Charlotte says, "I'm scared." Charlotte turns to her elders for advice. She asks Janet, "Should I consider myself a single mother if the father's around, but we are not together?" I don't know whether she knows Janet raised three children by herself.
>
> Janet says, "I would think yes because you are going to raise a child mostly on your own."
>
> "Yeah, so that's what I'll call myself, a single mother," says Charlotte with a decisive nod, as if with pride. "I haven't met the child, but I love it!" She then turns to Mary. "What was it like to be a mother?"

This is the first time I have heard Mary discuss her personal life with students. "I had my children in day care from the time they were three months old because I was a single mother too," says Mary. "From the time they were that little to the time they entered elementary school, I couldn't think about anything but them. It was like I had no other life but a life about protecting my children." Charlotte nods, and the circle is quiet. Janet tells us we are out of time and asks each of us to provide one word to describe the circle.

Several of us contribute. "Sweet. Mature. Babies. Nice. Maturity. Joy."

Though Mary says she does not know how to relate to girls, this heartfelt exchange about single motherhood transformed relationships within the group. According to Carol, Charlotte can be taciturn and have "a more tough exterior." But in circle she became more vulnerable. This was not a healing circle—none of the conflicts among the girls were mentioned, and no agreements were made—but after this second circle, Mary noticed a significant shift in how the girls related to one another:

MARY: The whole class calmed down. They started to support each other. I remember [one student] would say, "we're gonna make sure everybody in here does all their work," stuff like that. It didn't carry itself beyond a point, but it really did bring them into some sort of supportive group of each other.

ANITA: Did that happen right after circle? You could see a dramatic shift?

MARY: Yeah. I don't know if it was after the first [circle] or by the end of the second one, but yeah, it was very noticeable very soon.

Though the changes in behavior "didn't carry itself beyond a point," these initial small circles, which did not focus on the negative interactions between the girls but instead sought proactively to reveal their commonalities, produced changes in behavior typically achieved with reactive, healing circles. Principal Carol Warren feels such circles also support students academically as the girls had so much to say about relationships and becoming women. "They're itching to talk about this, so obviously how are they going to focus on algebra if they don't have a forum to talk about these issues?" For teachers, then, talking circles acted as spaces of healing as they deepened relationships with students, sustaining themselves through the tough work of teaching in a new, demanding program.

Staff circles. During their common planning time, staff used circles at various times throughout the year to discuss programmatic issues. But these circles often spontaneously became spaces of healing, airing tensions and fostering conversations about racial dynamics among teachers. According to Angela, one memorable circle unveiled some of her assumptions about Math Teacher William Johnston.

William Johnston is a third-year teacher—handsome with wide, alert eyes and a small gap between his two front teeth. His hair is locked and falls a little below his shoulders, and his posture is always erect. He is well-known for engaging students through stern, forceful lectures, even diatribes. Sometimes these are spontaneous interventions that occur during class time when he pulls students in the hallway to ask why they aren't working. Other times, he takes the lead during more formal interventions convened by all the teachers to talk to students one-on-one. According to William, childhood neighbors referred to him as "little Farrakhan," relating him to Louis Farrakhan, former leader of the Nation of Islam, because of his passionate and vocal personality.

Though I am on a first-name basis with almost everyone on the staff at the school, I often refer to him as Mr. Johnston rather than William. Around me his demeanor seems distant—he does not make eye contact when I approach him, and when I interview him, he admits that his manner can appear standoffish. But around students he is open, humorous and blunt. The son of a Caribbean mother, he says that many times when he's talking to young people, he feels like he's talking to the younger version of himself. "I was a street kid. I grew up in the city. I grew up to an immigrant, single mom, poor. Gangster friends . . . our [the students' and my] stories are somewhat similar. We speak the same language, listen to the same music; the kids live in my neighborhood."

As a result of his affinity toward young people, he left law school to become a teacher, hoping to disrupt the high imprisonment rates of young people, especially of color. "I didn't want to be on the punitive side. I wanted to be on the preventative side . . . I didn't want to be involved with incarcerating people that look like I do." When responding to disciplinary incidents, his sometimes brash communication style contrasts starkly with the more mild-mannered demeanors of Angela and Lucy, something he ascribes to cultural differences: "I feel perfectly at home with the students, so the things I can say, the things I can get away with, the level of aggression and forcefulness that I can command is probably different."

Principal Beatty led a circle with the Project Graduation staff to address what could be done to strengthen Project Graduation, especially in light of the difficulties of building the program on their own. When Angela received the talking piece, she expressed her disappointment that not all of the staff were on the same page about planning rigorous lessons. William got the piece and stated that he felt singled out in some of her criticisms, especially because there were only four teachers in the program.

There are marked differences in how the three content teachers manage and plan their classes. Lucy arrives at school at 5 a.m.; William has publicly stated that he is not paid to spend that much time at school. On the surface, such statements might communicate indifference on Williams's part, yet he pointed out to Lucy and Angela that just because he had a different approach did not mean he was any less dedicated than they were. He also talked about work that he was "not getting credit for," including mediations that he conducted between students. According to Angela, "He said to me, all these things that you just said, your emotions, even your language—'cause I think I swore once or something—you can get away with that because you're a White woman. I can't get away with that. I couldn't sit here in a conversation and just swear like you just did."

Although the circle was convened to discuss general concerns about the program, a discussion about teaching and learning in the circle led to a deeper conversation about race, privilege and assumptions. William reminded Angela about how being a White woman afforded her certain privileges that he did not have—namely, that as a Black man, he would likely have been evaluated more harshly had he used profanity in the circle. Angela admits that she had incorrectly assumed that William did not care about teaching as much as she or Lucy because of his quietness or body language during meetings. "I said to him, I took you not talking a lot as you withdrawing; you're isolating yourself in meetings, and I took that to mean that you don't care, and I hear now that that's not it. That opened my eyes to what you're going through and that you feel like the role you play with our students is different, and it is. It's important."

William tells me that during the circle he felt that his "zeal and motivation" were being questioned because he did not have the mannerisms of a "liberal White woman" that are necessary for professional success. When I ask him how he would define these mannerisms, he says, "In general, the more you nod and tilt your head, bat your eyes, grinning, perfunctory laughter, whatever White women learn. The faster we learn it, the better we fare, but I'm just not that guy." On the one hand, this characterization borders on stereotyping. On the other hand, William sheds important light on the differences between how his actions and those of Angela and Lucy are interpreted. In the circle, he wanted to make it clear that just because he did not act like Lucy or Angela did not mean he was not committed to his job: "I felt like my professionalism or dedication was being questioned, and I just made the point that just because I don't have the mannerisms of a liberal White woman doesn't mean that I'm not excited or I'm disengaged or anything like that. There's a lot of leeway that other people might have that I don't because of who I am."

So even while restorative justice evolved and was implemented only partially in Project Graduation, there were elements of healing circles embedded in talking circles. Restoration of relationships could occur naturally without the language or structure of a healing circle, allowing participants to give voice to critical issues that impact their pedagogy. Given that I observed Angela's, Lucy's, and William's comfort with engaging in conversations about race, class and power with one another on their own time, this exchange might have taken place outside of circle. However, circle acted as a catalyst for such dialogue. The talking piece provided William and Angela opportunities to engage in the issues that were most relevant on their minds. Had Principal Beatty solicited feedback about the program in a typical format, William, who later told Angela that he refrains from talking in meetings because he does not want to dominate the conversation as the only male, may not have responded to Angela's concerns with such candor. In circle, "there is a better chance that more voices will be heard. Just as some students are more reserved than others, some adults are reluctant to speak in a meeting. The circle encourages those people to say something" (Costello et al., 2010, pp. 96–97). As a result says Principal Beatty, circle "allows people to have deep conversation pretty quickly."

During that circle and after school, Angela and William resolved the conflict, and Angela was able to clarify that she had undervalued his role as a mediator, but she wanted students to see William as more than a person who engaged in interventions. "He feels like he can have different kinds of conversations with [students], but it ends up derailing academics, too." Despite the absence of regular healing circles to address staff conflicts, the principles of restorative justice—keeping one another accountable and attempting to repair harm in relationships—were practiced implicitly in staff circles, even if the implementation of the philosophy was only partial:

> He had said in [that] circle later on, "I have your back no matter what. You're on my team, no hard feelings." . . . It's been complicated, but we have tried to understand each other better and come from different places in a lot of this, but we've respected each other. We ended up talking and hugging after school, and it was so good when it was the two of us.

"WE DON'T WANT TO SUSPEND, BUT . . .": WORKING WITHIN A PUNITIVE PARADIGM

Though talking circles were foundational in strengthening relationships and preventing or addressing conflicts, one challenge of institutionalizing restorative justice from the bottom up was the larger, school-wide, punitive disciplinary culture—a culture that undermined program efforts to reduce suspensions. Project Graduation staff wrestled with how to discipline students who behaved well with teachers they knew within the program but poorly with adults in the rest of the school. Assistant Principal Nancy Lincoln says, "The only time we do a suspension [is] when it warrants involvement with the entire school." In fact, according to all teachers in the program, students were hardly ever suspended for behavior within the program. They were more responsive and deferential to teachers within Project Graduation than they were outside of it. These fractured responses possibly speak to the atomization of SLCs at BHS and the lack of a school-wide sense of community and mutual respect. As Lucy points out, Project Graduation students do not have the same kind of relationships with other teachers at BHS:

> The bad, the naughty stuff, the disrespectful stuff is not happening as nearly as much in our [program]. It's happening with our students in

different classes in a big way but not with us really because I think the circles have worked. They trust us as their teachers, but then they go out into the rest of the building, and they're treated like the "Project Graduation" kids, and it's bad . . . As far as discipline goes, it's always a problem in a big school, but what's unique about this situation is we really sort of don't have any power. The discipline stuff that we're having is stuff that we can control [and] we're going to try to use circle for. There's a big clash with the rest of the building that's very frustrating.

Though I was not at school on a daily basis, I am skeptical of the statement that disrespectful behavior does not happen in the program. Incidents of theft of cell phones and money were reported throughout the year within the program. Money was even stolen out of my wallet when I left my backpack unattended in the common area. I was witness to a number of moments when students spoke to staff in raised, heated voices, yelled in response to directives or walked away and slammed doors. I suspect that Lucy's statement that the "disrespectful stuff" does not occur arises from the subjective nature of what constitutes "disrespect." Aware of students' individual circumstances, a Project Graduation teacher might forgive behavior that would not be overlooked in the rest of the school. After all, staff members were sensitive to the fact that it was common to hear teachers around the building typecast "those PG [Project Graduation] kids" as troublemakers. Unfortunately, there was ample evidence for the stereotype: in the early part of fall 2010, there was a rash of fights in the building. According to Angela, every fight was started by or involved a student in Project Graduation. In such instances, program staff had to defer to teachers and administrators in the rest of the building, who automatically suspended students for behaviors such as talking back, walking out of class or fighting.

Throughout the year I continually heard the refrain, "We don't believe in suspensions, but we don't know what else to do." Part of the reason some students are not academically successful, says Study Skills Teacher Mary Spellman, is because there is not a clear set of consequences in Project Graduation or the rest of BHS when students skip class or refuse to do work:

There isn't a good consequence structure, so for example if kids are late from class, the teachers [outside of Project Graduation] won't let them go to class. They sit around there, then what's supposed to happen? There's no penalty . . . I think we started thinking—I know Lucy and Angela started thinking—they didn't want to have out-of-school suspensions. Then what were the alternatives? The problem with all the alternatives is that they are really labor-intensive to implement. We weren't clear on what was supposed to happen, and if you don't do that, then you get suspended.

And even though all teachers told me that suspensions do not truly keep students accountable for their behaviors, the general belief was that they were sometimes necessary to send a harsh message. Mary says, "I don't think we can afford to stop [suspending] . . . There is no penalty at all. That seems unwise. I don't understand that."

Assistant Principal Nancy Lincoln claims that because Project Graduation students already struggle with traditional school and with attendance, she doesn't like suspending because, "if we suspend them, they probably won't come back." I ask Nancy how she addresses students who repeatedly engage in problematic behaviors.

> I don't know. We're at a loss. We're all, what do we do? This kid works, takes care of family. After school [detention] is definitely a no-no. We're at a loss. What we're gonna do now is sit down with the teachers and sit down with him, and we gotta figure out something. We don't know . . . Every student is different, and we have to be creative.

For Lucy, discipline in Project Graduation takes one of two forms, both of which she finds ineffective: suspensions and quick interventions. In contrast to the earlier statement that egregious behavior does not necessarily take place in the program, Lucy acknowledges the difficulty in addressing conflicts that *do* occur: "I'm torn. I don't believe in suspension, but I also don't believe in what's going on here [in Project Graduation], which I try seriously to ignore all the negative things that are happening. If there's a fight to maybe do a quick meeting so that they won't hurt each other in the next class, but then there's no repairing. There's no consequence."

Angela admits that even as a proponent of restorative practices, she has not "embraced . . . wholeheartedly" the idea of never suspending students because sometimes she feels like "it's intolerable to [put up] with certain behaviors." William succinctly synthesizes all of the beliefs I heard about disciplinary approaches when I ask him whether suspension should be used as a disciplinary tool:

> I believe in everything as a discipline tool. Is it appropriate and will it be effective? Obviously suspending kids who don't come to school often or prefer not to be in school is going to be a gift in disguise, but not everyone views being forced out of school as a good thing. I don't necessarily buy that it's always a bad thing. Using it profusely without discretion is just as bad. The goal is to be creative.

In addition to the limitation of a larger, punitive school-wide culture on implementing and spreading a restorative discipline model, there was one other constraint: the necessity of long-term investment and faith in restorative practices given that antisocial behaviors—especially by those students in the program who had been disenfranchised during much of their schooling—did not necessarily change even after multiple circles.

ACTING IN A "CIRCLE WAY": LONG-TERM INVESTMENT IN RESTORATIVE JUSTICE

It is said that the purpose of circle is to "be in circle when you're outside of circle" (Boyes-Watson, 2008)—in other words, to translate the egalitarian practice of listening, speaking and committing no harm while in circle to one's day-to-day interactions: "The first lesson is that the Circle is not a technique or a program but a way to be. The Circle is a commitment to practice living the values of the Circle . . . The meaning of 'being in Circle' has expanded to refer to acting in a 'Circle way' or holding oneself 'in a good way' in one's relationships with one's self and others." (p. 84). Ideally, one should be in a circle at all times and carry oneself in a "Circle way" with all people. However, it takes time to learn how to act in a "Circle way" outside of circle. As discussed earlier there was sometimes a disconnect between how students behaved inside of the program versus in the rest of the school. The dissonance was not altogether unsurprising because the circle and the program were viewed by students as spaces in which they felt safer and more valued than elsewhere. Newcomers to restorative justice often pose a practical but difficult question: how long does it take for the practice to improve student behaviors? This is a particularly important question when working with students who have experienced multiple barriers in their schooling. The examples of two students suggest that it can take years before restorative practices repair relationships and transform behaviors.

One student who excelled within the program but experienced suspensions in the rest of the school was Senior Luis Rodriguez. Luis's home life and prior educational experiences provide insight into his behavior inside and outside of school, and in many ways his story encapsulates the struggles of other students I interviewed who shared narratives of drug abuse, physical and sexual abuse, homelessness, learning disabilities, exposure to violence, and years of experience with suspension and expulsion. In the following example, he engaged in harmful behavior immediately after participating in a powerful circle:

Today Angela and Lucy have invited Bridge administrators and staff members, as well as community members from all over Boston, to attend Project Graduation's symposium on the novel *Native Son*, by Richard Wright. This event is the culmination of a six-week unit on the book. The symposium begins with a plenary session in the choir room, a large space on the first floor of the school with four rows of amphitheater-style seating, royal-blue carpet, and a center stage at which Junior Tina Lewis sits on a wooden stool, reading her essay on the novel. She leans over with her elbow on her right knee. Her left leg is sprawled onto the floor, and her eyes do not leave the page. I pass a table of bagels, cream cheese, and orange juice and take a seat, noting about

30 adults—including all Project Graduation staff—and 20 students from the program dressed in suits and ties, neutral-colored slacks, and starched shirts. In contrast, Tina is dressed in her traditional uniform of baggy jeans, studded belt, colorful T-shirt and red head wrap. "I talk about this book so much that people have started calling me Bigger,"[1] she says. One might be confused about whether this is a compliment given Bigger's desperate, violent acts, but she has come to understand his character on a deeper level. She clarifies, "There's a part of Bigger in all of us, and I learned from this book to think before acting and not fall into a path that will only lead to destruction." The book has taught her about the pervasive influence of racism, and its impact on individual behaviors—but she has also learned about the choices she can make as one person, in spite of societal ills.

After the reading, Angela assigns everyone to a small talking circle to discuss the book with student facilitators. I am part of a group of a total of eight participants—an administrator, school police officer, community member, myself, two other students and the school nurse. We grab chairs and form a circle in a corridor outside of the choir room. Seated next to me is one of the facilitators of the circle, Luis. I have observed him in previous circles but do not know him. He is a thin Mexican boy whose curly black hair is pulled back behind a thin elastic headband. Though the class has been reading the book for the past six weeks, he confesses quietly, with an embarrassed smile, that he has not read it. I tell him he is OK and will do just fine.

Luis' co-facilitator, Thomas, another Project Graduation student, engages us in an intimate conversation about our own experiences with racism. He asks us to connect our stories to the themes in the text, particularly focusing on the impact of racism on both the oppressed and the oppressor. Thomas then passes the talking piece around after each of the following prompts: Do you know anyone like Bigger? When was the first time you remember talking to someone of a different race? For people of color, when did you first experience racism? For White people, was there a time when you thought something racist was happening, but you did not intervene?

The head school police officer, Sergeant Randolph Holmes, is a tall, approachable man with a youthful face that belies years of experience. He is African American, and says he experienced repercussions when he decided to marry a White woman. "Some of my family members were . . ." He trails off, squinting his light brown eyes. "It took them some time, but they finally began to open up and accept her. I think a lot of times we operate out of ignorance and fear because of our past experiences."

Luis is the last person to speak. He smiles, though I can't tell if it's a nervous, sardonic or happy expression. "The principal at my last school, whenever I got in trouble he would say, 'Your kind always messes up.' I asked him what you mean by 'my kind'?" Luis makes air quotes. "He's like, 'Hispanic.'" Several of us shake our heads.

Thomas gets the piece and for the final round asks, "Should *Native Son* be taught in schools?

The answer to the last question is a resounding, "Yes."

At the end of the circle all of us except Mr. Brady, the student support staff member at the school, grab our chairs and return to the choir room. Luis nervously approaches me with a black laptop bag and asks if it is mine. I say I am not sure who it belongs to. "I just didn't want anyone to take it," he says.

Students and adults from other circles slowly trickle in. Upon reconvening the entire group, Angela asks participants to debrief the circle process and their conversations. One White woman with silver hair pulled back into a ponytail says, "I've been in education 20 years, and this is the most moving event I have attended. To read such a powerful book and have students lead us in conversations about something as difficult as race . . ." She turns her head around and extends her arm to the students. "You all are truly impressive."

Once the event is over, Angela approaches me and looks exultant. "This is all because of circles! It's something we've been building over time. This is a process, and students are buying in." Carol walks up, and they excitedly share how students who are never on time all showed up. I marvel at how students have used circles to make relevant connections between an historic piece of literature and their lives. Carol and Angela hug, teary eyed.

Mr. Brady, the administrator from my circle, looks disgruntled as he returns to the choir room. His laptop bag has been taken. Luis stands behind him and says he discovered the laptop bag in the boys' restroom and turned it into the main office. "I swear I just found it there," he says, raising up both hands as if under arrest. Mr. Brady looks at him warily. One hour later Luis confesses to having taken the bag. He is suspended for five days.

Luis acted in a "Circle way" whenever I spoke to him throughout the year, within circle and in most—though not all—interactions I observed between him and teachers in Project Graduation. But minutes after a talking circle outside of the program, he committed a violation against a fellow participant. Why didn't Luis act in a "Circle way" once he left this circle? I approach Luis for an interview to find out, and he asks, "Am I in more trouble?" I assure him I just want to understand his perspective of discipline in the school.

He says he would be happy to talk to me as long as I take the time to get to know him. "Not that I don't trust you, but you know that way we can get to know each other better."

I tell him that I can meet him on the weekend as he has to work during the week. "We can meet for lunch. I will take you out as a thank you," I say.

He says, "How about you come over to my house, and my mom cooks for *you*?" I'm surprised by generosity, only because I barely know him, but the offer seems to signal his interest in sharing his biography.

It is a beautiful Sunday morning on my drive to East Boston, located by the Boston Harbor near Logan Airport. Luis's neighborhood is filled with the largest population of Mexican and Central American immigrants in New England and bustles with pedestrians shopping along sidewalks in front of dollar stores, barber shops, money transfer businesses and small bodegas decorated with native flags and multilingual signs. Identical three-story buildings, each painted a slightly different shade of grey, flank one another on opposing sides of Luis's street. In the entryway of his building, toys are strewn beneath a wide stairwell. The building feels as though it has housed many tenants over the decades. Because the apartments are not labeled, I call him, and he comes down and greets me with a large hug. His waxen hair spirals out from behind a headband, and his eyes are alert; he tells me he has only been awake for a few minutes. When I walk in two kittens scurry through the adjoining living and dining room. The space is darkened by drawn curtains. "You like my little home?" he asks.

"It is really warm," I say with a smile.

Over the next hour Luis describes a life story that parallels those of his peers; nearly all the students I interview in Project Graduation have a long history of school suspension, and Luis's story exemplifies how discipline and achievement are indeed "two sides of the same coin" (Gregory, Skiba, & Noguera, 2010) as his exclusion from school paralleled his disengagement from academics. At his previous high school, he was repeatedly suspended for five days at a time for anything from fighting to whistling songs that were associated with his gang, which he joined in fifth grade. He was once suspended for giving a teacher a nasty look. Suspensions provided a buffer between Luis and teachers who did not want to deal with his disciplinary issues. Like James, Luis was told that if he stopped showing up to class, he would pass. He says, "My junior year was basically spent here [home] because I would go one day and then I would get suspended again." He was finally arrested and expelled when, like Darius, he was found in possession of a knife he carried for his commute to and from school. He explains, "I'd rather feel safe than sorry."

Luis's need to feel safe is not surprising given that he has been exposed to violence from a young age not only in his neighborhood but near campus on his first day at Bridge, when a man wearing a bandanna put a gun to his face and threatened him because of the color of his baseball cap. The confrontation is a chilling reminder of the potential for students to face life-threatening circumstances only a short walk away from school. Luis says, "I said, 'If you're gonna shoot me, then do it then.'" Ultimately the man walked away. Luis sounds unfazed by the idea of dying. At the time, he did not tell any of his teachers about the incident. I tell him that what happened to him is horrible. He shrugs. "No, it's not horrible because I see it every day out here." In fact, he wanted to conduct the interview at his house because if we went to a nearby restaurant, he was afraid someone from an opposing gang would approach him and endanger me.

Luis first intrigued me during a talking circle months earlier when students were asked where they saw themselves in five years. He was normally jovial in circle, laughing along with his peers when someone cracked a joke. But that day he was serious. His face was pale as he said, "If I keep going the way that I'm going, I'll be dead." A few students chuckled. But there was no smile on his face. "No, I'm serious. If I don't change, then I will be dead." Angela has spoken to him at length about his near-death encounters, including the experience at the bus stop:

> [Luis felt like] 'Don't flash that thing and not use it.' It was this moment of, he didn't want to live with that dread anymore. It's almost worse to worry about it. Kill me, but stop with this threat of my death every day. He really says that; 'Every night I don't know if I'm going to die.' He's the only student I know that's in real retaliation; he's caught up in all this in a big way. It's really sad.

When I interview him a second time, I feel more comfortable probing him on the subject of how he feels about taking Mr. Brady's laptop, an offense that now seems trivial compared to other crimes he has alluded to but not been arrested for. When I ask him why he took it, he says simply, "I wanted it." He has written a paper for Angela in which he says that he has no regrets about taking it. He walked out of his suspension hearing because, he says, "I didn't want to hear what I did. I know what I did, and they kept bringing it back up, so I got up and left . . . I said, 'Just give me my days, and I'll go home.'"

This is not the first time I have heard the refrain, "Just give me my days." In my teaching days, the words seemed to express a student's desire to expedite the all-too-familiar process of punishment and avoid being shamed through lectures and disappointed looks. The phrase also sounds like a reference to a prison sentence. Luis has been suspended from school for years, and for him this is just another ritual. Angela says that something like a healing circle, in which students must sit face-to-face with whoever they have harmed, is far more difficult than leaving school. Luis tells me that Mr. Brady has always labeled him as a troublemaker, so I understand why he may not feel guilty about the theft. But in saying, "I just wanted it" and "Just give me my days," he is not truly held accountable to Mr. Brady for his actions. Mr. Brady said he would not press charges if the laptop was returned, and Luis was simply sent home.

To hear Luis express no remorse or accountability for the theft, and to hear him explicitly express a desire to resolve the incident through suspension, does not feel like a legitimate reparation of harm. I don't think his teachers would disagree. Angela made sure to communicate her disappointment about the incident to Luis. "We can't help but feel differently about our students after they do something like this . . . That's the consequence of this kind of stuff. You break trust with people. And he said it. He said, 'You're not going to look at me the same after this.'"

Angela was particularly disappointed that a circle way of being did not always permeate the boundaries of that circle: "He's been really successful in our program doing really well . . . It's really upsetting. And then he [stole] it [right] after circle. It just goes to show you the issues run so deep." Because Angela is familiar with Luis's background and gang involvement, she understands that restorative practices do not simply erase the impact of prior experiences of students or the obstacles they face once they leave the program or the building. The challenge of restorative justice is that the outcomes are not always immediate, and as a result it can be difficult for practitioners to remain committed to the practice or to convince skeptics—such as teachers in the rest of the building who experienced difficult interactions with Project Graduation students—of its success.

And Luis *did* experience success, graduating that year despite how far he had fallen behind, a testament to the relationships he built with each teacher. "[They all] say go to college. Mr. Johnston told me that I can be down with the hood and actually be somebody." It took time for Luis to come to trust each teacher. He felt that William "had a grudge" against him until he went to ask him for help. "[Mr. Johnston] said, 'I'm going to push you. You might get mad, you might want to beat me up but I'm going to help you get good grades." Learning the backstory of his teachers also pushed him to take their advice more seriously. "People walk all over Ms. Spellman. They don't know what has happened to her in the past . . . with her cancer . . . Before [that] I never used to take her seriously." He says that once she shared her story with him, he started listening when she explained how to use the credit recovery system on the computer, which allowed him to graduate on time.

Even Principal Patricia Beatty told him, "I'm going to help you graduate no matter what." Luis feels he has been successful academically because of the relationships engendered through practices such as circle. For him, Project Graduation is

> way better because I seen that I feel like I'm somebody. I'm a powerful voice . . . The first [circle] it was like, why am I here? It was taking me out of class, and I don't think that's what I wanted. But I actually kind of like it because teachers stop teaching for a couple of hours; they take the time to get to know us; they ask us what they want to ask. They want us to trust them, and not that many people trust people so that's basically a group. It's trust; everything we say is trust.

It only took a few months for Luis to begin trusting his teachers in the program. But the goal of restorative practices, says Angela, is to help students "navigate beyond the walls of the program," such that they would not even think of engaging in harmful behaviors outside of their own SLC. She operates on the faith that one day her students will be able to avoid conflicts in other spaces as well and that restorative justice provides at least a seed for more positive behaviors.

When I think of a person who epitomizes the positive impact that restorative justice can have on a student over a much longer period of time, I immediately picture Jaylen Robertson, a dark-skinned student with large, expressive eyes and dreads that fall below his shoulders. He dresses fashionably in sagging, black pants, a brown belt, a black T-shirt with multicolored shapes, black shoes with untied black shoelaces, and a black, zip-up cardigan. I have known him for three years, and he was one of the first students who regularly said "hello" when I came to visit his classroom in SLC A during his sophomore year. It was hard to observe some of his behaviors. Several of my field notes are peppered with moments in one of Angela's most difficult classes where he randomly would yell out profanities, engage in paper throwing as she lectured, sleep or refuse to do work.

> Angela is trying to get students in this large class of 30 students to focus, but there are several students talking. I am sitting in the back of the class behind a group of loquacious students. Angela says, "All talking needs to stop now, please."
>
> Mitch is talking to Bill about another girl. "She's got no titties. She's got no breasts."
>
> Laura and Jaylen are talking, and she says to him, "You're mad like, gay." Angela scans the room as other people engage in side conversations.
>
> Mitch says to Jaylen, "Jaylen's gay."
>
> Jaylen says, "You can suck my dick."
>
> Mitch says, raising the tone of his voice, "I'm not gay." Mitch says, "Ask anyone in this class. That kid grabs ass. That's all I'm gonna say. And it's not female ass. So guess the other one." Angela asks what people could write down in a notebook where they are taking down annotations.
>
> A student at the front of the class says, "Inferences."
>
> Jaylen mutters something followed by a loud, "Fuck!"

To address the side discussions and lack of focus in this large class, Angela organized a healing circle and invited parents and other teachers in SLC A. All parents were invited, and about seven showed up. During the circle Jaylen said, "I fall asleep in class because of how bad things are in here. I'm up at the door ready to leave before the bell rings." Once Jaylen's mother received the talking piece, she said:

> It's hard to hear that Jaylen is not being productive. This is the first day of the rest of your life. I take my hat off to you teachers because you're with my kids all day long, and I don't even want to see them that long

(laughter in the room) . . . This is collective responsibility and collective accountability.

Jaylen says he began to improve his behavior after the circle: "The reason I've been improving a little bit, well more, is because my mother came in, and that was really, like, it shocked me, because my mother, she never comes for anything." He says circle was the first time that he publicly owned up to sleeping during class and not doing his work. He cannot always be honest with his mother, and admitting his behaviors in front of a group helped keep him accountable. "[In a circle] I'm with a group of people, and I can open up. I have a lot of witnesses that prove that I'm being serious now." I did observe him steadily improve his work ethic over the year after multiple experiences in circles and one-on-one conferences with his teachers. Angela met with him at least once a month to keep him accountable for coming to school on time and completing his work. Several of these conferences included Laura and Roland, two of his friends from the same class who also needed support. During each meeting Angela, and sometimes other teachers, discussed agreements that had been made and whether they had been met:

> Angela starts by checking in about what goals had been set last week in contracts the students had written up. Jaylen says his goal was to get to school on time. Angela says, "The coming here on time—definitely not working." She laughs and he smiles. He also says he wanted to do homework but was not finishing it on time.
> "Is the issue about organization?" asks Angela.
> "I'm just lazy," says Jaylen.
> "I don't buy laziness."
> Jaylen reveals all the responsibilities he has when he gets home. "My mother always wants me to clean." Mondays from 6 to 10 pm he participates in a group to prepare him for college. Tuesdays he participates in basketball games from 6 to 8 pm and practices afterwards. Wednesday he has Bible study.
> Angela says, "A teenage boy in Bible study? That's really good. We respect that." He says on Saturdays he sleeps by 2 am so that he can sleep five hours and get to church on Sunday, but as a result he falls asleep in class.
> Angela suggests, "What if we try to do a homework club before school . . . I can bring breakfast." Jaylen says that his alarm goes off, but he turns it off. Angela narrows her eyes and says, "It's not about the alarm." He plays with a long gold rope chain, maintaining eye contact with Angela. I have never seen him listen so intently.
> She asks Jaylen how his grades are, and he says he doesn't know because he didn't look at his report card. Angela sounds surprised. "You were the most improved tenth grader—you went from an F to a B."
> "An F?" he says.

"That's good," says Laura. Angela says she is willing to help students "fight this battle" of getting to school on time; if they could come by 7 am, she would bring breakfast, and they could do homework. Both students agree to come, especially if there is breakfast.

Though he claimed that he was unable to complete his schoolwork because of "laziness," it was clear from his daily schedule—his dedication to religion, sports and ironically, college preparation—that this was untrue. Sitting in on this meeting, my own stereotypes of Jaylen began to be dispelled. He was more than a student who yelled back at Angela from time to time or tore up assignments. Angela was able to remind him of his own agency, asserting that his lateness was not due to the alarm clock. In one-on-one conversations he told Janet and Angela about his private struggles with family and the roots of his anger, which stemmed from not feeling nurtured at home. Over the next three years, he blossomed into a serious student and was offered a full scholarship to UCLA. His senior year he joined Project Graduation, where he continued to receive individualized attention in a restorative climate. Along with other BHS students, he also led circle trainings that I organized at Harvard, speaking to preservice teachers about how restorative justice helped him succeed and improve relationships with teachers.

It would be reductive to ascribe his success solely to the restorative culture at his school. Yet it seems clear that had he been suspended every time he used profanity or engaged in horseplay, he might have had a very different educational journey. After all like the other teachers, I am aware that restorative justice, like anything in life, has an evolving impact on students—some students might be immediately impacted after one circle, as in the case with the female students in Mary's class. Other students like Jaylen need years of support by the same group of teachers before feeling motivated enough to commit to their studies. The close relationships he forged with his teachers provided a foundation for his path toward graduation. He cites circle as part of his success:

> Circle showed me that my teachers care because some don't give a fuck. They don't want to be around students, but here we get to know teachers on a personal level. When people talk to you about your life goals . . . It's a good feeling because you build a relationship most people don't have with their teachers. It calms me down, and I can focus better because I'm not worried that teachers are talking behind my back.

It is long-term faith and persistence that push the staff forward as they continue the work. Despite occasional setbacks experienced with individual students, Angela has gained perspective on the overall academic progress of her students and how many have acquired a newfound commitment to education. The day after the *Native Son* symposium, Angela says wistfully,

We [the staff] all have a lot of love for this. I was on a huge high yesterday. I was like this is what I always imagined might happen . . . to me it's a culmination. [Circle] is intellectual; it's emotional; it's responsive to real student needs. I loved walking around and hearing the students talking about their real experience with race and racism and what they think about it. How often do people get to do that?

THE REVOLUTION

In the end, Rebecca and Angela fear that bottom-up implementation has not done enough to truly create conditions for a school-wide shift toward restorative justice. "I know Project Graduation is doing some restorative justice, but it has not infiltrated or it hasn't permeated the rest of the school," says Rebecca.

Angela agrees that implementation cannot be "top down only" but that teachers working from the bottom up do not have the capacity to "launch a campaign for restorative justice in the school."

Lucy believes restorative justice was effective in building relationships and addressing conflicts in SLC A because every adult in her SLC, including Rebecca Stern, was willing to participate in the circle process: "[Restorative justice] ended up becoming a big part of our small learning community, for every member of it, our administrators, our lead administrator. I think there has to be buy-in at the top, and I truly believe there has to be some accountability." Lucy believes that principals in new schools attempting to implement restorative justice must dictate its importance and that there has to be some top-down support in which principals say, "This is how we're using our comp planning time—deal with it," for teachers to ever try it.

In the spring of 2011, two and a half years after my initial visit to BHS, I make an appointment with Dr. Beatty to discuss the progress of restorative practices at the school. I am surprised to learn that in the fall, all freshmen students and their teachers will be introduced to circles. The school will then ramp up professional development so that 10th-grade teachers will be trained in restorative justice the next year, 11th-grade teachers the year after that, and 12th-grade teachers the following year. The impetus for this latest change came from an afternoon professional development in which Lucy talked about the use of circles in Project Graduation and SLC A. Dr. Beatty says teachers told her it was "the best professional development they had attended," and the buzz provided the momentum to implement restorative practices more systematically.

Just as it takes persistence for restorative practices to transform individual behaviors, it has taken time for the philosophy to spread to other parts of the building. Although Angela no longer works at the school—she has moved to California with her husband and newborn daughter—I know she would be proud to learn that restorative justice may soon undergird disciplinary practices in *all* of BHS, not just one SLC. In concert with Rebecca Stern, Angela exemplifies Emerson's contention that revolution can begin in one person's mind. Nevertheless, as Chesterton states, some agreement among like-minded people may be necessary to fuel a revolution. Dr. Beatty understands this delicate balance. I remind her about how she once told me she believes in "evolution, not revolution." She smiles, repeating, "Restorative justice is something I really believe in; it is the way to go." However, she has thought purposefully about how to spread the value of restorative justice and simultaneously honor the autonomy of teachers. She wants a democracy so that there is enough buy-in for a revolution toward restorative justice. Rather than enforcing a strict, one-size-fits-all model of restorative discipline for next year, she is advocating a "blended model":

> I don't sit in this office and decide how change should be done. I try to create structures for teachers where teachers are given some options and ideas and told things have to change. For example, to say to the ninth-grade teachers, "You're going to get trained in restorative justice. Based on the training I want you to create a blended model." If they say, "We are so thrilled with this, and we want to do 100 percent restorative justice," [and] as long as they can practically do it, I'm delighted, but I don't think they will. I don't think they're ready to do that.

Dr. Beatty is mandating a change, but she is also allowing for a blended model in which staff decide just "how much" restorative justice they want to use and how much traditional discipline (i.e., suspensions) they want to employ. The hope is that restorative practices will successfully mitigate conflicts and that teachers will eventually be drawn away from the traditional, punitive model of discipline. However, Dr. Beatty is aware that teachers may not be "ready to do that" and provides teachers the space in which to use their own discretion when handling student disciplinary matters.

Despite the persistent tensions between top-down and bottom-up approaches to seeding restorative justice, the practice continues to evolve at BHS—not only because of the imperfect implementation of circles by a few individuals but also because of administrative leaders like Rebecca Stern and Patricia Beatty. They have invested in the implementation of long-term change in school discipline through their own participation and leadership in healing, talking and staff circles. The "success" of restorative justice has been hard to quantify—in some cases students relate to one another better and do better academically, and in other cases students commit harm without being held accountable for their actions. Yet changing a school culture in which teachers do not want to suspend students but feel as if they have no other options, and in which students who get in trouble may say, "Just give me my days," takes time and commitment. The graduation in June provides a well-deserved opportunity to gaze on the young people in Project Graduation in their satiny caps and gowns and bask in all that they have achieved.

The day before graduation I go on Facebook to contact some students to find out when and where the ceremony will take place. On the newsfeed, Jacob posts:

> i graduate today
>   . . . nobody really knows how big of a deal this is for me . . . i never thought it would happen . . . but somehow it made it happen with help from others . . . ♥ for every 1 who kept me motivated i love yall.

Jacob, Luis and Jaylen graduated along with seven other peers from Project Graduation. Jacob and Jaylen went on to pursue higher education. After disappearing for several months, Darius returned to the program and graduated the following year. And perhaps this *is* revolutionary, after all.

NOTE

1. The protagonist of the novel.

6 "I Am Not Extraordinary"
Janet Connors and the Role of Community Members in Restorative Justice

I first hear Janet Connors's story in a talking circle in 2008. We are in a 10th-grade class at BHS, where teachers in SLC A have been using circles with their weekly advisories to build community. At this point I only know Janet as a fellow from the Center for Restorative Justice who grew up in Boston, comes to the school weekly to keep circles, and has worked in various capacities in the community for nearly 40 years. She is a broad woman, five foot ten, with short, salt-and-pepper hair and bangs that frame gleaming, green-grey eyes and a square, naturally flushed face. She ambles when she walks, her upper body slightly shifting side to side, right hand clutching a copper-colored cane that supports arthritic legs. She looks to be in her late 50s and is wearing a slate-gray T-shirt, gathered black pants, glossy maroon clogs, and several pieces of jewelry: a silver ring with a large, black opal on her left hand, a textured turquoise ring on her right hand, and long strands of amber around her neck. Hers is the only White face in this room of 20 Black, Asian and Latino students.

We have just shared our highs and lows of the week when math teacher Simone Forrester gets the piece. A tall, slender Black woman, Simone wears a track suit and fashionable athletic shoes. Her hair is pulled back in a wispy bun. She has told me that this year has been a struggle for her because of discipline issues but that she is starting to enjoy circles. She says quickly, as if just thinking of it, "Write a question that you might want to ask. Just take a minute." Students pass slips of scratch paper around the circle.

When I get mine, I press it to my knee and write, "If you could spend a day with anybody, who would that be and why?"

A student collects the papers, puts them into a hat, and Simone pulls out my prompt. After reading it aloud, a student asks, "Dead or alive?"

"Anyone you want," says Simone. She passes the piece to Janet, seated next to her.

"I would spend it with my son Joel, who was murdered eight years ago," begins Janet, "and I would spend it with him 'cause I miss him so much, and I would love to know what he looks like now. I would love to know what he feels now." Her lips upturn in a soft smile, and she gracefully meets all of our gazes. "I would love to know what he would be doing if he were alive."

Students continue to pass the piece and share their own answers; 10 minutes later when we are halfway around the circle, a student turns to Janet. "How did your son die, if you don't mind answering me?" He verbalizes what I imagine many of us are wondering.

"He was stabbed to death," says Janet. She stops and looks around to address the group, not just this one student. "He was livin' in an apartment on Columbia Road with roommates, and his roommate had fallen and hurt his back, and he got a prescription for OxyContin from a doctor. Then when he realized what that would translate to on the street, he got a second prescription. My son was also sellin' weed. These kids who killed him, there were four of them. They were Oxy addicts, and some of them actually were into heroin, too."

"How old was he?" asks one girl.

"He was 19."

"What was their race?" asks one boy. "Who killed him?"

Janet sighs and puts her hands on her knees. Students are not supposed to talk until they receive the talking piece, but they are enraptured, quieter than they have been since the circle began 20 minutes prior—silent, in fact. Janet says, "We're breakin' circle here, but if that's OK, I will do this." A few of us nod.

"They were all white kids, and they broke into the apartment 'cause they knew that there was drugs and therefore money in the house . . . They kicked in that door into the apartment too. They had guns and masks and knives. They went into the front of the house where most of Joel's roommates and his friends were hangin' out . . . They had asked them all to lay down, to get down on the floor, and they pistol-whipped one of Joel's friends, and when Joel wouldn't lay down, the kid stabbed him. He was stabbed in his heart."

Janet is speaking in a matter-of-fact tone. A few students exchange glances, raising their eyebrows, looking down, or straight into Janet's eyes.

"His friends were stuffing towels into his wound, and they called 911, and they were tryin' to give him CPR, but he died very shortly after gettin' to Boston Medical Center, and I only tell ya the details of it because his friends stayed there."

Here Janet's voice trembles ever so slightly. She shakes her head, looks up to the ceiling and then returns to the faces in the circle.

"That's how it happened, and I also tell you the details around it because neither my son nor his friends would have thought of themselves as drug dealers. His friend thought, 'hey [I] got a prescription and I could make some extra money. Oh, I'm sellin' a little bit of weed to my friends.'"

Janet's words are suspended in the air. It feels like this is probably not the first time she has shared this experience, and indeed I hear her recount it many more times in circles around Boston over the next few years. Her story is one of struggle, unanticipated grief, and the importance of loyalty and friendship. It has been shared intentionally to communicate the perils of something that seems as innocuous as selling weed. And for these young students, some of whom are close to the same age as Joel was when he died—and some of whom may be engaging in the underground economy to make extra money—it is a cautionary tale, though not an unfamiliar one. That very day other students talk about losing an uncle who was killed and a friend who was shot at a party over the weekend. What students have yet to hear, but will learn in subsequent circles, is how Janet has made her own peace: another story for another day, and one that she hopes can instill a sense of possibility about how to nonviolently address conflicts they face in and outside of school.

THE CONCEPT OF COMMUNITY

By all accounts, the rest of Janet Connors's story is extraordinary. After her son Joel was murdered at the age of 19 in January of 2001, she was the first person in Massachusetts to participate in a restorative practice called Victim Offender Dialogue (VOD), in which she met with—and forgave—two of the four men involved in the killing once they followed through on agreements to stay employed, attend substance abuse programs, and become mentors in their neighborhoods. Yet despite her remarkable story, Janet insists that she is "not extraordinary." She knows of dozens of female survivors of homicide who feel just as she does—that restorative justice is integral not only for their own healing but for the reparation necessary to prevent further violence in urban communities. Yet the very people from the communities most impacted by crime may be excluded from restorative practices: "Too often, the victims, offenders, and community members who are the primary subjects of the restorative justice movement, in that they are the ones who participate in restorative justice programs, are ignored voices within the larger movement" (Woolford, 2009, p. 21).

But what defines community? In the past the concept of community was limited to a geographic space in which it was presumed that people who lived in the same neighborhood shared social bonds and resources (Boyes-Watson, 2005). By participating in local organizations and religious institutions, these individuals became politically engaged in their communities through long-term relationships with fellow residents (Warren, 2001). However, the decline of civic institutions has led to a redefinition of the term: community can be ascribed not just to a geographic space but to one's relationships in many different contexts, whether in the workplace, school or among disparate networks of friends and relatives. Restorative justice theorist McCold (2004) differentiates between these *microcommunities*—those networks of relationships that we rely on for individual support—and *macro communities*, groups defined "by geography or membership" (p. 156). Both provide valuable networks of support for individual members; however, this portrait focuses on the role of *macro community* members in restorative justice, examining how Janet Connors, a parent and activist born and raised in Boston, has made inroads as a strong voice within the restorative justice movement in the city.

Although Janet's story is indeed extraordinary, this portrait provides lessons not only about her singular journey but about the benefits of, and barriers to, involving nonprofessional community members like herself in restorative practices. Through her community work and involvement in VOD, Janet brings the following to restorative practices in schools: an ability to communicate restorative principles with her narrative, firsthand knowledge of many of the students and their neighborhoods and a vision for how to maximize the potential of restorative practices in spaces beyond schools. While Janet exemplifies how community members are an essential and often untapped resource in urban schools trying to initiate disciplinary reform, her experiences additionally reveal the challenges of doing so when the field of restorative justice has become increasingly professionalized—disenfranchising the very people most affected by punitive education and criminal justice systems.

I begin by outlining Janet's journey as a restorative practitioner and community activist, tracing her interest in the philosophy to her upbringing, struggles as a working-class, single mom and finally through participation in VOD. Next, I transition to her work in schools, analyzing how these early experiences informed and strengthened circle practices in Boston. Finally, I discuss the limitations placed on noncredentialed community members in a movement that many fear is becoming led by people affiliated with universities and professional organizations, who are often geographically removed from the very macro communities they are trying to impact.

RESTORATIVE ROOTS: UPBRINGING, MOTHERHOOD AND LOSS

I am standing in front of Janet's house for the first time. This quiet street is lined with older one- and two-story homes, inhabited by community members she has known for decades. I have known her for one year and never imagined when I first heard her story that I would one day sit in her home to hear about her restorative journey. I tentatively asked whether I could write her portrait, sensitive to the fact that she may not have wanted to say more about Joel and her experiences with restorative justice than she already has; I was grateful when she quietly nodded and said, "That would be really validating for me."

She has invited me into her home for lunch so that we can conduct our interview in the most comfortable environment possible. The house is composed of two hues, a light blue complemented by a navy blue lining the edges of the triangular roof. I am not surprised by the blue because Janet is always bedecked with turquoise rings, bracelets and pendants. I also know she loves the water and swims every day to ease the pain from fibromyalgia and arthritis. I walk on concrete slabs across her lawn, calmed by the light tinkling of heart-shaped wind chimes dangling from the roof of her porch and the sweet, earthy smell of an incense stick burning on the window ledge by the front door. A sign below the metal doorknob reads, "Peace to all who enter here." Were this a stranger's home, I would be highly skeptical of the incense and the greeting. I would wonder if the person inside had a relatively easy life and therefore had the privilege of peace and the audacity to bestow it upon others. But because this is Janet's home, I accept this blessing with the respect for the discipline I expect it has taken for her to promote such peace.

As soon as I enter Janet encircles me with one of her signature, warm hugs. She is clad in a spectrum of blues—a turquoise T-shirt with a braided, V-neck, aquamarine, speckled oval pendant on a silver chain and a silver bracelet with deep-blue, interlinked circles. We settle in at the kitchen table and eat homemade tacos before I pull out my recorder and a list of questions. She folds her hands, leaning in, open to answering. Janet has lived in this predominantly working-class neighborhood her entire life and tells me how Dorchester morphed from a predominantly White neighborhood of Polish, Lithuanian, Italian, Jewish and Irish immigrants to one filled with African Americans and newcomers from Southeast Asia, the Caribbean, Eastern Europe and other regions around the globe. It is this geographic space she refers to most when using the term *community*:

> I feel very connected to Dorchester. I feel very rooted, and I've seen it go through many changes. When I grew up, it was a largely white community, and now, it's the most diverse community in the city. In some ways, I feel like I've traveled because I feel like the world came to Dorchester, and I've learned a lot through that. In the changes and as the changes happened, I learned a lot about justice and injustice about racism, about classism.

It is here in Dorchester that she participated in the Civil Rights Movement, living through the busing crisis that took place during desegregation. In prepping for our interview I read *Common Ground* (Lukas, 1986)—a Pulitzer Prize-winning narrative of school busing in Boston—and learned that several civil rights legends peopled this area at some point in their lives; Martin Luther King, Jr. lived in this neighborhood as a doctoral student at Boston University, Dorchester resident William Monroe Trotter worked with W. E. B. DuBois to found the National Association for the Advancement of Colored People (NAACP) and Malcolm X lived in neighboring Roxbury. Janet is featured in this book because of her involvement in an organization called Racial Unity Now (RUN), a group of working-class Whites from Dorchester who worked on, among other issues, reducing racial violence against Black families moving into formerly White neighborhoods.

Her connection to community—exhibited in over four decades of work with families and local nonprofit organizations—was modeled by her parents, who participated in civic and religious institutions. Her mother led the Cub Scouts and Girl Scouts and instilled in Janet the value of giving back to the community through their involvement with the Catholic Church. "My father was a cop. He worked on the harbor; he was the engine man on the boat. And he worked some as a mechanic if he had weekends off . . . So he worked a lot. But he was also a member of the Holy Name Society and all that sort of stuff," she says, referencing the Catholic organization that promotes public service. "So I think I got in terms of being part of a community and being active in a community I got that from [my parents]. But the left politics . . . we were raised Catholic and just sort of really believing everything that they talked about, about people being created equal, about loving thy neighbor, you know, that kind of stuff—and then seeing the contradictions in that as I got older. I think it's sort of what set me on a more social justice path."

Later into the interview, she looks to the side, eyes beaming before she chuckles. She says that her Catholic school upbringing presaged one of her core restorative beliefs: that everyone had goodness inside of them. "I remember the nun was drawing pictures on the chalkboard. They used to do it like a T-shirt, almost this is your soul, and your soul is pure, and then you make a mistake and you get a little Xs on your soul. But you can erase the bad, so it kind of goes in line with even the Catholicism that I knew growing up too." Janet grew up thinking that despite the Xs marked on the souls of people who commit harm, an individual can always return to her "core self," a phrase she borrows from Robin Casarjin, founder of an organization dedicated to developing emotional literacy in prisoners (Marxsen, 2003). This core self, which Casarjin defines as the "greater self," refers to a primordial goodness in all humans. Casarjin states, "We all possess an intrinsic wisdom, power, courage, peacefulness, and intelligence" (Marxsen). Says Janet, "I think that I always believed that most people have good in them. I saw in my father that there was an ugliness and a meanness to him, and there was also a goodness to him."

Janet's beliefs in restorative principles are clear when she talks about the "meanness" and "goodness" in her father in the same breath:

> He was an alcoholic, and he was abusive; he was physically and verbally abusive and actually to me sexually abusive, and he was physically and verbally abusive to my mom. He really was a Jekyll/Hyde kind of person—he really did have two personalities. So he could be very charming. I think I definitely get my laugh from him. I get my sense of humor from him too.

After this Janet begins talking about her mother. But I am temporarily stunned by what she has just said, unable to comprehend the ease with which she lists his offenses. It is remarkable to me that she would share the ugly details about her father's brutality toward her, her mother and siblings only to follow up by attributing one her most signature and wonderful qualities—her sense of humor and accompanying laugh—to this same man. Her laugh usually commences with a hiccup-like titter, as if her belly is gearing up for release. Very quickly the laugh turns into a throaty vibrato; close your eyes, and you hear a smile in her laugh. Open your eyes, and you see parentheses of laugh lines surrounding watery eyes. Now that I know where her laugh comes from, I wonder if I will hear it differently in the future.

With the birth of her son at age 19, Janet's experiences as a single mother propelled her into a lifetime of community work. Her father continued abusing her, staggering into her room smelling of alcohol, calling her "slut" and "whore." She left home and relied on welfare to support her family. Welfare workers looked in her refrigerator, checked in her closet and made assumptions about her, treating her and other single mothers she knew disrespectfully. Janet joined the National Welfare Rights organization and trained mothers whose requests for assistance were denied to be "assertive, not aggressive" in making their demands. In connecting her challenges with those of the women around her, she began to develop a broader awareness of class- and race-based inequity in her neighborhood, which led her to act on other issues that plagued her community. She began protesting the Vietnam War after 11 people she knew died during combat. She worked to oust a corrupt judge. She knew several families whose heat was turned off in the wintertime when they could not afford to pay their bills; she and a group of people walked around and turned their heat back on. She says, "It was through that time in my life that I learned that we have our own personal experiences and struggles but that they will always go beyond our own individual experiences and our own individual struggles."

Through her activism she became acquainted with restorative justice and says that she has implicitly practiced the philosophy throughout her career. She first heard the term as a volunteer in a prison busing program, where she provided rides to people visiting incarcerated family members. She learned specifically about circle practices in the 1970s as feminist groups began using them to bring people together to discuss different issues. In the late 1990s she worked with Roca[1] (Spanish for "rock"), an organization recognized nationwide for using circles to address the needs of young people and commit them to maintaining peaceful lives. It was there that she was formally trained in the circle process. Perhaps because she has used a similar process working with young children and families in various capacities throughout her career, she retrospectively refers to her work with children and families as "circles."

Along the way, Janet, like many community members around her, balanced being an activist with taking care of her family as a single mother.

Ten years after her first child David was born, Janet gave birth to Shana, who she says was always much more adventurous than her male siblings. "She was actually the one I worried the most about as a teenager; I never actually thought anything would happen to Joel. Because he was in a lot of ways naïve and timid. He used to call me . . ." says Janet, holding an imaginary phone, her voice falling an octave lower as she imitates his frequent calls, "'I'm going to the plaza. Now we're back from the plaza. Now I'm going here . . .'" As a child, Janet remembers him as clinging to her, seeking safety rather than treading into new territory. Tethered to Janet by a small rope, toddler Joel would bob amid dainty splashes in his neighbor's aboveground pool, floaties girding his thin arms, a foam belt snapped around his waist. "Then," says Janet, "all of a sudden he was 10 years old and jumping off some 10-foot tower. So he needed to take his time, but then he truly embraced things." I don't know what I was expecting to hear about Joel, and I have a hard time imagining what he was like. All I have known about him is that he was a good-looking young man with a square face, kind eyes, thick eyebrows and a thin line of light brown hair extending around his face at the edge of his jaw line; this I have seen from the button hanging from Janet's rearview mirror, a constant reminder that he is with her on her journey. I feel honored to be privy to these small bits of dialogue and the glossy light in Janet's eyes as she laughs about his "clinginess."

Joel, born one year after his sister, did not necessarily seek out conflict, but it was part of the context in which he grew up; he fought at school every day to defend himself because, according to Shana, "if you didn't defend yourself, you were a target every day." He ended up getting his diploma through City Roots, an alternative program for students struggling in traditional schools. He attempted to gain his computer certification but was unsuccessful. When he died he was a truck driver for a thrift store and a bouncer for an 18 and over club, jobs that did not satisfy his financial desires. "He *loved* money," says Janet of Joel. "He loved things. I saw him graduate from silver to gold to platinum in his desire for jewelry—not that he had gobs of it, he had one platinum bracelet—he paid $150 for his engine to be painted blue and for dashboard lights that you can make blue and green, stupid stuff," laughs Janet. She talks about his love of objects with a light, teasing humor, as if talking about "kids today" and their values.

Yet this need for objects also led to serious repercussions as Joel began selling marijuana. Janet did not want young people in the house smoking weed and told him he could drink in front of her when he was 21 but not before then. Seeking freedom, Joel moved out into an apartment with his friends at age 19. I am trying to be careful now, balancing questions about Joel's death with focusing on the restorative acts Janet organized in the aftermath. I pause, seeking no comfort in the interview questions I have typed below me. The words come out haltingly. "How long was he living there before he was—"

"Three months," she says, her voice low, difficult to hear. I nod my head, sitting in the silence before voicing further questions.

*

The four men involved in Joel's death were known for invading and robbing homes. On January 13, 2001, they broke down the door to Joel's apartment in search of drugs, money and equipment. "This was not the first home invasion they were a part of," says Janet. Joel was stabbed twice by two different men, but it was the first stabbing in the heart that killed him.

In the aftermath of Joel's death, Janet had to work through her own mourning and address the possibility of retaliation in her community. Circle became the vehicle by which to galvanize those impacted by the murder and keep the peace. Janet decided to hold a series of conversations with those impacted by Joel's death. The idea for the conversations came from a woman named Gloria, a friend of Shana's and a street worker[2] who was on the critical incident responders' team, the "trauma team for the community." She told Janet and Shana that debriefings were being used with families and friends to reduce retaliatory incidents following murders. Gloria first conducted a debriefing with Joel's family, including Janet, her ex-husband and his wife, David and his girlfriend, and Shana. She worked with social workers to sponsor two more conversations that would allow loved ones to express their grief. But Janet pushed the workers to add one more restorative piece at the end of the dialogue: accountability to ensure that no one would seek revenge. "I was *immediately* struck by the devastation of young people's lives in this. So I was immediately struck by not only Joel's death but also by their lives, those four lives getting screwed up, and also Joel's friends and Shana and David's friends and the effects that it had on them." Some of the effects included the desire to avenge Joel's death. But Janet was clear that no one else should be murdered "in Joel's name." I have heard her use this phrase for the past two years—"not in Joel's name"—and it is always said slowly, reverentially, in a low register.

Because I know that no one was killed in response to Joel's death, the dialogues around Joel may have impacted the community in a way that is not easy to quantify. Drewery (2004) notes, "From a psychological perspective, it is clear to us that there is a strong link between the process of the [circle] and the success and longevity of its outcomes. In other words, the process of the conversation has a major influence in producing psychological change" (p. 338). While you can quantify the number of people murdered in a year, how can you quantify the number of prevented murders? How does one prove a direct causation between structured restorative conversations and nonviolence? Janet has an inherent belief that these conversations, which took place over the course of 10 months, worked:

A lot of the kids said they really wanted to do something, but that because me and my ex-husband had been so strong in expressing our desire for nothing else to happen in Joel's name, that they had restrained from it, but that sometimes it was hard. One of the people on the critical incident team said, "If you really want to [retaliate], what [do] you do?"

And some of them said, "Well, I think about Janet"—some of them called me Ma—"I think about Ma." So there it was, restorative justice was coming back into my life, and I wasn't even completely aware of it at the time.

But restorative justice would enter her life in a much more direct way following her encounters with the sentencing process, which was confusing at best, arbitrary at worst. Janet thought these young men would go to jail for a very long time. Three of the four men involved in the murder agreed to plea bargains. Two of the men testified and received sentences of 8 to 10 and 10 to 12 years, respectively. The third would not testify and received a sentence of 18 to 20 years. This man was known in the community as a "predator, as a psycho," says Janet. During the trial, his friends and family yelled epithets at Janet and her family, taking no accountability for Joel's death. "But when you go into someone's house," says Janet, "and you kick in the doors, and you have guns and knives and masks then you're responsible for what happens." The fourth man—the one whose stabbing caused the wound that ultimately killed Joel—was acquitted of all charges. "Suddenly," she says, "my interest in restorative justice was very much stirred up again. It was really hard to accept that verdict. It was really hard to deal with the fallout in terms of my son's friends, my other kids and their friends, my nieces and nephews . . . it was really hard to deal with the fact that somebody had gotten away with murder."

After Joel's death, Janet wanted assurance that these men would not commit harm again. She decided that to truly attain justice, she would need to see the men as human to reach out to them and express her grief and anger:

> I remember writing in my journal even before the arrests were made: who is this monster, who are these monsters? And then I remembered within a couple of months . . . they weren't monsters, and that if I thought of them as monsters, I let them off the hook. Because monsters hurt people, and people aren't supposed to hurt people, so that really the way to hold them accountable was to hold them in their humanity.

Janet contacted a man who facilitated VOD, in which "the victim is able to tell the offender about the crime's physical, emotional, and financial impact; to receive answers to lingering questions about the crime and the offender; and to be directly involved in developing a restitution plan . . ." (National Institute of Justice, 2012). At that time, there were no formal channels for victims in Massachusetts to participate in such a process, so Janet advocated to become the first person in the state to participate in VOD. The process only works if the offender agrees to take responsibility for his actions, and when she reached out to Larry, the first man who pleaded to manslaughter in the case, he agreed to participate.

Janet worked with a mediator for nine months before the first meeting, where she learned about the striking similarities between Larry and Joel's lives and the roots of Larry's criminal behavior. She brought a memorial book of the first anniversary of Joel's death filled with artwork, jottings and photos of tattoos and tagging friends had made to honor his passing. She spoke with Larry about her upbringing, and he talked about how when his alcoholic father left, he began selling drugs at the age of 11. Both Larry's and Janet's children have lost a parent; his father died while he was in prison, and Jill, Janet's long-term partner, passed away shortly after Joel died. Joel missed his sister's wedding because he was dead, and Larry missed his sister's wedding because he was incarcerated. Both have grown up with similar values in Irish American, working-class homes. He admitted how his actions did not reflect these values and took accountability for the impact of his actions on his friends. "His brother is now using heroin. Some of Joel's friends are using heroin, and while they may have gone that way or leaned toward that anyway, Joel's murder in both situations . . . pushed them further in the direction of addiction as opposed to stopping."

In trying to make things right for herself, Janet needed to express her fury and sadness and hoped that the man would turn his life around. "I told him that he had a piece of my forgiveness," says Janet, raising her eyebrows, lines creasing her forehead. "He would get the rest of it when he walked out the door and caused no harm to himself, his family or our community." Prior to his release, Janet met with Larry and his mother to look at his childhood photos. She once again reminded him that he can save himself and "make good" on his life; Joel no longer has that option. "He has since written many letters to the facilitator talking about what a difference having that dialogue has made for him and how he really hopes he can really live up to what he needs to do."

Janet then met with another man, Roland, who she calls the "ringleader" of the group. Now out for a few years, he is the only one of the four who has written Janet an apology letter. He agreed to accompany her to Joel's grave. As she did with Larry, Janet urged Roland to consider his life outside of prison. In a restorative context, victims may ask offenders to "take steps to change their behavior, reducing the likelihood that new crimes will be committed: perhaps these victims will encourage the offender to participate in alcohol or drug counseling" (Umbreit, Coates, & Vos, 2007, p. 35). Indeed, Janet encouraged him to continue to participate in programs that addressed his substance abuse. Roland made four agreements: to stay in Alcoholics Anonymous, talk to young people so that they could learn from his mistakes, keep a job that was lined up for him in construction once he got out, and cause no further harm to self, family or community.

After their dialogue, they met once again at the cemetery with his parents and the VOD mediator. Roland read her a letter filled with phrases they had used in their last meeting, and she read a letter to him that amazingly used almost the same verbiage: "He also wrote a poem that he read that was about not being able to bring Joel back, and that's a shame he'll never be able to live down, but how he has his life and has to take it and make it the best that he can." Once he got out, he kept to his agreements, was a mentor on the block, and ran 12-step groups. Janet folds her hands together. Shafts of sunlight move across the kitchen, and she shrugs lightly, revealing that she sometimes sees this boy's mother at Joel's gravesite.

In May 2012, Janet sat side-by-side with Roland and Larry in front of a room full of restorative justice advocates and community members as part of an afternoon session on VOD. After all three shared their experiences with the dialogues, Roland and Larry both broke down crying, sharing how they thought of Janet every night, owing her their second chance at life. Someone in the audience stood up, praising Janet, extending his hand out to her and saying, "Everyone in the community is inspired by what you've done here. You lost one son, but you gained two." She winced ever so slightly. I suspected that this was an extreme overstatement and was aghast that anyone should say such a thing. Perhaps Janet makes forgiveness look easy; Roland and Larry both expressed amazement that she ended their dialogues by hugging them. Yet forgiving these men has been far more difficult than Janet may convey through her heartfelt, compassionate demeanor. A week later she and I meet for brunch at the home of Donna Flaherty, a teacher at Equity who both of us have befriended through the restorative justice work. I ask her how she felt about that comment. She sighs. "Nothing can bring Joel back. The fact is they are not my sons, and I wanted to say more about that, but the moment kind of passed." Nonetheless by asking the young men responsible for killing Joel to make agreements to better their own lives, she remains committed to her belief that the men can return to their core selves and a belief that Joel has not died in vain. And through her advocacy, Janet has changed institutional options for people impacted by homicide; Massachusetts penal policy now offers all victims the opportunity to participate in VOD.

WORK IN SCHOOLS: FROM HEALING THE SELF TO HEALING THE COMMUNITY

Janet's work continued in collaboration with local organizations. After Joel's murder, Janet found employment that connected her to victims of violence in the community. She worked at the Louis D. Brown Peace Institute as a survivor support and leadership coordinator, providing people who have lost loved ones to homicide with access to services and support networks. She then worked at Roca,[3] where she met Carolyn Boyes-Watson, director of the Center for Restorative Justice at Suffolk University. Carolyn worked with Janet to research the use of circles with families and invited her to become a fellow at the center to give her, says Janet, an affiliation that could help provide further credibility for her to do work in schools. Janet was drawn to working in schools because of the preventative nature of working with students at a young age and because working with young people provides her with inspiration after losing Joel:

> I get to see kids, especially in the community building circles, I get to see kids like being tender and wise . . . I think that helps when you live in a community where there is so much youth violence going on and where there are so many people sort of dogging on the kids . . . it really helps me to be in this community, to live in this community, to keep a positive outlook, to keep hope for the future for the kids.

And it is her decades of community work, as well as her unique experience with restorative justice, that have enhanced circle practices in the schools where she works. By connecting to young people through her narrative and utilizing firsthand knowledge of the students' social contexts and lives, Janet offers a vision for how community members can expand the scope of restorative justice beyond schools and into the neighborhoods where students reside.

Connecting to Students through Her Narrative

In sharing the narrative of Joel's murder, Janet connects with students who have experienced violence in their own lives and shows how one has power to respond to conflict in a positive way. According to Lucy Reed, English teacher at BHS, Janet offers a "counter narrative to the story that we always hear about revenge and feeling defeated: I mean I think all the students have been affected by her story and have found strength in her ability to move forward . . . she is affecting change in a way that's very profound."

Carol Warren, principal of Project Graduation at BHS, says that every time Janet speaks about Joel in circle students "immediately perk up" both because they have lost loved ones and because the tale about forgiveness is unusual:

> Many of them know more than one person who's been killed, and I think her pain really resonates with them . . . And it's really eye-opening for them, that they say, "Oh my goodness, here's this person who has lost a son, and she's not bitter. She's not angry. She's not going out and getting revenge. She's doing this other thing to find that sense of peace." I think for a lot of our kids they need someone to model how to find that sense of peace in a way that's nonviolent.

When facilitating healing circles with students in conflict, Janet employs her story to model how to handle one's anger, never minimizing the struggle it takes to combat feelings of vengeance, anger and frustration. Janet discussed this internal battle in a talking circle at BHS, where students responded to the prompt, "Discuss a time when you exercised self-control":

> Janet gets the heart-shaped talking piece and rotates it in her fingers for few seconds. "I was in the car, and I stopped at a stop sign," she says. "And people were crossing the street . . . one of the people crossing the street was a young man who murdered my son. It took everything in me to keep my foot on the brake." She lifts her hand, splays her fingers into a stop sign. "I had to tell myself, 'Keep your foot on the brake, keep your foot on the brake,'" she says hypnotically. Her voice dissolves into a whisper as she repeats, "Keep your foot on the brake." Several students look stunned, humbled.
>
> Up until now, the student next to me has been leaning back, his elbow on the table behind him, one leg dangling in midair. He pushes himself forward, leans on his knees and says, "I would have revved up the engine just to scare him." The class chuckles, and Janet eyes him with a slightly strained smile. It is as though she is lost in thought, once again behind the steering wheel, Joel's face dangling from the button on her rearview mirror, foot still on the pedal.

Janet makes it clear to students that the path to ending the cycle of violence involves daily struggle. She is not a beneficent being who calmly navigates an encounter with one of the men who killed her son; in fact she admits it took everything within her to keep her foot on the brake. Janet models how to talk openly about these emotions and shares important wisdom about trying to separate issues in one's life from how we interact with others and perform necessary tasks at school.

In one such healing circle, sophomores Lena and Antonio meet with Math teacher Susan Gabral. Days earlier they walked out of her class without explanation; Susan then followed the two students into the stairwell, where she put out her hands to prevent them from descending. A yelling match ensued as Lena and Antonio forced past her and insisted that they were going to the nurse as she told them to get to class. According to Susan, they have not done any work in her class since that incident, and whenever she asks them to put their phones away or be quiet during a quiz, Lena says things like, "Shut up. Don't even talk to me. I'm losing what little respect I have for you":

> Susan Gabral is a White woman, wearing a long-sleeved white shirt, gray slacks, and black flip-flops. Sunglasses rest on a head of curly hair pulled back in a loose bun. I have heard that she is a strict teacher, very effective, with no-nonsense routines. Lena and Antonia walk into her classroom with tentative smiles. Lena is African American, five foot six, of medium build. She has a square face and shoulder-length straight hair

parted in the middle. Antonio, a White student of Portuguese descent, is usually by her side. They are known for their dramatic flair, and can be friendly and personable, but also erupt into histrionics when annoyed by their peers or teachers.

They join Janet, Susan and me in a circle that is awkwardly formed around a rectangular student table. After a check in round, Janet asks Lena, Antonio and Susan to explain the incident from their point of view. Susan apologizes for her reaction in the stairwell. Next Lena apologizes for her statements in class. Then she states that because she and Antonio had strong a relationship with Susan at the beginning of the year, she feels that they were being picked on to show other students that there are no pet students in the class. She tugs at her ear and says, "I'm sorry I disrespected you . . ." She stares at the floor. "I want it to be gone. I don't know. I haven't been feeling right a lot, and I guess I take it out on the wrong people. I'm trying to stop that, but it's just like I can't."

Janet gets the piece and is quiet for a few seconds. She turns to Lena and explains that we have control over how we respond to conflicts, and that "we all have stuff that's going on out there. I think that's something that it's a lifelong thing to try and work on—control," she says. "Today for me, as you know, I have a kid who was killed eight years ago, so there are still days when I wake up going, 'Oh, I'm just so tired.' But I have to just acknowledge that that's where I'm at today but not let that affect how I'm going to be with other people today."

Though Lena initially apologizes, she states that she refused to go to class because she felt that Susan wanted to show that she does not have pet students. Lena does not go into detail about what is affecting her social interactions, but it is clear she is struggling to not "take it out on the wrong people." Janet then shares her narrative, communicating that everyone has baggage we bring into school; she reminds us of the fragility of life when she tells us it is the eighth anniversary of her son's death. But in addition she pushes Lena to take accountability for her actions and to not let that "affect how" she is "going to be with other people today." The reminder of what Janet deals with on a daily basis put the conflict at hand in perspective, providing a powerful lesson about the need to use self-restraint no matter what is happening in our lives. While another administrator or teacher certainly could have kept this healing circle and offered similar lessons, as a survivor of homicide, Janet's story holds particular weight with students, many of whom have lost loved ones to violence. Janet shows them that even after experiencing a tragic loss, she has to interact in positive ways in other areas of her life even when it is a daily struggle to do so.

For students, her restraint often invokes awe as they reflect on their own struggles and conflicts in school. In the portrait of BHS I discuss how Jaylen Robertson started high school academically struggling and repeatedly acted out in class—but ultimately built strong relationships with his teachers, graduated and pursued higher education. Jaylen spoke on the National Public Radio show "Humankind" about how Janet has impacted his life.

> How she can just forgive what happened it's just . . . I couldn't do something like that to be honest with you. Like Janet is so strong and the fact that she was able to open up to everybody in the circle and really tell what happened and to be able to trust everybody in the circle, it's just, I just find that heartening. I love the fact that she was able to do that 'cause I could never open up to anybody and talk about a death of somebody that's so close to me, especially if it's blood or my son. I could never do that. I really appreciate what she did because without her, I don't think I would even be in school.

Upon hearing the interview, Janet laughed at what she perceived as the hyperbole of the last line. But when Jaylen says, "I appreciate what she did," he refers to more than the fact that she shares her biography so openly: Janet has sat with him in multiple circles for three years in high school, working with him and his teachers to understand how to improve his behavior and excel in school. But she also has known him since he was four years old, when she worked with him and his mother in a nurturing program that aimed to help families parent their children by focusing on their assets. She then worked with him one-on-one again at BHS and knows the struggles he faces with his family, personal battles with anger and the sorrow he felt after getting arrested for breaking into a community rec center. It is not only her narrative but her firsthand knowledge of students that holds special sway with young people.

Firsthand Knowledge of Students and Their Social Contexts

Most members of macro communities have firsthand knowledge of the social context in which young people live and work. Having worked in the community for decades in different capacities—as a teacher and education coordinator in day care centers, program coordinator at a settlement house and as a family development specialist in an organization working to prevent the maltreatment of children—Janet has known several of the students and their families at both Equity and BHS from the time they were small children. "I worked with children and families and saw so many young people go in and out of lockup—young people I knew as little ones. I knew their best self, their core self, their good self, and I would see them come back out and be further removed from that." Her familiarity with how students could stray from their core selves, and her knowledge of students from other community spaces, provided her with a more comprehensive context through which to interpret and probe student behaviors.

This was exemplified during a meeting with a sophomore named Laura, who had been verbally sparring with her ex-boyfriend Jason in several of her classes. During a talking circle in Angela's classroom, Jason verbally threatened to hit Laura. The teacher told Jason that he could be suspended or he could participate in a healing circle with Laura. In a preliminary meeting with Laura before the healing circle, Angela and Janet asked about her prior relationship with Jason:

> We're seated in Angela's classroom, with four chairs surrounding a student table. Angela welcomes Laura into the room, and Janet yells out, "Hi, girlie! How are ya?" Janet has known Laura since she was a child and has sat in circles with her in a community program.
>
> "Fine," says Laura glumly, embracing Janet with a side hug.
>
> Laura is White, petite, with curly, dyed-black hair pulled back in a high bun. She is wearing gray winter boots pulled up over flannel pajama pants, and her hands are tucked into a zipped-up, turquoise hoodie. In class, Laura is rambunctious, sometimes aggressive when she feels threatened. Here, she sits conspicuously quiet, answering Janet's questions with a simple yes or no. However, she does reveal that she and Jason used to "talk" or go out. Janet asks, "In that circle the other day, what happened?" Laura speaks quickly, rambling a bit as though what she is saying is redundant.
>
> "I had the talking piece," she began. "I was going to say something to add on to what he said. Then he said, 'No. I'll punch you in the face.' And then I was like, 'Then do it, like really.'"
>
> There are details missing from the truncated story, but for now Janet asks Laura if the root of the conflict might be that she is upset about their breakup. Laura says, "Maybe, but I don't like him anymore."
>
> Janet says it's OK that she is angry but that "it's what you do when you're angry." She asks Laura to think about why Jason yelled at her and says, "Hurt people, hurt people, that's a saying. When people feel hurt, and you kind of get really defensive, and you lash out to the point where you don't even remember . . . That can't really let either of you off the hook for an angry response." Janet's voice gets quieter.
>
> "I get a sense from you and from knowing a little bit about you from before, from over at the youth group, that you got some hard stuff that you deal with in your life. Is that true to say?"
>
> Laura slowly nods. Her eyes harden. "Yeah."
>
> "That hurts and that makes you mad. Sometimes you're carrying that anger around with you into other places that you go. Is that fair to say?"
>
> "Yeah." The two talk intimately, as though Angela and I are not there.
>
> "I'm sorry you have to go through that Laura."
>
> "That's OK." Laura's voice is soft, and her gaze has not strayed from Janet's face.

"It's not really OK, but I'm sorry that you have to go through that. It really isn't OK that you have to go through some of the stuff."

I feel myself tearing up. As an observer, I have felt frustrated watching Laura act out on occasion in class. Janet confirms her goodness, however, despite these actions. Laura seems bent on not crying, and as a result I feel like crying for her.

In the beginning of the meeting Laura insists that she no longer has feelings for Jason. She is reticent about why she has angry outbursts in class. Yet the tone of the conversation turns serious as Janet seems to touch on the heart of the matter. Angela and I do not necessarily know the exact circumstances Janet alludes to in this moment. But the reference to "the hard stuff" Laura has dealt with elicits an emotional response in all of us. Janet touches on these delicate issues without compromising confidentiality and validates Laura by insisting that it was not OK for her to experience such pain in her life. The subtext is that Janet knows inside Laura is a loving person who does not want to yell at others. But she reminds Laura that no matter what her circumstances, she must always be accountable for what she does with that anger. She continued working with Laura throughout the year, helping her to understand why she took out her anger on certain people and to explore where the anger was coming from.

Having known students like Jaylen and Laura since childhood, she is able to acknowledge, through intimate knowledge of their personal lives, how difficult it is to deal with anger in productive ways. But in addition to acknowledging individual accountability, Janet is familiar with larger systemic and social forces that impact student behaviors, such as poverty, violence, lack of access to health care, and poor schooling. Indeed many restorative justice advocates insist that the only way to achieve true justice is to situate harms and crimes between individuals in a broader context: "It is necessary that facilitators and community participants make attempts to connect such conflicts to their structural conditions so the restorative justice meeting does not merely ameliorate the immediate problem while leaving the broader conflict unaddressed" (Woolford, 2009, p. 115). Another of Janet's contributions as a community member, then, is her understanding of how students' actions are related to broader systems that need changing—both because of her experiences living in her neighborhood and because of her experiences with VOD, when she came to understand the circumstances of the lives of two men who murdered her son.

Structural Understanding of Student Behaviors

It has been difficult to acknowledge and unveil the structural conditions that impacted the men who killed Joel—especially because Janet had worked with families and young people her entire life and was part of the very system that was failing youth. "I began to also question like where did we fail them? . . . How do we get kids who can kill other kids?" Janet counts herself among those who let these young people down; she is part of the "we" that has produced kids who can kill other kids. "I felt some responsibility as an adult who lives in this community that where this is going on that this happens, not a direct responsibility, but I don't have a direct responsibility for slavery either, but I have some responsibility in it. You know what I mean?" This last question gives me pause. It is easy as a researcher who has not experienced such a loss to agree, but I am dumbfounded by the insight Janet displays, indirectly implicating herself in a system that did little to offer these young people opportunities to prevent them from living a life of violence.

The first system that she feels failed not only her own children but the youth involved in Joel's murder was the education system. Janet was all too familiar with how the school system was broken, unable—or unwilling—to accommodate the needs of young people who did not fit into a prescribed profile of docile, self-motivated students:

> I do feel like the schools *failed* them [my children] . . . So I think that influenced my work in the schools now—the fact that I have seen Boston Public Schools fail not only my own kids but other kids too, and that I know through my own kids and through other kids that there are strengths that aren't always tapped in a traditional school setting.

None of her children graduated with a diploma in a traditional manner. Joel received his diploma in a nontraditional school. Her oldest son David had hyperactivity and attention deficit issues, but Janet could not get him the services he needed. When she advocated on his behalf, she was told that his behavioral issues should be dealt with at home and not at school. He ended up quitting and took his GED. At the age of 15 Shana wrote a play that was produced by the Boston Center for the Arts. Even with such talent, Shana struggled in school because of standing up for what she felt to be right, which meant talking back to teachers if necessary. She dropped out and got her GED.

Shana continued to experience institutional barriers while pursuing higher education. After Joel died, Shana was two months late with her paperwork for financial aid at the University of Massachusetts. She spoke with an administrator and explained that her brother had been killed. Says Shana, "The first thing she told me was it was your responsibility to get that paperwork in." Shana had to work five years to pay off the tuition from that semester, even though she did not receive a single credit. Her education was delayed for half a decade, but she says that such barriers are common in her neighborhood. Though Shana has been academically successful, eventually graduating from the writing program at Goddard College in Vermont, Janet's disappointment in the education system was further cemented after her daughter's experiences.

Janet and Shana also witnessed how social services did not address the needs of young people. Shana's very good friend had been the caseworker of the first young man, Norman, who stabbed Joel. This friend tried to convince a judge not to release Norman from a day reporting center, where he was court mandated to appear daily. But because of an overflow of cases, the young man was released from the reporting center and killed Joel only a few months later. Says Shana,

> My friend who was his caseworker really argued that this kid, who was 16 going on 17, did not have anything stable. His mom was on drugs. He was on drugs. He wouldn't show up. He was so obviously not in control of his life. He needed *help*. Even if that help meant coming to this building every day where he would be monitored until he could get some drug services or something, that would help him.

Shana's caseworker friend was with her when she got the call that Joel had been killed, and he was devastated; the system had allowed another young person to fall through the cracks. Each of the men involved in the murder, says Shana, had been failed by the education system as well as social services. All were addicted to drugs and had relatives or parents who were addicted to crack. None had participated in preventative programs that might have addressed their substance abuse issues.

Janet's familiarity with these community issues helps her analyze how student behaviors can be related to broader systems that need changing. She feels like most students "don't really have an understanding" of why they live in neighborhoods that are poor, why it is not unusual for young people in their schools to drop out of school, or why a number of their peers or family members may one day end up in the criminal justice system. For her, restorative justice helps students move beyond resolving their own conflicts: as I will discuss in more detail in the final chapter, it helps develop a critical understanding of other factors that impact their problems.

Says Janet:

> [Students] just feel like they're thrown into the set of circumstances because of the race and class that they are, because of the neighborhoods they live in, because of the way it is as opposed to trying to understand why it is the way it is and being an agent, being able to talk about it and be an agent for change.

When I ask whether she thinks restorative justice moves beyond healing interpersonal conflicts and can truly change structures, she says, "If restorative justice was *the* way the structure worked, then it would change." She envisions circles being used beyond schools in community centers, hospitals, juvenile justice facilities and other neighborhood spaces. And she sees parents and other community members as valuable assets, people who could be trained to lead a restorative justice movement that she fears may be "co-opted by the larger system." For her, working with and for the community is not only a desire but a responsibility. "I'm always going to give to community because I received from community and I do believe in a reciprocity." Ultimately, Janet shows how community members can contribute greatly to the success of circle practices in schools—through their experiences, commitment and awareness of the social conditions and forces that shape how students behave and achieve in schools.

CHALLENGES TO COMMUNITY INVOLVEMENT: THE "McDONALDIZATION" OF RESTORATIVE JUSTICE

While Janet exemplifies how community members can enhance restorative practices in schools, her experiences additionally reveal the limitations of doing so when the field of restorative justice increasingly requires accreditation—even though "for all intents and purposes restorative justice developed as a community based movement established in direct opposition to the large-scale, institutional way of doing business" (Erbe, 2004, p. 293). Janet says she has struggled with two notable—and interlinked—barriers to community involvement in restorative practices in schools: "evidence-based" school reform efforts that seek to take individual successful initiatives and replicate them large-scale and the ever-increasing professionalization of the field.

The first problem that concerns Janet is what she calls the "obsession with evidence-based practices." "I'm so sick of that phrase," she says. "It's like, what evidence [do] we have that zero tolerance works? Sometimes doing the right thing is just about doing the right thing." Since 2001 when No Child Left behind was reauthorized, federal research funding has been primarily tied to stringent standards based on the assumption that "randomized, controlled field trials" provide the most rigorous evidence of what can work in education (Biesta, 2007, p. 34). Funders often want proof that using restorative justice leads to higher test scores or school attendance. But, says Janet, a quantitative relationship cannot really convey the long-term outcomes associated with a process that can, as I discuss in the portrait of BHS, take years to impact students:

> That is the problem for me all with evidence-based outcome measures and that sort of stuff. In many arenas there is not necessarily a direct cause and effect. [Restorative justice] is really an accumulation of things over time and letting it grow inside of yourself into what you want it to be. That's why I hate all of this talk about outcome measures and evidence-based practice because I feel like people are then going to try and work toward the outcomes just like they teach to the MCAS.[4]

When I remind Janet that I too am trying to provide evidence of the outcomes associated with restorative justice, she smiles. "At least you're not tying restorative justice to test scores." Whereas it is true I am specifically employing a qualitative approach to show *how* restorative justice works, I am also doing so to explore whether it *does* work from the vantage point of participants. But Janet does help me think critically about what we mean when we ask, "Does it work?" Answering the question should involve rigorous conversations about the purpose of education and what kind of competencies we want our students to take away from their schooling. For Janet, the process is much too nuanced, cumulative, and intangible to be evaluated by math or English scores.

The demand for evidence-based initiatives is closely linked to the demand for professionalization in the field of education. After all, many grants that fund reforms such as restorative justice require administrators and practitioners to have degrees. This necessitates the involvement of lawyers, academics and other professionals in the process—to the exclusion, Janet fears, of local community members. Woolford (2009) confirms, the "long debate over whether it is better to have local laypersons facilitating restorative justice, or whether specific training is required to ensure appropriate restorative practice, appears to have been won by the latter group" (p. 160–161). For Janet, the move toward professionalization is not new; decades earlier she witnessed bottom-up efforts such as community mediation get taken over by professionals from the criminal justice system. "I don't have any college degrees myself, but I've had some experiences myself where I've been part of some grassroots effort to make some change, and then it gets co-opted by the system so community mediation just becomes another kink in the system as opposed to a real alternative."

In addition to her concerns about professionalization, Janet has reservations about another consequence of evidence-based outcomes: the tendency to try to scale up and standardize programs or, in her words, "McDonaldize" successful restorative models. At Equity High, for example, law students from Northwestern University worked with community members to pilot a peer justice program with the very intent to duplicate the model throughout Massachusetts. Doing so, she says, ignores the fact that at its core, restorative justice is meant to be community specific, catered to the needs of the people who have been harmed as well as those who have committed harm in settings such as schools, businesses, prisons and hospitals. By depending on funders who demand that participants have degrees to duplicate a model, Janet feels that scaling up of programs simply perpetuates the exclusion and devaluing of community members and their knowledge. "So I get a little bit nervous . . . again it's not that I don't think there should be standards . . . it's just that I want to honor all the experience that people have." She pauses for a few seconds. "And I want their culmination—even though they didn't walk across the stage and get a piece of paper—but the culmination of all their experiences to be valid as much as that piece of paper that some people hold."

While Janet shows how community members without degrees can gain entrée into restorative justice work by connecting to local institutions such as the Center for Restorative Justice, in some cases such an affiliation can actually be a double-edged sword. "There are some places where having that affiliation gives credence and validity . . . like maybe with administrators in schools or something like that, but then there's some places with regular community folks where it's like, who is that someone from this university, and universities have screwed over communities before. So it's a real mix sometimes for me." Thus aligning community members with institutions can provide a challenge as they straddle working with professionals and people in the neighborhood. She feels like more community members would become involved in restorative practices if restorative justice organizations were geographically located in urban neighborhoods. In fact, she dreams about turning her own house into such a center. "I sometimes have fantasies about this house having a living quarters and center . . . So I do have a vision for that." Through her work she remains accountable to giving back to the community that has sustained her and shows how members of macro communities can advocate for folks who may not otherwise speak up about the harms in their neighborhood.

Recruiting community members without higher education into the restorative justice movement can be difficult for other reasons: they may feel alienated and overshadowed by their credentialed colleagues. "I believe restorative justice is not something that people necessarily need to have degrees to do. I am a case in point," she says, pointing to her chest before she shrugs. "In fact, I think it would limit who would step up from the community if we started requiring that people had degrees." Janet sometimes feels threatened and "class conscious" because she has to compete with credentialed lawyers and graduate students for professional opportunities. "It's not that I have a limited vocabulary by any means, but I do sometimes get intimidated by big words by references to theories and things like that." Janet has watched people with credentials—who did not necessarily have the experience or skills that she had—supersede her professionally and take credit for her ideas:

> I would teach people something and then I would see them say it . . . and they would get the credit. And so then I would wrestle with myself around my own sense of validation, my own sense of recognition or lack of recognition, and then knowing that on some level that was actually the ultimate thing, *the* ultimate. To have your teachings get carried on . . . I think that one of the reasons it becomes a struggle for me is because I feel like I'm always trying to prove myself.

Janet's struggle has been both emotional and financial: after 40 years of work and dedication to the community, she has no retirement, a situation she may not be facing had she earned a college degree. Still, the community she serves comes to her aid; when she won a national restorative justice award and could not afford to attend the reception, friends and colleagues pitched in for her airfare and hotel.

Janet feels fortunate that in many spheres, her decades of experience working with youth and families, affiliation with Suffolk University and personal experiences with restorative dialogue have provided access to professional opportunities in schools. But she worries that "the heart and soul of some endeavors" such as restorative justice have been overshadowed by the necessity of degrees, which do not always equate to "quality and standards." Having the certification from an organization such as the International Institute of Restorative Practices, for example, does not guarantee one can be as influential or successful at keeping circles as Janet is. This is not to say that she does not understand the value of degrees—just that she feels that people who do not have such credentials are excluded from a process that is supposed to be inherently egalitarian:

> I know that people put in a lot of hard work to earn those degrees, but I think that [other] people put in a lot of hard work and have other learning experiences that are just as valid and equivalent and that that often gets overlooked and overshadowed. So I would hate to see [that] happen for restorative justice because I feel like it's a real place where, one of the principles and values is that every member has something valuable to contribute.

Targeting and hiring members of the community, she says, necessitates a different set of standards by which to evaluate candidates. What that looks like would depend on the context. Janet thinks it requires some simple creativity to figure out how to incorporate community members who do not have degrees in to restorative practices. "I just don't want to cut regular people off." Then, almost as an afterthought she says with a laugh, "And I don't want to cut myself out either."

VISION

Today the concept of community transcends geography. But geography is still important. Enlisting and training parents from macro neighborhoods to lead reforms such as restorative justice is particularly important in Boston because of busing; students who feel supported in schools do not always feel connected to adults in their neighborhood and vice versa. As Janet shows, community members can bridge the divide between students' home and school lives, bringing a special sensitivity through their personal relationships with young people outside of school. Helping students address the roots of their behaviors inside and outside of school through restorative justice, says Janet, can help community members reclaim their neighbor-hoods. "I would love to see cadres of people in neighborhoods trained to be circle keepers, so when something goes down in the neighborhood, the neighborhood takes care of it. My justice is very much tied to my commu-nity and to justice for my community."

Janet has indeed sought justice outside of formal institutions, especially in light of the failure of such institutions to serve young people such as her children and the men who murdered Joel. Her connection to the people around her—her sense that restoring justice in her own life helps restore justice in her community—pushes her forward in the work. She doesn't ever want to retire. "I'll always do this work in one way or another," she says, sharing that she wants to write a memoir about her work in the community and experiences with restorative justice.

Some ask, do all community members have to have experienced a loss such as Janet's to contribute to restorative practices? Can restorative justice be as successful with teachers who are not in macro communities? Roger Françoise, a teacher who teaches restorative justice at Equity High, says, "Yes, I think it can, but it's really hard to find that amount of experience. It gives it just a different weight entirely. I mean her presence is just really about it, period . . . I feel to a certain point we may have fallen back on or rely too heavily on Janet's presence in order to set the tone, but if she wasn't here, it would have been much harder." Although it "may have been much harder" to do restorative work without Janet, she does not think someone has to have experienced the trauma she has to be able to connect with young people. *All* community members can offer vital and intimate knowledge that can relay the importance of restorative justice; she is, she reiterates, not spe-cial. "I am not extraordinary," she says with characteristic humility. "People may not have gone through what I have, but that doesn't make their experi-ences any less important, or any less useful, for young people."

In March 2012, Janet speaks to this assertion and her revolutionary vision for restorative justice. She, myself and two students and two educa-tors from BHS and Equity have convened in her living room on a Satur-day afternoon for a roundtable conversation on restorative justice. Paul, a friend and board member of the *Harvard Educational Review*, records the conversation and plans to condense the transcript into an article for a spe-cial issue on the school-to-prison pipeline. We are comfortably seated in a circle, resting in armchairs and holding mugs of tea and plates of pizza. The room is rectangular, covered with an oriental rug, surrounded by art-work, photos—of Joel, family and friends, Janet as a bouffant-wearing teenager—and illuminated by sunlight that spills into the room through white, chintzy curtains. We blocked out an hour for the conversation, but we are already an hour and a half in; the more we talk about restorative practices—their promise, the pitfalls and, yes, the outcomes at both of the schools—the more we have to say. She says,

There is a place for the grandmother [in the movement]. There is a place for the mother. There is a place for my neighbor. And that's what restorative justice really is because it is not just about restoring things back into balance for that one person or for those two people who have some kind of interaction. It's about restoring things back into balance for the larger community and that nothing that we do is just about us. Everything that we do affects other people.

Janet exemplifies how communities are rich, untapped reservoirs, filled with individuals typically overlooked, anonymous people who can often impact students more than credentialed professionals and who are no less extraordinary than Janet.

NOTES

1. For further information about the organization and its impact on youth in urban communities, see Boyes-Watson (2008).
2. A street worker is a social worker who works with youth on the streets, particularly those who are prone to participating in violence.
3. Based in Chelsea outside of Boston, Roca is an organization that uses circles to "take on a unique and pressing challenge: helping to alter the life trajectories of America's most high-risk young people—the young people that are involved in crime, engaged in dangerous behaviors, have rejected help, have dropped out of school and are simply too difficult for other programs to serve" (Roca, Inc., 2013).
4. Massachusetts Comprehensive Assessment System, or the state standardized test.

7 "Turning the Paradigm on Its Side"

Youth–Adult Power Dynamics in a Student Apprenticeship Model of Restorative Justice

Built in the 1920s, the Johnson Education Complex looms at the intersection of a rotary that feeds into six surrounding streets, lined by two- and three-story houses with hanging pots of flowers and shrub-dotted lawns festooned with occasional shrines to the Virgin Mary. The building reaches back for what looks like a full city block; it is no wonder that five years ago, this behemoth building was split into the three small public schools—the Academy of Future Engineers, the High School for Health Professions, and Equity, a school of approximately 300 students. In front is a fenced-in oval lawn with benches, bushes and two sprawling trees with braided, multiple trunks on each side of the green. This looks like the all-American comprehensive high school with its three-story, red-brick façade, inlaid Greek columns and triangular pediment on the roof. A giant flagpole looms out of the center of the lawn, the flag waving in what seems like slow motion.

At the top of three sets of stairs at the entrance are a set of double doors adjacent to a message marked in jagged letters: "After 9 a.m. ring this bell." Once buzzed in, I enter a foyer with the main office door to my left, an unattended metal detector a few paces ahead of me and, a few feet beyond that, the closed doors of an auditorium. Hanging from the ceiling is a blue and white satin banner that reads, "Relationship, Rigor, Reflection," what I later discover are the three core principles of the Equity mission. Next to the metal detector, a white piece of chart paper is displayed on a tripod, reminding students of less lofty expectations they must follow as members of the school:

- Remove all hats and hoods.
- Turn off and put away all electronics.
- Remove any metal objects.
- Unzip/open bags for checking.
- After signing in:
  - Go to locker.
  - Go to breakfast.
  - Wait for the bell.

The directives sound like those at any school, not one that touts a social justice mission manifested in, among other things, its use of restorative justice. But this is not necessarily surprising; a school environment rooted in social justice does not necessarily preclude basic rules about cell phones or bag checks.

I am on my way to the law and justice course, a core elective in which students are trained in the restorative practice of circles. I have heard that the youth play a central role in disciplinary matters by suggesting how students who break rules can repair the harm. When I enter the classroom, Mark Cooper, a lawyer who visits the school to teach this one elective, is moving chairs into a circle. Because this is his only course, he teaches this class in the room that officially belongs to another teacher, Donna Flaherty. The classroom is spacious, with four wall-length windows and walls stocked with books on shelves. Rectangular student tables have been pushed to the sides of the room. The white walls are covered with posters of Che Guevara, National Women's History Month, a "How Big Is Africa" poster in which Africa is filled with maps of Alaska, Europe, the United States, and China and a poster with the slogan "Unfortunately, History has set the record a little too straight." The posters befit a school named "Equity," especially as I'm about to observe a healing circle, a practice that is inherently structured to be equitable for all participants. The circle to come provides an ideal exploration into the themes of social justice that resonate beyond these poster-filled walls.

Mark Cooper is a bespectacled White man who looks to be in his late 20s. He wears a tie, dress shirt and slacks. Nearly all of the 15 students in this daily class are Black, and the rest are Latino. Ten students sit in the circle, and a few choose to sit on the periphery of the circle, heads down on desks with headphone wires hanging from their ears like IV lines. Mark opens the healing circle by reading the details of this week's "case," a word striking in its association with the criminal justice system. The case involves two students from this very class—John and his friend Tania, who sits opposite him in circle. John wears a loose-fitting T-shirt, black jeans, and black sneakers. He has a round face and high cheekbones, small, heavy-lidded eyes, and a light beard of scruffy tufts of hair. Tania is taller than him, with rich brown skin, large baby cheeks and straight, shoulder-length hair parted down the middle.

One week earlier when Tania skipped school, she asked John to swipe her ID into the school attendance system to make it appear that she was present. A school administrator caught John and provided a choice—the two could either get suspended or participate in a healing circle. Their ability to choose a traditional disciplinary option versus the less punitive one was indicative of the school's larger movement toward embracing a new paradigm—restorative justice—that seemed to align with its vision of fostering leadership in its students.

Mark begins by asking Tania, seated directly to his left, why she thinks this incident has been brought to circle. He passes her the talking piece. She explains that she was not really skipping because she was visiting her deathly ill friend in the hospital. She looks at the floor often, speaking slowly and sighing. Her reflective tone shifts as she says sharply, "It's not like it's that big of a deal. John could've gotten away with it but he was just stupid and got caught." She says these last words loudly, directing a stony gaze at John.

Students laugh. One says, "Oh snap!" I am taken aback that she seems to show no remorse and that it feels she has righteous indignation toward John despite the fact that he got in trouble for trying to help her out. John hangs his head, and she returns the piece to Mark.

"This is a safety issue," says Mark. "As your teachers, we are responsible for you when you are not at home. It's called *in loco parentis*, which literally means, 'in place of the parents.' I'm going to pass the piece around now to see why the class thinks this case has been brought forward."

Here students who have been quiet come to life, challenging Mark's rationale that this is a safety issue. Marco, a short, thin boy in an oversized T-shirt and cargo pants says, fire in his voice, "If you all are so interested in our safety, then how come whenever you decide to suspend us, you send us home in the middle of the day even if our parents aren't home? How come you get to choose when you're concerned for our safety?" Marco seems to speak from personal experience and addresses Mark as "you"—a symbol of adults in general at the school.

Several students chime in, "Yeah!"

Another student gets the piece and asks, "How come when there was a fight in the cafeteria that cop pushed up one of the kids against the wall for no reason? How is that being concerned for our safety?" The observations are astute, exposing the contradictions of a school that uses restorative practices but still relies on campus police and practices of suspension.

Mark gets the piece and waits a few seconds before putting responsibility for the problem back onto the students. He offers a counterpoint: "These are all good points. But what have we taught you at this school? You can either sit here and make these observations and be dissatisfied, or you can try to find a way to change what it is that you think is unjust." The circle has turned away from John and Tania to a larger discourse about disciplinary inequities and the hypocrisy of arbitrary adult concerns about safety at the school.

Meanwhile, John's head is still down. I can no longer see his face. Rather than feeling restored, he looks depleted. He tells Mark he is sorry in a dry voice, and Tania says, "I know what I did was wrong, but then again I've never done it before, and it's not like I didn't have a good reason." The bell rings, and as the class leaves, a fight breaks out in the hallway between students from another class. Students begin running in different directions, adults chasing after them. Hearing the disgruntled student voices in the circle, and now seeing the burst of violence in the hallway, it feels like little has been accomplished today, that the students don't take restorative justice seriously—or at least when it is applied to rules that they question. I also presume that John is probably not a fan of circles.

However, a month later I'm surprised to see Mark accompanied by John and Tania at a meeting I am attending with Joseph Daniels, assistant chief operating officer of the Boston Public Schools. We are a group of 10 researchers, professors, students and lawyers who are here to try to convince the district that revisions of the district discipline code should include alternatives to zero tolerance, such as restorative justice. We run the meeting as a circle, so that Mr. Daniels can understand what restorative practices looks like. It is in this meeting that John uses what he later calls his "great analogy" for describing restorative justice:

> Restorative justice is like recycling . . . [when] the student gets suspended, you just throw him away. [They] get suspended and they never get to understand what happened. They go through that process, but they're just thrown away. And then they go on this little boat that takes them all across somewhere, which is like the school-to-prison pipeline. They go through this little process where they just get thrown away, and they're gone and they're locked away forever. But if they go through the restorative justice system, that's like recycling; the bottle's being recycled. Now the bottle can go through this process to be reused, and [be] put back in the community, instead of being thrown away like the traditional thing. It's recycled and put back into the community, and it's understood what it did and why it did it, and the harmed party gets to understand what happened as well.

That day, John's impassioned and poetic description of restorative justice, along with his knowledge of the school-to-prison pipeline, altered my hasty characterization of him as unengaged, quiet and morose. As if by fate, the day I return to Equity in September 2009, the fall after this healing circle, I see John and Tania after school. "You're the recycling guy!" I exclaim to him. His face radiates with a smile that is at once bashful, knowing and proud. He and Tania are now seniors and co-teachers in the law and justice class. They also keep healing circles with fellow students throughout the school. I am curious about how the two, who appeared so defeated in circle, have become some of the strongest student proponents of restorative justice, so much so that they now apprentice peers in the model.

SHIFTING PARADIGMS OF POWER: ADULTS AND YOUTH IN "EQUAL PARTNERSHIP"

This portrait examines the complex dynamics that played out at one small school implementing restorative justice, where practitioners strove to carry out a mission of youth empowerment by offering students input in disciplinary matters. Once I spent time in the school, I learned that John and

116   *"Turning the Paradigm on Its Side"*

Tania were not the few, exceptional leaders who could apprentice others in restorative justice, nor were they simply star students cherry-picked to sit at the decision-making table with adults to advocate for district discipline changes; many law and justice students could have done the same. According to Mark this is because he and other teachers have worked to foster leadership skills in the student body in an effort to trouble the traditionally hierarchical relationship between students and faculty—one in which adults have power *over*, as opposed to power *with*, youth. Says Mark,

> We need to rethink schools almost from the bottom up, and we need to turn, at one point—I said to Carolyn Boyes-Watson—we have to turn the paradigm on its head in terms of that youth–adult dynamic. She said, 'Let's not turn it on its head; let's turn it on its side.' . . . [Right now] you can see a vertical alignment with adults at the top and students on the bottom. Her point was turn it on its side, which I think is a great image. Now it's adults and youth in equal partnership. The arrows instead of being one way from adults to students, it's a two-way arrow, where there's dialogue both ways between students and adults.

The opening vignette however reveals some of the core tensions of carrying out this ideal of adults and youth "in equal partnership"; circles at Equity worked to dismantle traditional power dynamics between adults and youth and allowed students to interrogate and challenge hierarchies within the school and in society. At the same time, traditional power dynamics— between men and women, adults and youth, straight and gay students, immigrants and American-born students, and differently abled students versus those without disabilities—were also reified when certain voices were silenced in circle through students' body language, comments or laughter— a struggle teachers grappled with as they sought to assert traditional authority by "doing discipline" in circles.

To situate the tensions inherent in equalizing power between students and teachers, I begin by showing how the effort of turning the youth–adult paradigm on its side was embedded in the school's design, from its mission statement to its hiring practices and curriculum planning. Next I trace how this paradigm shift continued as students worked with teachers and community partners to create an apprenticeship model of restorative justice. Finally I analyze how the two components of this apprenticeship model—talking and healing circles—simultaneously challenged and reified traditional power hierarchies, creating dilemmas for teachers grappling with how to discipline students in seemingly egalitarian circles.

A SOCIAL JUSTICE MISSION: YOUTH AS "AGENTS OF POSITIVE CHANGE" ALONGSIDE ADULTS

The High School for Equity was founded in 2005 when the district, like dozens across the country, broke underperforming comprehensive high schools into small schools through an initiative funded by the Bill and Melinda Gates Foundation. Parents, teachers, community members and students from the former Johnson High School—the building where Equity is housed—put in bids for their own theme-based small schools; Equity was one of three chosen out of ten submissions. Central to the purpose of the school was to "foster the growth of social activists who can identify problems" and ultimately become, as Mark reminds students in the opening vignette, "agents of positive change" (from the Equity Mission Statement). The hundreds of hours of planning the school resulted in the "Equity Family Handbook," a 140-page document that articulates the mission, academic expectations and courses offered.

Staff members enacted the mission early on, when they invited students to work alongside faculty members to craft the programming and curriculum at the school. Equity graduate Donald Beckham was one of these students and says that although the mission of the school was largely in place before students got involved, once the bid for Equity was accepted, teachers and administrators wanted students to have a "hands-on experience" in shaping their education. He says, "I attended a lot of meetings over the summer to plan the goals of the school and help with the hiring of teachers and even Principal Stephen Dobbs." This kind of student engagement is what attracted Stephen to the school in the first place. "It was incredible to come to a community that had already thought very deeply about what it wanted its school to look like," he says. "And that was incredibly inspiring to meet these teenage designers of the school, so we've tried to kind of keep that ethos alive."

Budgetary restrictions and staff dissension have somewhat limited the scope of the implementation of the mission. The Equity handbook offers two electives, law and justice and research action for change (RAC), as examples of courses that embrace the social justice mission by allowing students to have voice in the discipline process and conduct research projects that "make meaningful statements about the world." Humanities Teacher Roger Françoise, who also currently teaches law and justice, taught the RAC course for the last two years. He says, "Students did anything from making documentaries to doing surveys, to writing up research reports on all sorts of topics—homophobia, domestic violence, immigration, teen depression, anorexia, poverty overseas and global warming." Yet, the RAC course was cut after two years due to budget constraints.

In addition, there were rumblings among some staff members I spoke to who believe they had no say in how restorative justice was introduced or implemented and that student misbehaviors were rampant in certain classes. These teachers, as well as some visitors to the school who I spoke to, felt that students were allowed to "get away" with behaviors that hindered the learning process in their classrooms. Although most of my time was spent in the law and justice class where restorative justice was taught, I spoke with other teachers from different content areas who had some experience with circles. One teacher says he is part of a cohort of teachers at the school who have taught for 10 to 20 years and who are "not as excited about doing something new," like circles. He sat in three healing circles with students who had cursed him out in class, and one who had thrown a chair at him during one lesson, but found that restorative justice did little to address or improve the behaviors:

> I've got no interest in doing any further circles. I've heard the traditional model [of discipline] actually called the traditional or adversarial model of discipline. Guess what? Sometimes your students are your adversaries. They're not there to learn from you. Some kids come in here, they view you as the enemy and they treat you accordingly.

Thus not all teachers were enthusiastic about the switch to a restorative model of discipline; based on behaviors exhibited by certain students, they, too, felt that some young people are "adversaries."

One student teacher from the 2009-to-2010 school year suggested that other teachers felt similarly about social justice initiatives at the school. He contributed to an education blog by stating that even though the mission statement is "beautiful, with nods to Paolo Freire, Nelson Mandela, and Mahatma Gandhi . . . it wasn't so great for students who were already disenchanted by the generally negative atmosphere of their school." He doesn't clarify what he means by "negative atmosphere," but he does suggest a lack of cohesiveness among the faculty around the social justice mission:

> I found that only a handful of the teachers believed in the mission. Consequently, the ones who did often struggled to make community partnerships and actually motivate the students to engage in any kind of activism. The biggest symbolic defeat came midway through the year when we asked students in our class what social justice was and none of them had an answer.

Reading these words, I understand the skepticism, remembering how I felt upon leaving the first circle, when swarms of students surrounded a fight in the hall on both sides. Perhaps this is what the teacher means by "negative atmosphere." Yet his explanation also excludes the many students and teachers who have enacted the mission—who not only know what social justice is but explicitly engage in efforts to study and fight for issues of equity. This includes a core group of students who started a social justice club and worked with a fellow doctoral student at the Harvard Graduate School of Education to engage in a participatory action research project— creating surveys, gathering data and analyzing student input around what future direction the school needed to take. Perhaps the most notable long-term social justice-oriented project was the student campaign to bring restorative justice to the school.

Campaigning for Restorative Justice

The concept of restorative justice was introduced at Equity in 2006 in an unlikely place: a science class. It was Equity's second year of operation, and

Chemistry Teacher Raymond Porter wanted to integrate the science curriculum with the school vision. He says, "I decided to bring forensics into my chemistry class, [and] it was my initiative to look for a law school that would be interested in collaborating with a high school whose focus was social justice." He discovered a social justice program at the Northeastern University School of Law, directed by Susan Maze-Rothstein. Susan teaches a legal skills in social context class, in which "law students plan and execute a social justice project" (Northeastern University School of Law, 2006). After law students helped conduct a mock trial that used forensics evidence in Raymond's class, Susan commissioned interested Equity students to work on an extracurricular project, one that was unrelated to science but relevant to social justice—that of editing a plan for a youth court based on restorative justice in Anchorage, Alaska. The court was real, and still in the process of being developed, so students at Equity were recruited to help draft the court plan and offer the perspective of high school students.

Susan's law students and youth at Equity discussed creating a two-pronged peer mediation program in Anchorage; a youth court was modeled on the premise of a blended model of a traditional court and a restorative model of justice. For example, if a student damaged school property, this was defined as a "victimless offense" because a school-wide rule was broken and the harm occurred to a few select individuals. In such a case the student would face a group of peers in the Youth Court, but the punishment would not include the traditional suspension or expulsion; rather, the peers would demand that some form of reparation be made. If, however, a harm occurred between particular individuals—say if two students got into a physical fight—this conflict would be referred to a healing circle instead.

After providing input on the Alaskan program, Equity students galvanized their peers to bring such a model to their school, where administrators had issued 145 suspensions and six expulsions in 2006 and 2007. Says Principal Stephen Dobbs, "The culmination of that experience [was] the kids really said, 'Wait a minute. Like we need this in our school and in our communities.'"

Equity graduate Donald Beckham describes a school environment marred by fights and arguments when it first opened in 2005. "There were a lot of conflicts in school . . . part of the problem was we went from being a large school to having everyone [at Equity] on the same floor, so it was easier to run into someone you had a problem with." He was skeptical of whether or not circles would reduce conflicts at the school, but he says students were open to the restorative model because the project did not involve "outsiders or people who are coming from a random school that are coming to our school and then trying to regulate how we do things. If it was done like that, then students would have [had] more reservations." A core group of 15 students worked with Susan's legal students at weekly after-school meetings to address how to alleviate such conflicts at Equity.

Donald says, "We were in connection with the Northeastern School of Law, working with them, really going in depth about the details of the program and how exactly it was going to work at our school—how [to] get the students to communicate—because half the time the conflicts were based on miscommunication."

This new program offered students the opportunity to make decisions in equal partnership with adults and allowed them to, as Mark states earlier, turn the traditional adult–youth paradigm on its side. Science Teacher Raymond Porter says students became motivated once they learned about the potential for putting the school's mission to create agents of change into practice. He says they began to understand that "the need for justice and the influencing of justice [could] begin with them at the high school level: those students began to reach out to the teachers and the administration for the need to have such a permanent entity that would give them a sense of empowerment while also being fair to their fellow students."

Mark Cooper, the law and justice teacher who originally came to Equity as a lawyer to teach students about constitutional law, first learned about the use of circles and restorative justice during these preliminary after-school meetings. Interested teachers and youth sat together in circles Friday afternoons to become acclimated to the process. Mark noticed that students who were the most "rambunctious" in his class—which he says was initially more of a "traditional classroom"—acted differently in this space:

> I'd stay after school. I was an observer at that point . . . I'd see the same kids in circle, and they would be different people. They would be respectful. These were kids often in my class who wouldn't listen to each other or to me. Suddenly I would see them listening to each other. I remember thinking as a teacher, that's one of the biggest challenges.

As Mark points out, students who did not listen to him or their peers in the more traditional structure of his classroom were able to display the restraint needed to follow the rules of the talking piece in circle. Such youth participation and engagement encouraged Mark and affirmed the need for him to incorporate circles in the law and justice class.

The amount of time, energy and people necessary to facilitate healing and community circles made it nearly impossible to funnel resources into running the Youth Court as well. Because law and justice teachers thought they were less labor-intensive to implement, circles became the primary model of restorative justice at the school. And students in the law and justice class—the incubator for restorative practices in the school, where youth were trained in facilitating circles with students and teachers at Equity—would continue to turn the youth–adult paradigm on its side as restorative justice was implemented, working to wrest power out of the hands of adults training them and creating opportunities for more student leadership and engagement in the process.

"IF THERE'S RULES, THEN WE DON'T WANT TO DO IT": YOUTH EMPOWERMENT IN RESTORATIVE PRACTICES

The turning of the youth–adult paradigm on its side continued as Law and Justice Teachers Mark Cooper and Donna Flaherty learned about circles alongside their students. Northeastern law students and Janet Connors visited the classes weekly to facilitate talking circles and model the process. Yet Equity Senior Shannon Thompson tells me that she and her classmates were not fans of the talking piece or the content of talking circles. After all, she and her classmates were not part of the same cadre of students who rallied to bring restorative justice to the school; rather, they were part of a course (law and justice) where practicing restorative justice was a requirement. At that time, an intern from Northeastern University named Lauren visited Donna's class to apprentice the students in circle. What emerged, says Shannon, was an adult–youth dynamic that seemed unbalanced:

> [Lauren told] us, "There are no rules to circle, but here are the rules."
> And we all said, "Well, if there's rules, then we don't want to do it," because it was described to us that we would get to run our own circles, but when she was there, she ran the circles and talked about what she wanted to talk about. We couldn't relate to it, so we didn't want to do the circle. Everybody shut down, except for some of the kids who talked just because. As time progressed and we kept rebelling against her, she became more frustrated and started showing up less frequently. At one point, we didn't even know where she went—I guess she got fed up with us. So we got thrown into [keeping circles] and learned as we went along.

The "rules" that bothered the students included using the talking piece, which teacher Donna Flaherty enforced as a nonnegotiable, and speaking on the topics provided by the keeper, in this case, Lauren. Without explanation Lauren stopped showing up after the protests. The fact that Shannon and these students rebelled could indicate their petulance or immaturity. But it is also possible that the ethos of the school—that of encouraging students to raise their voices—inspired the behaviors of students who refused to do as they were told. Indeed according to Donna, Shannon was part of a core group of students in the class who were "committed to social justice and sucked the rest of the kids in the class in" when expressing dissent. "That was a tough class," she admits with a laugh. "They really rebelled against the structures in an amazing way. I had to let go of my power and control . . . They were the teenager that I was. They were smart and amazing, and they wouldn't shut up, but they always had a rationale to back up what they were saying." In having to let go of her "power and control," Donna found that students actually lived up to the expectations of having ownership in the process; her positive spin on behaviors that might have angered another teacher ("they were smart and amazing, and they wouldn't shut up"), and self-identification with the behaviors prompted her to ask students to choose topics and co-keep weekly circles with her to truly "turn the paradigm on its side."

At this point, says Shannon and Donna, students quelled their rebellion and began to appreciate the value of circle. Donna says, "It became clear that them leading the circles was the most important thing."

Shannon says one conversation in particular "ignited" student interest in circles—a circle on feminism, where students discussed the role of women in the household. "One student made the comment the woman's job is to cook and clean and other things. The females in the class all said *no*," says Shannon, her voice rising, "and that's how our class became more vocal, and we started talking more." Shannon says she tried to pick topics that she knew would "get to the class"—in other words, provoke discussion. "We kept talking about topics that we wanted to talk about. Anything you can think of, we talked about as a class because we're similar people, [and] as we were doing it, it just flowed. There was no problems with it." It was this kind of engagement that deepened Shannon's interest in talking circles and inspired her to volunteer to become co-teacher of the class the next year. Like John and Tania in the opening vignette, she went from questioning the process to becoming a proponent of circles and restorative justice. This change in dynamic could be related to multiple phenomena: students speaking up against the process they disagreed with, the school environment and mission that promoted student activism, and the teacher that supported, rather than berated them, for their opinions.

It is also possible that the ideal of turning the paradigm on its side was practiced most by the individual law and justice teachers whom I observed rather than majority of teachers in the school who did not have to practice circles regularly. Equity graduate Patricia Davis was also a student in Shannon's class but says that "it's a stretch" to say that students in that class were outspoken because they were influenced by the social justice mission of the *entire* school. "The only people who I can say who try to groom me to be an activist were Ms. Flaherty and Mr. [Roger] Françoise," she says, referring to the other humanities teacher who teaches law and justice. "You can tell when people have a passion and care for the students versus those teachers who are just there to get paid."

Though Donna and Roger encouraged students to speak up when they thought a situation was unjust, Patricia says she and the other students, including Shannon, might have spoken up without encouragement simply because they had a "problem with authority": "[We thought,] don't come here and point your finger at me and tell me what to do . . . We were smart. But we were not a group of good girls." When I ask her for specific examples of how she and her peers in that class spoke up about issues that bothered them, she mentions that they started a recycling program and wrote and collected signatures demanding that two different instructors teach them more.

In fact, the idea for the latter action emerged out of a talking circle. Says Patricia, "One student said, 'What do you do when your teacher doesn't teach anything?' And Ms. Flaherty said, 'Petition.' And this boy in our class, he actually said, 'This needs to happen.' So we did it."

Because Donna could interpret the students' outspokenness and refusal to cooperate in circle initially in positive ways, the shift in the power dynamic in circle ultimately led to an equilibrium based on a mutual understanding: Donna would grant students ownership of the process, and students would acknowledge her authority to enforce the talking piece as a basic rule of circle. Thus the paradigm continued to turn on its side during the implementation of Equity's apprenticeship model of restorative justice, which was set up such that students would ultimately keep healing circles with their peers. Community partners such as Janet Connors and the Northeastern law students first apprenticed students and law and justice teachers in the class together; students facilitated talking circles with peers within the class; law and justice students were sent out to the rest of the school to keep healing circles; and finally students in the course were offered the opportunity to co-teach the class the following year. I observed numerous circles in which senior co-teachers worked alongside adults, sharing ownership of the circle and offering insights into how they came to appreciate the circle process. The first talking circle in September—one year after Lauren the intern was at Equity—exemplifies the mutual power sharing that took place among co-teachers and adults in circle.

> I knock on the door, and Janet smiles and gets up to let me in. The student desks have been pushed to the sides of the room. I sit in an empty seat next to Janet, look to my right toward the female student who is speaking and spot and smile at Donna. We have corresponded through e-mail, and this is the first time I am meeting her, but I recognize her from a restorative justice training I attended. She is a White woman in her mid-30s, wearing jeans and a black Equity T-shirt with the slogan, "One justice for all!" Her cheeks are a natural pink hue, and she has a round, friendly face. She has curly, brown hair whose tendrils sprawl out of a ponytail set high on her head. Her nails are painted a rebellious black. In her 30s, she looks like a cool older sister. Besides me, Janet and Donna, there is one other male adult—a student teacher— to my right, and 17 students in the circle. The group is ethnically diverse, with Black, Latino and Asian students as well as one White student.
>
> The student keepers, Shannon and Abigail, are seated almost directly opposite of me. After introducing herself, Abigail explains the purpose of circle. She says restorative justice is being used as a replacement for suspensions, and that circles work well: "Most of the time relationships are mended, and you have better relationships with teachers." As if placing herself in the juniors' shoes, she says, "You're probably gonna

think they're [circles] dumb and stupid . . . I hated them at first . . . but we talk about everything." To emphasize her point, she says that teachers heard about sex and all kinds of things that they probably did not want to hear about.

Donna raises her eyebrows and nods with a smile, before clarifying, "We can talk about a variety of topics, but I am a court-mandated reporter, and if you're talking about hurting yourself or others, I have to report it." Abigail stops talking for a moment as if considering what to do next.

Janet suggests, "Should we do highs and lows?"

They nod and Abigail says, "Now we're going to say our highs and lows of the week. I'll start." She says that her high is seeing her grandma, and the low is that it is going to rain. She passes the piece to the right, and students answer with a number of responses: seeing my uncle come back from Iraq, getting a scholarship, I can't find a job, it's going to rain all weekend.

The turning of the adult–youth paradigm on its side was evidenced when co-teachers Shannon and Abigail took ownership of the practice, planning and facilitating circles such as this one as equal partners with Donna and Janet, who nudged the process along and clarified the norms along the way. Abigail affirms that circle is an engaging and useful practice by stating that "you have better relationships with teachers" and that you can talk about any topic you like. This sentiment could have been conveyed by Donna or Janet alone, but as seniors Abigail and Shannon are closer in age to their classmates and therefore better able to offer convincing anecdotes about the power of circle; Abigail anticipates the skepticism of her peers, admitting that she thought the circles were "dumb," trying to convince them to try the practice on. Janet provides guidance by suggesting the circle begin with the highs and lows of the week. As Abigail communicates that students can talk about "everything," Donna interjects by reminding students of her role and responsibility as the teacher—if someone is thinking of committing suicide, for example, this information will not be kept confidential. The two adults and two youth engage in a delicate balance of providing input and leadership in the process and deferring to one another. Thus the apprenticeship model provided co-teachers an opportunity to deepen their knowledge of restorative justice by apprenticing their peers and to feel further empowered in the process as they worked side by side with adults. Shannon tells me it feels like everyone is equal in circle even if there are adults or teachers present because "there's no restraint on what you can say . . . as long as it's not on a disrespectful level, there's no problem with it." When students *did* engage in dialogue considered to be disrespectful, adults had to make tactical decisions about when to speak up and when to let students regulate one another.

TURNING SOME PARADIGMS BUT NOT OTHERS: POWER DYNAMICS IN CIRCLE

Law and justice teachers attempted to create a space in which youth had as much voice as they did, where students determined what issues would be discussed and facilitated circles as keepers. After all, as an egalitarian space, circles are supposed to provide every participant with the chance to contribute to the community as equals and in fact are intended to disrupt the traditional power hierarchies—such as those between students and teachers—that shape how we interact with one another. But in circles, social dynamics around race, gender, class and other dimensions also can undermine the goals of creating more equity, reinforcing social privileges (Cook, 2006). At Equity, for example, there was a gendered aspect of talking circles in which clusters of boys[1] in both law and justice classes could silence or marginalize male and female students in circle through body language, comments or laughter—complicating the notion of circles as equalizing spaces. While the youth–adult paradigm often could be turned on its side in talking circles, *other* power paradigms sometimes remained intact; in this section I share examples of circles where students reified[2] traditional power hierarchies between men and women, straight and gay students, immigrant and American-born students and differently abled students versus those without disabilities.

Reifying Traditional Hierarchies

As part of their grade, students in the law and justice course were required to keep at least one talking circle on a topic of their choice. As mentioned earlier, they did so only after Janet, Law and Justice Teachers Donna Flaherty and Roger Françoise and the senior co-teachers of the course modeled the process for a few weeks. Students discussed subjects like relationships, their favorite music artists and fondest childhood memories—but devoted an overwhelming amount of talking circles to serious topics such as violence, gangs, suicide, abortion, homophobia and racism. This further necessitated that keepers reinforce the talking piece to address the often volatile issues that prompted multiple people to talk at the same time. In one circle in Law and Justice Teacher Roger Françoise's class—in which boys outnumbered girls two to one—boys enacted traditional gender roles through comments made in the circle on racism:

> There are 19 of us in the circle, but because of the limited space in the middle of the classroom, the chairs are huddled together in what resembles a long oval. Monica is a shy Latina student who has passed the talking piece nearly every time I have observed. Today she is keeping the circle as part of the course requirement. She has short, brown hair, bleached blonde at the tips. Her skin is light brown, and there are

multiple piercings on her face, including one on her eyebrow and one by her lip. Roger, seated next to her, reads an opening quote: "Wisdom comes when we call things by their proper name."

Monica unfolds a piece of paper and reads the first prompt. "Why do you think racism exists in this day and age?" Monica has a Spanish accent; a few boys remark that they cannot understand. Lincoln, a student to my right and one of Monica's friends, chuckles and asks her to "speak in English." A few of the boys start laughing, and Monica smiles, looking down. She passes the piece to Roger. Roger is Haitian American, the son of immigrants, and in his mid-30s. He is a few inches taller than myself, casually dressed in jeans, a white, button-down shirt with rows of purple dots, and black dress shoes. His hair is cut short below his ears and a bit longer everywhere else. He wears a goatee and often looks to the side when talking, taking long pauses before answering. I get the sense that the pauses are both a result of his way of speaking, being thoughtful about articulating what it is that he exactly is trying to say. He restates Monica's question, perhaps trying to redirect the boys' teasing.

As the piece is passed, a few students mention how racism is still apparent in the language people use. "You still hear the N-word used today," says one boy. A few comment about how Black people can say the word, but White people can't.

"When we use it, it basically means friend," says Lincoln. Jamison, a student who has a small voice like Mike Tyson's, begins to speak.

Romero, a Black Latino student who covertly checks his phone every few minutes, mimics Jamison's voice along with a few other boys, part of a group of six who are engaged in constant side chatter. "It's sad that racism still exists today," says Jamison. "Even in this day and age, my uncle was murdered in the South. In some ways things haven't changed all that much in 50 years." Roger nods in commiseration, and some of the boys continue to chide each other quietly on the side. I can't tell if they have heard what Jamison has shared. All but two of the female participants pass the piece.

Monica gets the piece and does not answer her own question. There is still a low-level buzz from this group of six boys elbowing each other with private jokes, and after Roger narrows his eyes at them, they quiet down. Monica grips her paper and stares at it, looking to Roger. He steps in as a co-keeper, prodding, "Should we do another round?" She nods and hands him the piece.

"Thank you for sharing that, Jamison. I think we all have to think about the impact of history and how it still plays out today. When I'm with black friends, we sometimes use language that we wouldn't use around other people."

"So you say nigga?" asks Romero. Suddenly the boys who have been chatting are attentive. Romero says, "How can you tell us not to say it when you say it yourself?"

Roger does not admit to using the word, but his lack of a denial suggests that he has. "You have to be careful who you around because if I am sitting in a bar around a whole bunch of White people and they overhear me, they might get drunk and think it's funny to say the word, and then you have a mini race riot on your hands."

Romero leans in, saying, "Yo, pass the piece!" But there are many people ahead of him. I overhear some of the boys talking about marijuana. One boy accuses another, "You don't get high!"

When Romero gets the piece, he says, "I understand what the N-word meant back in the day, but if I choose not to say it, it is not going to change things. When I use the word, I can give it my own meaning."

I continue to hear a lot of cross talk among the boys. Lincoln says, "I was so hungry in the middle of the night!" When I turn toward the boys, I see Romero making a gesture toward his friends; he flits his tongue in and out between two fingers shaped in a V, a reference to oral sex on a woman.

I get the piece and say, "Even though people think words don't impact people, they definitely do. And actions also impact people." I ponder whether to derail a conversation from a talk about race to what I've just seen. My decision to speak up about the sexual gesture is fraught; was I perpetuating a youth–adult dynamic in which I called upon my power as a grown-up to essentially discipline him for his action? "Romero, I just saw what you did and it really grosses me out."

Lois, traditionally one of the more vocal females in circle, says, "I saw you too." It takes him a minute to understand what I'm referring to, and then he starts laughing, covering his mouth. He says, "Oh! I didn't know."

Lois whispers to Monica, "We should do a circle on sexism."

This circle above encapsulates much of what I witnessed in other circles: young people interrupting each other, teasing, pushing boundaries by challenging their teachers and sharing insightful, honest anecdotes from their lives all in the same session. It offered powerful opportunities for students to revert adult–youth power dynamics, as with the exchange about the word "nigga" between Roger and Romero. Their calling out of what they define as adult hypocrisy harkens back to the first circle I saw in Mark Cooper's classroom, when students questioned why adults who were concerned about young people's safety sent them to the streets during suspensions. Teacher Roger Françoise does not shirk away from such conversations and welcomes the opportunity to connect to his students by being vulnerable among them. He tells me, "Circle is the time to have the ability to let your guard down. If you're interested in getting through to your students, then you'll try it on." He uses the language of restorative justice practitioners (*try it on*) to describe how circles can allow teachers to connect to students in different ways.

Roger balances ignoring some of the side conversations in this circle with helping Monica to facilitate, a role that was new and not altogether comfortable for her. "Ideally circles would include more conversation, more people participating, and less of the side chatter," he says. Despite his "side chatter," Romero seems genuinely engaged by the conversation, offering insights into how he has the right to appropriate the N-word when he says, "When I use the word, I give it my own meaning." He is passionate about racial issues and even stops bantering with his friends long enough to yell out, "Yo, pass the piece!" so that he can contribute to the discussion. Yet Roger is worried that the ongoing commentary of some of the boys in the class is "costing the voice and input of everyone else," especially the young women who compose a minority.

After all, the boys in the class dominated the conversation, and their banter involved various assertions of masculinity—talk of sex and mockery of a high-pitched voice—that reinforced traditional hierarchies between native-born English speakers and immigrants, and men and women. From the beginning a few of the boys tease Monica because of her accent, and she consistently passes the piece, not responding to prompts she herself has written as per the norm. This may just be because she is shy, but it is also possible that spotlighting her status as an immigrant—telling her to "speak in English"—alienates her from ever trying to participate. That she is also a woman being chided for her language skills by young men also could have played a role in her reticence. Some of the boys then go on to tease the young man with an effeminate voice, reinforcing traditional notions of what manliness sounds like, right before he shares a story about how his uncle was murdered in the South. He does not flinch during the teasing and laughs or brushes off the continued mimicry of his voice throughout the year, but the treatment he received went against the core principles of circle.

Many students I spoke to stated that the most disruptive behaviors in circle were often displayed by boys trying to perform to gender expectations. Junior Jared Simpson has been involved in restorative justice since it was first introduced at the school three years earlier. He has sat in numerous circles and was recruited by the principal to provide input on the peer mediation program. Tall and lanky, he admits that he defies easy categorization; half Asian, half Black, artistic, laid-back but competitive in debate competitions, most of his friends are girls, and he is comfortable sharing his thoughts in circle. "I'm not a person that generally fits in with society, preconceived ways of what it takes to be a man." He doesn't think that boys are inherently incapable of contributing seriously in talking circles, but he does find that when some young men are grouped together, circle can feel like "a bunch of testosterone, and everyone's trying to be the alpha male":

> I know females tend to, they like to talk and listen more than a male would. You know, I can't even lie, even myself. Even though I don't believe in those preconceived thoughts, I can't lie. I do some of the

same things that other males do . . . It bothers me when no one listens because then it defeats the purpose of circle where it's respect and we're actually paying attention to you.

Jared's analysis of women aligns with traditional, albeit stereotypical, beliefs in their superior emotional intelligence. When Josephine Garrett and Melanie Gipson, each a student in a different section of the law and justice course, tell me that a group of boys in each class often joke around during serious circles, I ask them why.

> JOSEPHINE: It's their egos, and they're not used to sharing about their feelings.
> MELANIE: They want to be hard.
> JOSEPHINE: (tapping Melanie on the arm and smiling) You know it!
> MELANIE: Everybody got [to be] this type of macho man, be tough in their brains. It's crazy. They have a problem talking about sexuality, people being gay. Why would you care? You're not sleeping with that person.

Josephine and Melanie are mindful of the fact that the behavior of some boys in circle is colored by the need to conform to the model of a heterosexual "macho man," a masculine, "tough" person who always has to "be hard." Melanie also points out how such behavior manifests in conversations about gay people, something I witnessed in multiple circles and often by the same students. For example, Jonathan Davis, a student in Donna's class, made numerous comments about homosexuality throughout the year. It is hard to distinguish when he is being ironic in circle, trying to grab attention or being serious. In one circle when responding to the prompt, "Should a man who has conceived a child with a woman have a say in her decision to abort the pregnancy?" he says,

> The man should have the choice because even if he didn't want the child, [he could] tell [his] daughter about how men are only after sex. And if you have a son when he's young, you can teach him baseball and other things. Except if he's gay.

He scrunches up his nose when he says "gay," and a few people laugh. When I get the piece, I try to probe the consistent reference to gay people or the word "gay" by students in so many circles I have sat in on, ignoring the rest of Jonathan's comment. "We throw this word around in a negative way, and I don't understand the big deal. Some people are straight, and some people are gay. I'm not sure why it comes up so much."

A few students pass the piece, and one student assures me that when they say "gay," they don't mean it in a bad way. Another says, "Gay people say things that are gay too, so why can't we?" As with Romero, I am aware that I may be shaming Jonathan—perhaps alienating him or shutting him down, perpetuating an inequitable adult–youth dynamic through my mini lecture. However I also want to call out heteronormative and homophobic comments that have emerged in so many circles.

Melanie tells me that during a circle on suicide that she kept, Jonathan said, "I wouldn't care if my friend committed suicide if he was gay."

Because none of the individuals from either group of boys agreed to be interviewed, it is difficult to draw any conclusions from these snippets of dialogue; the boys could be performing to heteronormative expectations, suppressing their own struggles with sexuality, expressing genuine feelings of disgust toward homosexuality or none of the above. Whatever the case, it is always possible that such commentary can marginalize or silence other students. Lester Ruiz, a student in Donna's class, says that he sometimes "gets pissed off" when he witnesses students laughing at one another in circle. "I know for myself when other people's over there laughing, I don't feel like talking because I feel offended by someone else that would be laughing when I'm talking. And most people in the circle do feel that way."

Melanie, the student who kept the circle on suicide, says that the one thing she would change about circle is people joking around about certain topics such as homosexuality. She says after people make "ignorant" remarks, some students "wouldn't feel comfortable saying anything after that":

MELANIE: I asked the question, what would you do if you knew someone was gonna commit suicide? People were saying dumb stuff like if it's not my friend, I wouldn't care. Some people actually wanted to commit suicide in that class before, but they didn't feel comfortable saying that to everybody because they knew—

ANITA: You know that about some of the students?

MELANIE: Some of them said it. And they was pissed off at the fact that the whole class was insensitive. People said I wouldn't care. They can commit suicide; they're not my friend. If someone wanted to commit suicide, let them commit it.

ANITA: Why do you think they act like that?

MELANIE: I think it's to show off. They think it's cool, but it's not. You're 17, 18, 19, 20 years old; you should not be talking like that.

ANITA: Is it more boys?

MELANIE: It's the boys.

Melanie suggests that boys who make comments that are "insensitive" are, in a sense, performing; they do it to "show off" but in the process may alienate students who have been most impacted by the topic of the circle. In fact, these boys simply may be behaving in developmentally appropriate ways, performing their gender in a space that may not be altogether comfortable to them—a space where they may feel vulnerable talking about such weighty topics.

It would be shortsighted to suggest that boys are incapable of engaging in circles on serious topics or to presume that groups of boys inherently reify traditional power paradigms in talking circles. In fact according to Donna, Roger, Janet and several students I interviewed, the very group of boys who engaged in banter, laughter and side comments that potentially marginalized certain voices also kept some of the most powerful circles. Over time Roger saw that although some of the male students like Romero could detract from circle by not listening and making gestures, they clearly wanted to participate and had the capacity to engage in critical dialogue around important issues. A week before Monica's circle on racism, Romero listened intently during a talking circle on the value of education and waxed passionately about how he has consistently been underestimated by teachers, stating, "I have advanced scores on MCAS,[3] but they've put me in all the easy classes and special education for no reason."

Roger responded by trying to connect Romero's personal experiences to historical and institutional factors that affect many students of color. "That's probably because of the history of racism and education in this country," said Roger. "And the fact that there are a lot of White teachers who don't know how to teach Black students because there are differences in how Black teachers and White teachers talk. We learn about this in graduate school. This is a well-known topic." In the conversation, Romero and Roger engaged in critical analysis of the racial hierarchy in this country and how schools replicate the oppression of young people of color through structures such as special education identification. After class, Romero hung back and continued to talk to Roger about his experiences with the education system. Thus, some of the very boys who engaged in behaviors that showcased masculinity—and teased people who didn't behave similarly—were quite capable of contributing to a critical discussion in a respectful way.

In January Janet tells me about a circle I missed in which Jonathan and his friend Russell kept a circle in Donna's class. They asked students what Malcolm X and Martin Luther King, Jr. would think if they saw how the N-word was used today. Their leadership as keepers of the circle provided other students with fresh opinions on their capacity to contribute to thought-provoking conversations. Says Jared, the young man who says boys try to act "alpha male" in circle,

> We were all thinking, "Oh my God, this is going to be horrible" . . . And it was actually one of the best circles we've ever had . . . It was around Malcolm X and standing up for your opinions . . . We kind of thought in our own heads, 'OK, these two are going to say something stupid, so we're not even going to listen to them.' But after that circle when [Jonathan] and Russell had led it and hearing some other thoughts on

the questions, it kind of made me think. I'm like, 'Wow, so they actually do have deeper thoughts than just . . . surface-level type of things.'

Donna says Jonathan and Russell are two of "the sharpest thinkers in the class" but that they hide behind façades as class clowns, perhaps even saying things in circle simply to provoke laughter or frustration. It is little surprise then that Jared expected the two young men to "say something stupid." Instead, he is surprised to learn that he has underestimated his peers because of their prior behavior in circle, that they do have "deeper thoughts" than they may let on.

Jerome Sterling, who describes Jonathan and Russell as two of three boys in his class who often make fun of people in circle, concurs that their circle on the modern-day usage of the N-word was stimulating. "They did a good job," he says. "They took it seriously." When I asked him why he thinks they behaved more "seriously," he tilts his head to the side and says, "What changed? I guess the fact that they were doing it, so they wanted respect this time." Indeed many of the times that all students, not just the boys, were given ownership of circles, they tended to adhere strictly to the norms of respecting all participants and honoring the talking piece. Thus the very individuals who helped perpetuate certain paradigms of power—such as those based on gender and sexuality—also could turn such paradigms on their side when given the opportunity and power to shape the conversation in circle. Nonetheless teachers did assert their authority and disciplined students in circles who blatantly disregarded the norms of circle. In the next section I explore how adults tried to respond to disciplinary moments in circle without reinforcing *another* hierarchy, that of adults asserting power over young people.

NOTES

1. Girls certainly made comments or gestures that marginalized individuals, but there was a consistent pattern that emerged among groups of boys in both classes in talking circles—although not, as I discuss later, in healing circles.
2. By reify, I mean *made real*—to "regard (something abstract) as material" (Webster's, 2015). Students enacted power dynamics by potentially marginalizing traditionally disenfranchised groups (women, immigrants, etc.) verbally and silently through gestures.
3. This is the state assessment.

8 Doing Discipline in Circles
The Developmental Challenges of Restorative Justice

Roger and Donna state that disruptive behaviors in circle are not the result of complete disregard for the process; rather, they identify developmental challenges of teenagers acclimating to the process. Donna confirms that she initially wanted and still would "like for [circle] to always be perfect" but now understands that teenagers are developmentally at a different place as they are "by nature chatty": "When I sit in circles with adults, everyone is very respectful and quiet, but it's also . . . we're all professionals sitting in a circle. We know how to hold our tongues and be appropriate. I kind of think that the talking and the buzz sometimes in circle is not necessarily a bad thing." Although the assumption is often that being "appropriate" entails holding one's tongue and acting like "professionals," Donna acknowledges that teenagers like to talk and that their side conversations are not always "a bad thing." Thus I observed Roger and Donna responding to disruptive behaviors in circle in multiple ways: by sternly, often calmly, reminding students of norms, flashing irritated looks, ignoring some of the "buzz" and cross talk and, on only a few occasions, by asking students to leave, as Roger did in a circle in early October on race:

> Two students have just asked the circle to talk about a time when they were treated differently for their race. Roger has the piece and says he is "scrolling" through his mind to find a quick example. Damien, a baby-faced student with a brown, wavy ponytail, is seated to my left. As Roger thinks, Damien smiles at a girl across from him, interlocks his fingers together over his mouth and begins tweeting softly like a bird. Roger looks at him briefly, and Damien drops his hands.
>
> "One time me and my girlfriend were paying for items at a convenient story in a largely white area. The cashier dropped the change in the air so as not to touch me," says Roger, lifting his fingers in the air and separating them in reenactment. Students raise their eyebrows or cluck their tongues. Students share stories about police profiling.
>
> "One cop stopped me the same time every day—for walking while Black," says one young man. John says that cops handcuffed him instead

of a young man who had robbed him. Raven says that she was trying to check out [Alice Walker's] *The Color Purple* and [Sapphire's] *Push* from the library, but a volunteer kept following her as though she was going to steal the books. Amidst these revealing anecdotes, Damien cops his two hands together, and makes another chirping sound—the noise is subtle, so much so that I'm not sure how long it has been going on.

Roger says to Damien calmly, "Go ahead and step outside."

"Should I get my things?" asks Damien. His tone is innocent.

"Yes," says Roger.

After school, Roger says that Damien was "acting like a jerk" by making bird noises for at least 15 minutes. Even still, he says, "I felt bad about that [sending him out]." Roger wrestles with when and how to step in to discipline students in a circle because this is his first year teaching law and justice, although he was not unfamiliar with restorative justice prior to stepping into this role. A former film student, he worked on a documentary on the philosophy years before teaching at Equity, interviewing people such as a woman from Cambridge who was trying to get federal courts to recognize restorative justice as its own legitimate form of justice on reservations. He has been intrigued by the prospect of how restorative justice in school disciplinary matters contrast with its use for criminal offenses. "It was just a different experience to interview people who lost loved ones in vicious crimes and were using restorative justice for healing and to see how to translate that process in schools where the gravity around it is so different," he says. For teachers expecting circles always to be without such distraction, such experiences can be—and for Roger were—very frustrating. "[I first thought] is it that these kids just can't be quiet and sit in circles, and how disrespectful! And it's really not that at all. It's just so different, and it's different for students, and it just takes a lot to build that culture." Like Donna, he acknowledges that students may be acting inappropriately given the nature of circle—it is "just so different" from other spaces in school and requires time and patience to "build that culture."

He and Donna point out—as did students I interviewed—that excluding students from circle for their behavior simply replicates zero tolerance notions of punishment through expulsion. During my observations, students were probably kicked out of circle only 15 percent of the time. Yet the disregard for the talking piece and the difficulty in having students take all circles seriously frustrated a group of eight students who met in a weekly restorative justice club after school on Fridays to discuss how to improve circle practices. In a meeting mid-January, students say they want to discuss why some peers in Donna's class are being "childish and disrespectful" in circle. Mark Cooper facilitates the meeting, and we sit in circle and respond to his question, "Should people who are not being respectful be kicked out of circle?" This space offers an opportunity for youth–adult dynamics to be turned on their side as students contribute to their vision of what restorative practices should look like. Jared Whitman sometimes feels Donna did not assert her power enough and kick students out for not respecting the talking piece, but by the end of this meeting, he understands her philosophical reasons for doing so. "Some of us, I think I told her at one point we need to take these people out because they're just making circle worse. But even though she knew they made circle worse at times she held onto the values that it's a non-exclusionary thing, which is actually respectable."

In fact the consensus among all the young people I interviewed was that regardless of the disciplinary problems that arose in circle, no student should be singled out or alenated from participating. The feeling was that excluding any students perpetuated a power differential between young people and adults that was antithetical to the egalitarian nature of circle. For example, in one circle in Donna's class, Jonathan and two of his friends, Russell and Peter, laughed whenever Jennifer, a young woman with a speech impediment and the keeper that day, had the talking piece. When she spoke they would erupt into giggles, and Donna told them several times to stop. Russell said, "We're not laughing about *that*." At times Jennifer laughed with them. Jackson, who participated in that circle and is also a member of the restorative justice club, finds himself continually irritated with this group of boys. "It's not funny to be making fun of [Jennifer] like that because she also has a hearing problem in one ear. And for her to have to be made fun of that way must be hard for her." When I asked why he thinks she laughs, he says that she does it to protect herself, that it is a "concealing laugh." He says, "She's laughing to keep the circle going. She don't wanna put her feelings in the circle." Donna tells the boys to stop laughing multiple times, but part of the issue with calling out such behavior and circle is the possibility of derailing the entire conversation. Jackson says, "I know we could say something, but it's like when we say something, they [the disruptive students] say something. The circle just gets thrown off. If we were to say something, it would get more distracting." Jackson points out how sometimes spotlighting rather than tactfully ignoring certain behaviors or comments deemed disrespectful can further compound disrespectful behavior.

Ultimately, teachers tried to turn *all* paradigms on their side—to avoid the reification of hierarchies based on age and gender, sexual orientation and other factors—by maintaining a low profile, with the expectation that doing so would force students to demand respect from one another. To maintain an equilibrium between youth and adult power, Donna and Roger did in some instances step back to provide student keepers with opportunities to do discipline in circle. In one circle on judgment in Donna's class, keeper Frank Myers reads a quote about how we shouldn't judge because we shouldn't think that our way is the better way because we don't know what people have been through. He asks if people agree or disagree, but students are confused and ask him to reread the statement. He reads it two more times, and asks, "What do you think of the quote?" Most everyone agrees, offering perfunctory responses about how we shouldn't judge others because we don't know why they behave the way they do. The next round, Frank asks how people can be impacted by judgment.

Ramona, a petite Latina girl with black-frame glasses, erupts into fits of giggles, shoving her face into her hoodie as if to contain them. "Ramona, stop," says Donna sternly.

"Why does she keep laughing like that?" says the young man next to me. Ramona mutters an apology. Several students say one of two things; judging negatively can lead to someone's low self-esteem; conversely, judging negatively can lead one to have "thick skin" and inspire one to "prove people wrong." A young girl named Sasha talks about how when she got pregnant, her brother told her that she would never finish school and would end up "a statistic"; this inspired her, and she has surpassed him by graduating. Meanwhile, in addition to Ramona's bursts of giggles, there are pockets of side conversations springing up—either from Jonathan and Irving, the boys to the right of Donna, or the people near Ramona. Frank rises by the time the piece has come to Donna—it feels as though he is asserting himself somehow, trying to stand up against the noise or let people know he is the keeper. After a few moments, the class quiets down. As the keeper of the circle, Frank institutes his own form of discipline and asserts the role of the talking piece through his body language and silence—and Donna feels that this is ideally how small disciplinary matters should be handled, with students checking one another just as much as she does:

> My vision of it is for us to all just be equals and for me to not have to be that discipline person at all when I'm in circle. That's what I tell the kids . . . this should be you all respecting each other and expecting this quiet from each other. Sometimes they're amazing, and sometimes they're very challenging, but that's teenagers—you know what I mean? But almost always I'm not the only person ever asking for quiet. There are kids who will hold the piece and say, "I'm not talking until I get respect."

Donna offers a vision of restorative justice where she does not have to be the "discipline person at all," where students internalize restorative principles and keep one another accountable to the norms of circle—where the youth–adult power paradigm is truly turned on its side. Yet she admits this ideal is not possible if students begin acting "out of control"; at that point she becomes authoritative—though not authoritarian—and steps in to quiet the class down, ask a student to leave or even break up the circle.

What one defines as "out of control" is subjective, and can differ according to the teacher, or even differ day to day according to a teacher's level of tolerance. Even with his initial interest in restorative justice, Roger entered uncertain about what level of control he could and should assert during the process and believes there are no cut-and-dry answers: "[Circle] can always go in many different directions, and so you got to be comfortable with some of that, but then you also got to be willing to try and take control to whatever extent, whatever makes sense." He goes so far as to say that sometimes "you really do need to take it [circle] by the reigns the entire time because it's fragile. It's fragile, and it's hard to build that culture if you're uncertain about it in the first place." His comments about teachers needing to be both flexible about circle going in "many different directions" and being able to "take control" illustrate the ongoing tension that can occur when they allow students to truly engage one another in honest conversations.

This does not mean that adults saw a contradiction between honoring student voices *as well as* asserting one's presence as an elder. For example, though Principal Stephen Dobbs did try to set himself on equal footing with students—in circle he always presented himself as "Stephen"—he fundamentally believed that adults had a responsibility to upset the egalitarian nature of circles when it was necessary to offer their wisdom:

> I've heard it said from young people and adults alike, like when you enter the circle, you're all equal, which I love that. However, when I enter the circle, if there's an elder in the circle, I just simply refuse to think of myself as on equal footing with this elder, and so that's just one small example of like this is a big piece to unpack. It really is because, again, I think there's a danger in sort of romanticizing indigenous culture and saying we were all the same and we were all equal. No. There also was authority; there also was deference.

Stephen's commentary also includes an analysis of how indigenous practices can often be misinterpreted or romanticized by people who only emphasize how circles should provide everyone with an equal voice. In fact, he points to an important element of indigenous restorative practices that is often not emphasized in the literature in restorative justice: the existence of "authority" as well as "deference" to those who are older than us. Janet made sure to assert such authority—not only her own but the authority of the indigenous cultures from which talking circles have emerged. During a circle where students continued to talk over one another, she became so angered she used profanity—the only time I heard her do so in front of students:

> Since we're not using the talking peace, I'll just chime in . . . You can treat this like something serious, or you can treat it like bullshit. When we talk over other people and circle, we insult not only those people and ourselves, but the traditions of native people. Circle is a gift given to us by indigenous cultures, and for indigenous peoples, circle is like going to church. So when we talk over each other here, it would be like going to church and swearing at the preacher.

In this way even the power of history and culture was called up as a way to enforce students to keep to the agreements of using the talking piece and to remind students of their individual and collective responsibilities to honor each other and indigenous traditions. Students took these agreements much more seriously in healing circles, which offered a more direct connection to the restorative principle of repairing harm than talking circles.

HEALING CIRCLES: PARTIALLY TURNING THE PARADIGM

In healing circles students learn that restorative justice involves more than sitting in a circle and talking about topics that they care about. Roger says the "applicable situations [in healing circles] are probably the most important" aspect of restorative justice at Equity "because [students] have a connection to the people that are involved typically because they know them from being around the school." By "applicable situations," he refers to those incidents of harm adults choose to refer to healing circles, such as interpersonal conflicts among students or between students and teachers. As he notes, students can understand their peers in ways that adults cannot, and many of them know the participants, or have engaged in similar behaviors, so their wisdom and solutions resonated with students who committed harm. Nevertheless the turning of the paradigm on its side occurred only partially in healing circles because adults ultimately determined which incidents should be referred to circles and which should be handled with suspensions. In this section I begin by discussing how healing circles are planned. I then reveal how students provide key leadership by planning and keeping healing circles in equal partnership with adults. Finally I analyze how in spite of the attempt to grant disciplinary authority to students, adults acted as arbiters and gatekeepers to the restorative process, limiting the true possibility of turning the youth–adult paradigm on its side.

Planning Circles

For a healing circle to take place, a teacher or administrator had to write up a referral and send it either to Roger and Donna—who discussed it with their law and justice students—or to Mark Cooper, who presented the incident to the restorative justice club that met on Fridays. Once any of these adults volunteered to take on the case, their students convened a *planning circle*, the precursor to a healing circle. Planning circles forced students to discuss the relevant details of the disciplinary incident, identify the harmed party and the person who committed the harm, script questions for each round of the subsequent healing circle and brainstorm possible agreements in advance.

However students were not truly in equal partnership with adults in all aspects of healing circles, including planning circles. Teachers still determined what incidents were referred to in circles—although students did request healing circles from time to time—and thus the turning of the paradigm was limited by the adult decisions about what constituted a circle-worthy offense. As shown in the first planning circle of the year in Roger's law and justice class, students did not always agree with these decisions:

It is Monday afternoon and John is keeping the first planning circle. There are about 18 students present. John begins by asking everyone to report their highs and lows. It is Karina's birthday. This class claps for her and says happy birthday. Everyone or almost everyone participates in the circle including Monica. John begins by reading incident report which documents the case: "Two students were caught horseplaying in the cafeteria, and one put the other in a headlock. It was loud, and one student could not hear the other say to stop and that he was in pain. The boys are friends and shook hands in front of an administrator to say that they will not do it again. In lieu of suspension, they have agreed to attend a healing circle."

John asks students to respond to the report. A few students pass, with nothing to say, and Tania is the first to speak. "I think this is dumb," says Tania. "Those two guys are friends. I saw them in the morning talking to each other, and they already squashed it, so why are we wasting time having a circle on this?"

Other students chime in about how "stupid" and "unnecessary" this case is. Ironically, the incident is called a "case," reminiscent of language from the court system, and in this circle, students discuss, among other things, their disdain for this word. They decide midway to call the case a "situation" instead.

As the keeper, John is the last person to get the piece. "This case makes me mad," he says. "Circle is supposed to be a way to fix a problem, but they don't even really have a problem. They were just horseplaying. I'm a guy. We always horseplay. It's not a big deal."

Janet and Roger push back; Janet says that the incident was referred to circle, and so we have to plan for it. Roger says we should treat this as an exercise because none of us have done a planning or healing circle before, and so if anything, we can learn how to do it by taking on this case. Also he says that sometimes something may not have been squashed by now. Janet says that sometimes it seems people may have resolved an issue, but they may have only superficially done so. She asks, "I guess what I'm asking is, do you still think you can keep the circle even if you don't believe that it's fully necessary?"

"Yes!" says Tania emphatically, as if the question itself is an insult.

During the third round where students are to come up with questions to ask in the healing circle, Jonathan says, "Are we still talking about this?"

Robert says, "Can we talk about something else?" The bell rings before the class can finish—but it feels like they have hardly begun to unpack how to plan the healing circle.

After class Roger and Janet approach Tania. "As a co-teacher you really need to be on board with the process," says Janet.

"OK," says Tania quietly, nodding her head and staring to the side.

"Your negativity can really harm the process because if you don't buy into it, other students won't," adds Roger.

John walks up behind Tania to join the conversation. "You both need to model some inherent faith in circles," she adds, addressing both students. "If you talk about how stupid it is, other students will follow your lead."

"Did you see that, Anita?" says Tania to me as we leave the class. "Any time I express my opinion, I get shot down. That's why I have to keep my mouth shut. They say this is the school about social justice, but then they never hear what we want to say."

Because it is the first planning circle, there is some understandable confusion as to the purpose of the circle. Tania's comments are reminiscent of the first circle I witnessed with her and John more than six months ago. The arguments that brewed up during this circle call attention to the tweaking that must take place as the school continues its program of restorative justice. Tania feels her voice was ignored when she questioned the necessity of a healing circle. Handled by administrators, students were given only one option to address the incident: to plan a healing circle, even if they would have ignored the incident entirely because they saw the two friends speaking cordially in the morning. Tania also points out that discipline occurs in a random fashion—that horseplay happens all the time and is not punished. She points out the need for consistency in the application of rules and expectations. Yet her input does not change the process. Adults were still setting the agenda. Thus, though students were able to assert their voices during healing circles by sitting face-to-face with people who had experienced and could offer suggestions for resolution, their suggestions were not always heeded.

Healing Circles

After the planning circles one or two students (alongside an adult such as Janet or Mark) conducted a healing circle with all the involved parties in an empty classroom during the law and justice class. The following exemplifies how students were able to truly work in tandem with adults by offering their skill set to their peers:

It is Friday after school, and the restorative justice club has planned a healing circle with Jason, a student who vandalized school property after a verbal altercation with another student. We meet in Donna's classroom where John, Tania, her boyfriend Michael and I begin rearranging chairs into a circle. Jason, a lanky, White junior with soft, boyish features, strolls in wearing yellow sneakers and a baseball cap. I have a hard time imagining him busting a hole in a wall by the library, the offense that has brought him here. He and Tania exchange familiar smiles, and Jason greets Michael with a casual handshake and hug.

Mark Cooper arrives with leftover pizza from a moot court competition. Five other juniors who are part of the restorative justice club also show up. Tania begins circle by asking Andrew why he punched the wall as opposed to the student he was mad at. In a low tone Andrew says, "I just thought it would be better to take out my anger on the wall than on a person."

Mark says, "Tania, I just want to clarify the question. It's probably always a good idea to take out one's anger on an object than a person. Can you explain what you meant?"

Tania nods. "I just mean that if he had it in him to control how he felt by not hitting another person, then couldn't he draw from that same strength in the future and not hit a wall." She turns to Andrew. "You could have gotten your aggression out in a different way. Why didn't you go rap or do something else?"

Andrew shrugs and bites the corner of his lip. "I didn't even think about it. I was just in the moment, and the wall was right there."

Says Mark, "Going back to the earlier point, I just want to point out that it's probably hard to do things like dancing or writing when you're in the moment and angry."

Jackson points the talking piece at Andrew. "I used to punch holes in the wall too."

"Me too," says Michael.

"What are some things Andrew could do to make up for what he did?" She removes a piece of paper from her pocket and unfolds it. "We came up with these ideas. It's really up to you which one you want to do. You could help the custodian fix the wall. You could start a krumping[1] club after school to give back to the community, or you could do a combination of both."

"I'll do a combination," says Andrew. Tania says she will ask an administrator to set up a time where Andrew can work with the custodian. We also suggest that Andrew can hold the club the same time that we have this after-school club (Friday afternoons) so that we will be there to see that it is actually happening. Tania is going to make a file for this case in which she will keep all the questions she asked today. We also say it would be nice for Andrew to come once he has finished all of the hours and share his reflections on the experience. After we are done, we move the chairs back, and Michael and Andrew put on a spontaneous display of krumping.

In this healing circle Andrew explains the root of his anger not only to students he does not know but also to two friends—Tania and Michael.

There are aspects of the restorative meeting that also borrow from indigenous practices; in New Zealand, Maori community members hold circles called *hui whakatika* (Wearmouth, McKinney, & Glynn, 2007), which begin and end with prayers and some form of hospitality, such as the sharing of food. These circles also invite participants close to the person (like Tania and Michael) who committed harm so that he/she feels supported through the process. This healing circle begins with the spontaneous sharing of food (leftover pizza) and ends positively as Andrew performs with his good friend Michael. In providing a space for Andrew to show his talent, the circle also resembles a *hui* in which student interests are intentionally incorporated in the circle setting. For example, in one *hui* a young rugby player had crashed his mother's car into a neighbor's garden (p. 198). The circle conveners organized the circle at a local rugby club and invited the boy's close friends and family members to keep the student accountable and still honor his talent.

As the facilitator and someone familiar with Andrew, Tania is able to suggest a remedy that correlates to his particular interest in crumping. Tania takes responsibility for ensuring that the agreement will be met. While Mark and I, the adults in the room, have offered her insights, we did not craft the circle questions or put forth the remedies. In fact students could choose a remedy that adults did not agree with; Maria Longfellow, one of two administrators responsible for discipline in the school, disagrees with the outcome of the circle with Andrew. "If it were up to me, he would be responsible for paying the $400," she says. "His parents say that they don't have the

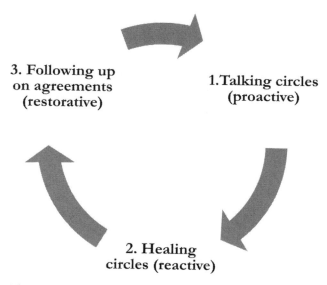

Figure 8.1 The Restorative Discipline Feedback Loop

money; that's fine. Then he should have to work at the school to make up for the repair." But he did not have to, and students remained autonomous in that decision. Because students drafted and planned the circle and were responsible for ensuring that agreements were met, the student–teacher paradigm began to be turned on its side.

Despite this autonomy, adults remained decisive arbiters in the process, and so the turning of the paradigm was only partial. Initially administrators and students decided that students faced with suspension have the option to participate in a circle instead. But Samuel Amos, the other administrator in charge of discipline in the school, acted as a gatekeeper in the restorative process: he often suspended students without giving them another option because he was not convinced that restorative justice works, though he has said he is "open to it":

> The only issue that I have with the circles is that I am not impressed with how the loops get closed, so students can use it to avoid being accountable 'cause they can go to circle, say anything, then it's gone. And I don't get a report back saying here's what was agreed, so because I don't get that accountability piece, I have no idea if the student's actually going to do their part. For example, a student who's coming to class with suspension will do a circle to avoid being suspended by me. They'll do a circle and say, "OK, I'm going to do A, B, C, D" and never does it.

Samuel rightly points out that there is a lack of accountability in the circle process—the third step in the restorative discipline feedback loop (see Figure 8.1). For example, Tania never followed through with Andrew; he never fixed the hole in the wall or started a krumping club. Though the reflective nature of circle may have prevented him from damaging property again, Samuel has no evidence of what took place. "Right now we don't know what happens when it [circle] happens. And even for me who buys into the process, that's an important part for me. I can't tell anyone that it [restorative justice] works." And this only perpetuates fewer referrals to circles and fewer opportunities for such evidence, which creates a cycle of inertia: he does not always offer students the option to participate in circles, so he never has the opportunity to see the outcomes or even convince other teachers that the process "works."

According to the most vocal student proponents of circles—the co-teachers and members of the restorative justice club—the administrators at the school were not fully committed to healing circles:

TANIA: They're half doing it . . . it's like, "We don't want to put the time and effort in so we're just going to do it our way and then let them have it their way too to satisfy them."

ANITA: Who's the "them?"

TANIA: Us that do it. All the people that promote it . . . I think they're still suspending kids. They're suspending them, and then they tell them to come back and do healing circle, and I don't think they have yet grasped the fact of its circle OR suspension; it's not circle AND suspension. It's circle or suspension. And they haven't grasped that yet.

ANITA: Why do you think that it? And who is the "them"? Is it the principal? The administration?

TANIA: The disciplinary administration.

Tania suggests that the disciplinary administration in the school uses circles to appease or "satisfy" students who participate in or "promote" the process. The very people in charge of discipline, says Tania, have not "grasped" the use of healing circles to reduce suspensions—they do not offer students the opportunity to participate in the restorative process except as an add-on to punitive practices; they do not understand that students who commit harm should have the option to participate in a "circle or suspension," not a "circle and suspension." But both sides seem right; there was no mechanism for keeping students who came up with agreements to hold one another accountable, and administrators did not always lend their support and participation in the process. A former special education teacher who was thrust into his role, Samuel balanced a number of responsibilities and says he has been overwhelmed with "handling everything" related to suspensions. As a result, restorative justice took a backseat among his priorities. The tensions between student autonomy and adult support speak to a larger institutional issue of implementing circles school wide—an issue that will be discussed further in the next chapter.

COMING FULL CIRCLE: EMPOWERING YOUNG PEOPLE

John, who once felt chastised as a participant in a healing circle, is now one of the most active student advocates of the practice in the city. He recently joined Principal Stephen Dobbs to talk to legislators at the state house about their program. John's vision of restorative justice is that it should be popularized in schools across the country, which he shared with state lawmakers. But he also emphasizes that restorative justice should be measured in multiple ways:

Circle is not just . . . about getting students to stay in school so they don't get suspended. It's more about making peace in their community . . . Because in order to get an education, you have to have peace between you, the students and the teacher. If there's a problem between you and the student, then you gotta fix that. And just getting suspended doesn't really fix that, it just probably makes the problem even worse because now you just think about that person is all this and that, and you're not really focused on school. But if you go through the restorative justice system, then you and that person become either friends, or you can just fix that problem that you had.

In talking to John, it does seem that he has a higher standard for restorative justice than perhaps some teachers at Equity, who might gauge the success of restorative justice solely on whether students recommit infractions that bring them to circle in the first place. It is not enough for John to go to a school where there are no disruptions, particularly if such peace comes at a price of students being together in community. To him, circles are not *just* about reducing suspensions. They are not just about reducing the number of fights in the building. This is deficit framing. John has an asset-based framing of circles. They build community. They build understanding. They teach communication skills. Some students are interested in football or poetry or math. John's interested in peace. Circles may be an asset for the community, but they also have provided a mechanism for John's personal growth and practice of peace building.

Student empowerment and input into the process provide an abundant source of confirming evidence about the power of restorative practices—as well as its limitations when things don't work. As Tania pointed out, if teachers are not on board, it can't work. Listening to student voices is not always comfortable, but it is almost always illuminating. As teachers see their students opening up in new ways in both talking and healing circles, they may be more open to the power of the circle process as the new disciplinary paradigm.

The opportunity to engage in a new way of doing discipline—in which students get to work with other students to come up with solutions to problems—seems to epitomize the quest, perhaps still hazy, for social justice at the school. And even if the paradigm of power between youth and adults has not turned completely on its side, in both process and outcomes restorative justice offered many other students practical life skills and leadership opportunities. The apprenticeship model provided Tania, Shannon, Patricia, Roland, Josephine, Melanie, Jared and others the power to question and shape the process. And the confidence with which students assert themselves and speak about restorative justice at community forums around Boston suggests that the practice is not an exaggerated panacea that will fade out of existence as quickly as it has come onto the national landscape.

NOTE

1. This is a type of street dance.

9 The Bridge to Equity
Lessons for Implementing Critical Restorative Justice in Urban Schools

When a fellow researcher heard about my research, she scrunched her face up in hesitation. "One criticism I've heard about restorative justice is that it puts the onus of responsibility for actions completely on individuals," she said, "without acknowledging the structures that impact those behaviors." I thought about her comment and why I dismissed it. As practiced at Equity and BHS, restorative justice was employed to keep both individuals *and* institutions accountable; teachers were very explicit in teaching their students about the school-to-prison pipeline and how alternative forms of punishment could disrupt the phenomenon. Restorative practitioners aiming to reduce racial disparities in school discipline must be familiar with the institutions in which they are operating to create lasting, system-wide change. After all, as Hereth, Kaba, Meiners, and Wallace (2012) state, skeptics often wonder "whether harm can ever truly be healed or restored in a context where structural inequality is the pervasive norm" (p. 257). At BHS and Equity, practitioners were motivated to reduce this inequality by educating and inspiring students to act against phenomena such as the school-to-prison pipeline.

And while it may be obvious that students should learn about their own agency in tandem with how larger forces shape their environment, I realized that much of what I have read about restorative justice left off this key component: the *critical* aspect of restorative justice. That is, the most crucial similarity between Equity and BHS speaks to my theoretical framing of these schools as progressive sites: adults at both places self-consciously attempted to disrupt the school-to-prison pipeline by teaching students to critique the larger structures and institutions that shape behaviors.

So in comparing and contrasting the lessons learned at both BHS and Equity, I revisited my four original research questions: *What roles did students, educators and community members play in the implementation and practice of restorative justice? How did participants make meaning of the purpose and outcome of circles? What strides were made in replacing punitive disciplinary practices with restorative ones?* Finally, *How was*

race explicitly addressed or not addressed during the implementation of
restorative justice in an education system where students of color are dis-
proportionately punished?

The two years I spent at BHS and the one year I spent at Equity answering these questions revealed more commonalities between the schools than
dissimilarities. The notable differences manifested themselves in the form,
rather than substance, of restorative justice at both schools. As the portraits reveal, there was a special emphasis on youth-led circles at Equity
versus teacher-led circles at BHS. Students, teachers and administrators at
Equity understood circles within the framework of restorative justice, while
at BHS many actors—excluding Angela, Lucy, Rebecca and Patricia—were
unfamiliar with the definition or philosophical basis of restorative justice.
Finally, there was a more formalized mechanism to implement restorative
justice at Equity through the law and justice course, whereas teachers and
administrators at BHS engaged in more impromptu circles with individual
students in addition to planned talking circles.

Overall, however, the lessons at these schools paint a larger picture of the
challenges and potential inherent in practicing restorative justice at urban
schools. As teachers and community members worked to create more equitable structures for dealing with discipline, they faced common constraints
on implementing and sustaining the practice while still employing a transformative approach that sought to fight inequity writ large, not only in their
classrooms.

COMMON CONSTRAINTS: RESOURCES
AND FLUX IN URBAN SCHOOLS

In both schools restorative justice was initially piloted in one part of the campus rather than school wide: in an SLC (Unit A and Project Graduation) and
the law and justice course at BHS and Equity, respectively. The implication
of this choice was that the practice was essentially sequestered and created
some misunderstanding for those not intimately connected with the practice
and philosophy. According to adults in Project Graduation, teachers outside of the program often viewed their students as troublemakers who were
not punished enough for behaviors such as arguing, swearing or tardiness.
Because the restorative philosophy did not permeate the entire building,
there was friction between program efforts to handle matters restoratively
and the school-wide reliance on more punitive tactics. As BHS Teacher Lucy
Reed points out, "The discipline stuff that we're having is stuff that we can
control [and] we're going to try to use circle for. There's a big clash with the
rest of the building that's very frustrating." This friction ultimately made
sustaining and practicing the philosophy—in its most authentic form, not
"halfway" as Equity student Tania puts it—extremely difficult.

Administrators and teachers at both schools reverted to suspensions to abide by school-wide rules that were not consistent with the restorative justice program. At Equity there was a flowchart to handle tardies—students who failed to show up to weekly detentions or Saturday school ultimately could be suspended for going to class late, an ironic punishment for students already missing instructional time and one that many students in the law and justice class found contradictory to the mission of the school. When I asked Maria Longfellow, an administrator who handles disciplinary matters at Equity, what the goal of suspension was, she said, "The goal of suspension is to keep the kids in school and keep the suspension rate down." The idea behind this statement is that suspension deters students from getting suspended, a notion that was inconsistent with the restorative philosophy of keeping students accountable and *in school* for their actions.

The schools shared other limitations, including the inability of teachers and administrators always to keep students accountable for agreements that were made in circle. This constraint was related to a scarcity of time or lack of staff members who could follow through with individual disciplinary incidents, a challenge that calls into question the sustainability and effectiveness of restorative justice in urban schools strapped for financial and human resources. But the more overarching constraint was the instability at both schools. The urban education context—so often marked by high administrator and teacher turnover, cyclical reform efforts aimed at improving achievement and a general state of flux as schools that underperform close or are reconstituted—significantly impacts the longevity of any initiative, including the move away from punitive to restorative discipline. As the editors at *Rethinking Schools* (Christensen, 2011) note, "At far too many schools, commitments to implement restorative justice occur amid relentless high-stakes 'test and punish' regimens—amid scripted curriculum, numbing test-prep drills, budget cutbacks, school closures, the constant shuffling from school to school of students, teachers, and principals."[1]

The schools in this study were no different. As discussed, the administration at BHS implemented a number of structural changes each of the three years I was present. This resulted in students and teachers sometimes shuffling to different parts of the building or taking on new positions. In the span of five years, the administration split the school into SLCs; the SLC I originally observed was dissolved, and its students were reabsorbed into other SLCs; and Project Graduation was formed to accommodate students on the verge of dropping out. In 2011, Patricia Beatty left BHS after having been a principal for seven years. This is longer than the current estimated average tenure of principals in urban schools—five years (Hull, 2012)—but her absence, like the absence of any leader, may have impacted the momentum of the restorative movement, although in what way remains to be seen. Principal Dobbs also left his position at Equity abruptly in 2010, taking a job in DC, where his wife had found employment. Though I did not conduct interviews once I left both sites, Janet and the teachers in this study with whom I remained in contact told me that despite these changes, circles continued to take place at both schools.

The most dramatic change in school environment was the ultimate closing of Equity the year after I observed there, in 2011. The closure was part of a district-wide move to restructure underperforming schools. Equity students rallied to keep the school open, attending public forums with signs and prepared speeches but to no avail. With the school closure came the diffusion of years of energy and momentum behind the restorative initiative. Roger Francoise says he only hopes that the energy behind the movement filters out to wherever students and faculty end up. Thus district policies that abolish underperforming schools like Equity hinder the ability for restorative justice programs to hold real traction at any one place.

THE POTENTIAL OF A *CRITICAL* RESTORATIVE JUSTICE

Despite these limitations, restorative justice served a similar and crucial purpose at both sites. Practitioners at BHS and Equity used restorative practices not only to try to keep students accountable for their behaviors but also to create space for young people to analyze critically the political and economic structures that contribute to these behaviors as well as the very phenomenon the practice is being used to counter—the school-to-prison pipeline. Some theorists refer to this as *transformative* restorative justice, a justice that "creates conditions for pursuing forms of personal and, perhaps more importantly, social change" (Woolford, 2009, p. 17). Open to reflecting on race relations among one another, with students and in interviews, these teachers exemplify how restorative justice can complement a much broader teaching philosophy—one that values and emphasizes the need to understand how power is divided in this country.

This study was shaped by my preoccupation with race, which no doubt influenced the responses of my participants. Nonetheless, every proponent of restorative justice in this study discussed his or her own racial identity in interviews without my prompting them, unusual given the well-documented challenges of getting teachers in training—the majority of whom are White and female—to engage in thoughtful, vulnerable discussions about race (Ladson-Billings, 1996). New teachers often state that they are colorblind when it comes to teaching students of color in particular; Pollock (2004) explores at length how educators are in fact "colormute"—silent on any discussion of racial differences. She suggests that this has potentially dangerous consequences in urban schools, where the racial divide is apparent in inequitable outcomes for students of color. In such a context teachers must at minimum be aware of their own social and racial locations and at best use their classrooms to help fight racial inequity. Restorative justice allowed Equity and BHS teachers to do both.

As Angela shows, she and William were able to discuss their own social and racial identities—particularly how each is perceived when and if using profanity—during a staff circle. Circle was a forum for her to connect English content to critical and current social issues. Likewise at Equity, nearly all White teachers who practiced circles reflected on how they were perceived because of their race and on how their classrooms reflected larger issues of social issues. Janet says, "I know, when I walk in, they might say, 'Oh who is this old, White lady anyway?' But I'm not like afraid or intimidated by that, and I know that if I'm just myself, I'm going to be able to build a relationship with them." Although confident she could connect to students, she was still aware of her own privilege as a White person. "I have always lived and worked in this community, so I've always been able to build connections and relationships across racial lines and ethnic lines, and I think a lot of it is in acknowledging that I do have privilege and that there are some experiences I can't understand, but in sharing that there are some, I can." The White teachers I interviewed grappled with issues of race but were not intimidated to address them—all emphasized the necessity of relationships in working across racial lines. Equity teacher Chris Morgan says,

> Early in the school year I didn't have the relationships. It was interesting, I think, gender and racial issues with me being a White man working in this population . . . You can be the White male teacher who just busts heads, who basically plays out power structures in the classroom, who says, "I'm in charge, and if you blink wrong, you're screwed." That's a typical way that not just White males but many teachers take with this population. "I'm in charge. I've got the power, and screw you." They're trying to dominate, and that doesn't work either because you don't build any respect, and the kids' behaviors only get driven underneath.

Chris ultimately went to Janet to help him use circles in his classroom—to participate in a transformative approach to discipline so that he would not "play out power structures"—another example of how adults at Equity tried to turn the paradigm on its side. The willingness of these teachers to engage in such discussions paved the way for a critical restorative justice, eliciting conversations where young people questioned the distribution of power along racial and gender lines; at Equity students devoted more than half of their talking circles to racism, sexism, or homophobia.

This race consciousness also manifested itself in the content of teachers' courses. Educators at both schools forged connections with community organizations, inviting them into their classrooms for trainings and lesson plans on the impact of racism in our daily lives. At BHS both Angela and Lucy taught students about the school-to-prison pipeline, even inviting me to do a circle on the topic. They also invited the group Reflect and Strengthen[2] (R & S) to come into her classroom once a week to facilitate circles; the members of this all-female organization use their time to teach students about institutionalized, internalized, ideological and interpersonal oppression, or the "4 Is of Oppression." After they reviewed the meaning of internalized oppression, Angela used the time to connect classroom literature to themes about power and oppression, discussing how in Orwell's *Animal Farm* the pig leaders did not have the best interest of all the animals in mind. Mindy, an R & S member, talked about how crack and cocaine are criminalized differently, noting that you can have a much smaller amount of crack rather than cocaine but be penalized with much longer sentences:

> Mindy asks, "What do you notice is the difference between who uses crack and who uses cocaine?" A conversation ensues about how cocaine is normally used in richer neighborhoods by predominately White people. "Who do you normally think is perceived as using drugs?" she asks.
> "White people," says Laura.
> "You think White people are seen as doing more drugs?" asks Mindy.
> "Yeah, because the crackheads you see are White, and I see White people using drugs in my neighborhood," she says.
> "So what you see depends on what neighborhood you live in," says Mindy.
> "That's true 'cause around my way, it's Black people I see," says Genovive.
> Georgia starts talking about the prison industrial complex and what that term means. After explaining it, she says, "Do you get it?"
> "Yeah we get it," says Paul.
> Mindy laughs and says, "Yeah you're just saying that, so I'll move on."
> "Nah, nah, we get it," he says.

Though all students did not necessarily always "get it"—the "it" being theoretical concepts about power, inequity and the "prison industrial complex"—Angela invited guest speakers to touch on these concepts throughout the year to reinforce them, always connecting them to English content. Mindy engaged students in a discussion where they reflected upon the area "around their way" and how racist messages are subconsciously transmitted. By discussing the differences between crack and cocaine sentencing, she touches upon how minorities are criminalized more often and more severely for similar offenses committed by Whites, connecting individual student acts to larger institutions such as the criminal justice system.

On another occasion, Angela invited an educational consultant from Amherst to facilitate workshops about race to prepare students for a public discussion on *Native Son*. A short, Black woman with eyes set close together, Angelika Hamilton stood in front of a class of 20 students—all students of color save one—explaining that she worked in a housing project to help young authors publish their books. Now she wanted to talk about the history of racism to help students understand the novel. "I'm going to talk about internalized oppression," she said. "How we get certain messages as people of color." She began the lesson by explaining that there is a dominant group and a target group in every society; the dominant group (i.e., Whites, heterosexuals, and men) find ways to demean and ostracize the target group (i.e., people of color, homosexuals, and women):

> Students split into groups and write down stereotypes of people of color: "We are one race, ghetto, not hard workers, non-educated, and useless; people of color are always up to be in sports or the entertainment business."
>
> Angelika asks if someone can come up with one word to "sum up the flavor of the descriptions" of people of color. Alex says that the message is that White people are superior. "So what word would describe people of color?" asks Angelika.
>
> "Inferior," he says.

Similar to R & S, Angelika asks students to connect their personal experiences with racism—in their schooling and personal lives—to the racism they see in society. Ultimately students led conversations about racism in circles, inviting community members to participate and discuss racism in *Native Son*. Such conversations spurred students to reflect on how they could change structural conditions once they left school—several students at both schools, for example, told me they wanted to become lawyers to change the criminal justice system.

Leadership was also crucial in supporting such conversations. BHS Principal Patricia Beatty sponsored a series of open-ended workshops after school, in which teachers could propose sessions and lead discussions on a topic of their choice. One teacher led a workshop on the challenges of working with youth who are coming out of the criminal justice system, focusing on their recidivism rates. The speaker was a young White female teacher with long hair, thin, wiry glasses and a soft-spoken demeanor. She wore a blazer and used a PowerPoint to talk about her research on the criminal justice system and interviews she had with incarcerated youth and their mentors. She stressed that she had more of a theoretical background on the topic as she had studied this while a student at the Kennedy School of Government at Harvard. Rebecca Stern, along with five teachers and one administrator, attended. Participants then began sharing stories of individual students, exchanging ideas about how to intervene in their lives. One teacher said, "We're missing an important race and class analysis here," raising the issue of how race intersected with the punishment of working-class students of color.

The whole time I was there I marveled at how astute the observations were and how freely teachers exchanged ideas about touchy topics—race and class—that otherwise go undiscussed in many schools. In this context circles provided one more place for critical thinking. As Janet states in her portrait, students "feel like they're thrown into the set of circumstances because of the race and class that they are, because of the neighborhoods they live in, because of the way it is as opposed to trying to understand why it is the way it is and being an agent, being able to talk about it and be an agent for change." Being made aware of the "circumstances" that can oppress people, suggests Janet, can hopefully lead a student to do more than get angry or frustrated—to act, to become "an agent for change."

This critical restorative justice is necessary not only to create agents of change but for the survival of restorative justice as a truly effective means of addressing injustice. Breton (2012) cautions proponents of restorative justice against zooming so narrowly on person-to-person harms at the expensive of truly addressing, and rectifying, historical and structural harms, such as the colonization and genocide of indigenous peoples:

> If the restorative justice movement fails to address the People-to-People issues and the crimes embedded in our history, it will risk losing credibility in this country, as it seems to have already done in Canada. Many First Nations now reject restorative justice, and precisely on these grounds. The core vision of going to the roots of harm and doing what it takes to make things right is experienced as empty rhetoric, invoked only when colonial power structures deem it advantageous to do so. Instead of working toward wholeness for Peoples, restorative justice functions as another tool of colonizer institutions, whose goal is not healing but for one People to conquer and dominate another. Restorative justice is simply used to make the violence of the criminal justice system—the colonizers' control-by-fear device—seem more humane. (p. 45)

Breton notes that restorative justice can be a way to make the current "colonizer institution" of prisons seem "more humane," which ultimately alienates people from the alternative paradigm altogether. Similarly, practitioners in schools may be at risk of alienating others from employing restorative justice if they use it as a "more humane" way of addressing person-to-person harms but fail to address institutional norms and practices that perpetuate inequity in schools—including high-stakes testing, scripted curricula, and cyclical school reform efforts fueled by corporate entities and curriculum companies.

Whether or not restorative justice practitioners in schools disrupt the pipeline for individual students remains to be seen; the stories in these pages suggest that restorative justice increases opportunities to intervene in student academic trajectories but does not always improve student behaviors. While it is laudable to keep our young people in schools rather than on the streets when they make mistakes, the buy-in of skeptical teachers—and there are a lot of them—is difficult to achieve if students continue to remain in conflict with peers and adults around them—especially if no reparations are made for past offenses and the larger issues of injustice in the education system go unaddressed.

In short, restorative practitioners at these schools were not *just* interested in reforming individual student behaviors. They saw restorative justice as part of a larger social justice agenda and related the overrepresentation of minorities in school suspension to the disproportionate criminalization of people of color in prisons. To them restorative justice is not only a reactive response to harm; it is proactive, a means to chip away at institutional practices and norms that separate, ostracize and demean students—practices such as suspension and expulsion that are so ingrained in practitioners minds' that we fail to dream of a harder path, an admittedly more time-consuming way, to discipline our young people.

NOTES

1. See http://www.rethinkingschools.org/archive/29_01/edit1291.shtml.
2. This is an organization created by survivors of homicide victims. Janet's daughter Shana was one of the founding members.

Epilogue

In the fall of 2012, I began teaching middle school English in a disciplinary alternative school. The school serves students who have been suspended for primarily two reasons: behavioral problems or the sale or use of drugs, namely marijuana. I took the job with the hopes of envisioning how restorative justice could be applied in such an environment. I quickly realized that while the program was structured in restorative ways—equipped with high-quality teachers who had been teaching at the school for nearly a decade, educators who were passionate about not only improving student behaviors but inspiring students to excel academically at their home campuses—it was not the place for the kind of restorative justice work that took place at BHS and Equity—or so I thought. The main difficulty was the short amount of time that students spend at the school; a student who earns daily points for staying in dress code and following instructions could be out in as soon as six weeks.

Yet, as discussed in this book, for restorative justice to work there has to be an existing community to be restored to. Because students from all schools in the district could join the school at any point in the year, classes were constantly in flux as old students left and new students arrived. It was difficult to sustain the long-term bonds necessary to build a restorative community. Therefore when harm took place at the school—when students fought one another, stole, hid my keys or called me a bitch—there was often not a sense of restoration. The philosophy was that students were still learning to make better choices and that tomorrow was a new day. The hope was that incrementally they would improve over time, and some did.

While intellectually I knew I should not take student misbehaviors in the classroom personally, the environment depleted me. It seemed counterintuitive to deal with student misbehaviors by putting all young people who had been kicked out of school in the same room. Day after day I heard many of them talk about who had robbed whom, who had threatened to fight someone on Facebook and what the best type of marijuana was. Students who had little experience with such issues would enter the classroom and began posturing, mimicking the most vocal students. I saw a young man who refused to follow a police officer's directive to leave the cafeteria get taken to the ground with a chokehold. I began to feel that my work as one teacher in one classroom was not enough, that all my years of research and observation around restorative justice needed to be applied in a way that could bring about more structural change to impact students from a much earlier age.

At that time I stood much in the same place I began as a first-year teacher—struggling with issues in the classroom, observing some students like Martin cycle in and out of school and feeling unequipped to intervene in their academic trajectories. Having studied the difficulties of shifting paradigms around discipline, I found myself viewing students at the discipline school negatively. Old resentments crept in; I dreaded working with some of them. When I felt disrespected I kicked them out of class. I felt like a failure. Was I someone who studied the theory of restorative justice and could not practice it with real, flawed, hurt and vocal young people? These are questions I continue to grapple with as I continue my journey. But the job also humbled me and connected me to the teachers in this study in a profound way. I understood much better the challenges of their work to empower young people, honor their voices, and handle the frustrations of a circle gone wrong, of agreements not being met.

Still I look to Martin and Janet for inspiration. Janet flew down for the Restorative Justice Collaborative of Houston's first conference and spoke as our keynote; when I visit Boston I drive to Dorchester, and we drink tea in her cozy kitchen. Martin is out and holds a job. I read his updates on Facebook. He came to my baby shower and calls me from time to time to check in. We have dreams to talk to other people about our experiences as teacher and student, to work alongside like-minded educators to innovate disciplinary practices at local schools. And indeed those dreams are coming true; in the spring of 2015, the Restorative Justice Collaborative of Houston held our second annual conference, "Young People in the Shadows." The opening panel of the day featured the voices of young people from the last 15 years of my career, including Martin, Luis Rodriguez—one of the young men featured in the Equity portrait, who flew down from Boston to speak— and two of my current students in the restorative justice program. It was both surreal and beautiful to see students from my past and present come together to inform the community about their experiences in the school-to-prison pipeline.

Martin talked about having warrants out for his arrest even after he was released from jail, all because of truancy tickets from his days in high school. Luis talked about how having a son turned his life around and how he probably makes more money now as a truck driver than many of the teachers who told him he would end up doing nothing with his life. Finally, one of my students talked about the multiple warrants out for her arrest due to truancy and the hundreds of dollars in tickets she is attempting to pay off as she raises her young daughter and tries to graduate. While they painted a dismal portrait of an education system that failed them, these young people also offered solutions and inspired participants to do one simple thing when dealing with "students like them": listen.

The restorative justice student leaders at my school are now training probation officers, counselors and assistant principals all over the city. They even lead talking circles at the discipline school where I used to teach, both to support the students and keep them accountable when harms occur. They have taken on the charge of Miguel and Jose: they are indeed "starting a movement." Janet continues to keep me updated about the challenges of doing restorative justice at BHS, other schools and in prisons. "This is my passion," she tells me. "I can't imagine not doing restorative justice." Despite my frustrations with a system failing so many of our babies, I recollect the lessons from Janet, Equity and BHS and shore up my granules of faith—in the possibility of overhauling schools and prisons, repairing harm, restoring relationships and, finally, in the goodness of most people.

References

Adams, C. (2008). Safer saner urban schools: The story of West Philadelphia high. *Scholastic Administrator*, 36, 6–8.

Advancement Project. (2009). *Key components of a model discipline policy*. Retrieved October 4, 2009, from http://www.stopschoolstojails.org/content/model-discipline-policies

Advancement Project & Civil Rights Project. (2000). *Opportunities suspended: The devastating consequences of zero tolerance and school discipline*. Report from a National Summit on Zero Tolerance, Washington, DC.

Alexander, M. (2010). *The new Jim Crow: Mass incarceration in the age of colorblindness* (Rev ed.). New York: New Press.

Allard, P. (2002). *Life sentences: Denying welfare benefits to women convicted of drug offenses*. Washington, DC: The Sentencing Project.

Amstutz, L., & Mullet, J. (2005). *The little book of restorative discipline for schools: Teaching responsibility, creating caring climates*. Intercourse, PA: Good Books.

APA Zero Tolerance Task Force. (2006). *Are zero tolerance policies effective in the schools? An evidentiary review and recommendations*. Washington, DC: Author.

Aronowitz, N. (2014, March 9). School spirit or gang signs? 'Zero tolerance' comes under fire *NBCNews.com*. Retrieved February 3, 2015, from http://www.nbcnews.com/news/education/school-spirit-or-gang-signs-zero-tolerance-comes-under-fire-n41431

Bazemore, G., & Umbreit, M. (1998). *Conferences, circles, boards, and mediations: Restorative justice and citizen involvement in the response to youth crime*. Washington, DC: Office of Juvenile Justice and Delinquency Prevention.

Berg, S. (2008). *The Illinois Negro code*. Retrieved from http://www.chroniclesmagazine.org/2008/01/18/the-illinois-negro-code/

Biesta, G. (2007). Why "what works" won't work: Evidence-based practice and the democratic deficit in educational research. *Educational Theory*, 57(1), 1–22.

Blackmon, D.A. (2008). *Slavery by another name: The re-enslavement of black people in America from the civil war to World War II* (1st ed.). New York: Doubleday.

Blumenson, E., & Nilsen, L. (2002). How to construct an underclass, or how the war on drugs became the war on education. *The Journal of Gender, Race, and Justice*, 6, 61–109.

Boyd, T. (2009). Confronting racial disparity: Legislative responses to the school-to-prison pipeline. *Harvard Civil Rights-Civil Liberties Law Review*, 44(2), 571–580.

Boyes-Watson, C. (2005). Community is not a place but a relationship: Lessons for organizational development. *Public Organization Review: A Global Journal*, 5, 359–374.

Boyes-Watson, C. (2008). *Peacemaking circles and urban youth: Bringing justice home.* St. Paul: Living Justice Press.

Braithwaite, J. (2001). Youth development circles. *Oxford Review of Education, 27*(2), 239–252.

Braithwaite, J. (2002). *Restorative justice and responsive regulation.* New York: Oxford University Press.

Breton, D. (2012). Decolonizing restorative justice. *Tikkun, 27*(1), 45.

Brown, R., & Severson, K. (2011). Enlisting prison labor to close budget gaps. *The New York Times.*

Cameron, L., & Thorsborne, M. (2000). Restorative justice and school discipline: Mutually exclusive? In H. Strang & J. Braithwaite (Eds.), *Restorative justice and civil society* (pp. 180–194). Cambridge, UK: Cambridge University Press.

Casella, R. (2003). Zero tolerance policy in schools: Rationale, consequences, and alternatives. *The Teachers College Record, 105*(5), 872–892.

Cavanagh, T. (2009). *Book review: Working restoratively in schools.* Retrieved from http://www.restorativejustice.com/Book%20Reviews.html

Charmaz, K. (2005). *Constructing grounded theory.* Thousand Oaks, CA: Sage.

Christensen, L. (2011). The classroom to prison pipeline. *Rethinking Schools, 26*(2). Retrieved on January 1, 2014 from http://www.rethinkingschools.org/archive/26_02/26_02_christensen.shtml

Cook, K. (2006). Doing difference and accountability in restorative justice conferences. *Theoretical Criminology, 10*(1), 107–124.

Costello, B., Wachtel, J., & Wachtel, T. (2010). *Restorative circles in schools: Building community and enhancing learning.* Bethlehem, PA: International Institute for Restorative Practices.

Cotton, K. (2001). *New small learning communities: Findings from recent literature.* Portland, OR: Northwest Regional Educational Laboratory.

Cregor, M. (2008). The building blocks of positive behavior. *Education Digest, 74*(4), 31–35.

Creswell, J. (1997). *Qualitative inquiry & research design: Choosing among five approaches.* Thousand Oaks, CA: Sage.

Culos, C., Bohanon, H., Carney, K., Piggott, T., Hicks, K., Anderson-Harriss, S., et al. (2006). School-wide application of positive behavior support in an urban high school: A case study. *Journal of Positive Behavior Interventions, 8*(3), 131–145.

Daly, K. (2002). Restorative justice: The real story. *Punishment & Society, 4*(1), 55.

Denver Public Schools. (2008). *Policy JK—student discipline.* Retrieved from http://ed.dpsk12.org:8080/policy/FMPro?-db=policy.fp3&-format=detail.html&-lay=policyview&File=JK&-recid=32883&-find=

Dickson-Gilmore, J., & La Prairie, C. (2007). *Will the circle be unbroken? Aboriginal communities, restorative justice, and the challenges of conflict and change.* Toronto: University of Toronto Press.

Dignity in Schools. (2009). *Fact sheet: School discipline and the push out problem.* Retrieved from http://www.dignityinschools.org/files/DSC_Pushout_Fact_Sheet.pdf

Drewery, D. (2004). Conferencing in schools: Punishment, restorative justice, and the productive importance of the process of conversation. *Journal of Community and Applied Social Psychology, 14,* 332–344.

Edutopia. (2006). *90 percent: White teachers.* Retrieved from http://www.edutopia.org/90-percent

Edutopia. (2010). *Restorative justice in youth court: Alternatives to suspension.* Retrieved from http://www.edutopia.org/blog/youth-court-restorative-justice

Eaton, S., & DeLauri, L. (2010). *Building equalizing schools within inclusive communities: Strategies in the classroom and beyond that redirect the school to prison pipeline*. Cambridge, MA: Charles Hamilton Houston Institute for Race and Justice at Harvard Law School.

Eber, L., Lewis-Palmer, T., & Pacchiano, D. (2002). *School-wide positive behavior systems: Improving school environments for all students including those with EBD*. Tampa: Research and Training Center for Children's, Mental Health, University of South Florida.

Erbe, C. (2004). What is the role of professionals in restorative justice? In H. Zehr & B. Toews (Eds.), *Critical issues in restorative justice* (pp. 293). Monsey, NY: Criminal Justice Press.

Fasching-Varner, K., Martin, L., Mitchell, R., & Bennett-Haron, K. (2014). Guest Editors' Introduction. *Equity and Excellence in Education*. Retrieved from http://www.tandfonline.com.ezp-prod1.hul.harvard.edu/toc/ueee20/47/447(4).

Gavrielides, T. (2008). Restorative justice—the perplexing concept: Conceptual fault-lines and power battles within the restorative justice movement. *Criminology and Criminal Justice, 8*(2), 165–183.

Geertz, C. (1973). *The interpretation of cultures: Selected essays*. New York: Basic Books.

Gilliam, W. (2005). *Pre-kindergartners left behind: Expulsion rates in state prekindergarten programs* (FCD policy brief). Cambridge, MA: Schott Foundation.

Giroux, H. (2001). Mis/education and zero tolerance: Disposable youth and the politics of domestic militarization. *Boundary 2, 28*(3), 61–94.

Green, J.A. (2009). Changing past student discipline practices to create a district-wide discipline plan. *Education and Urban Society, 41*(4), 457–468.

Gregory, A., & Cornell, D. (2009). "Tolerating" adolescent needs: Moving beyond zero tolerance policies in high school. *Theory into Practice, 48*(2), 106–113.

Gregory, A., Skiba, R., & Noguera, P. (2010). The achievement gap and the discipline gap: Two sides of the same coin? *Educational Researcher, 39*(1), 59.

Hansen, T. (2005, September). *Restorative justice practices and principles in schools*. Saint Paul, MN: University of Minnesota, School of Social Work: Center for Restorative Justice and Peacemaking.

Heaviside, S., Rowand, C., Williams, C., & Farris, E. (1996–97). *Violence and discipline problems in U.S. schools* (No. NCES 98–030). Washington, DC: U.S. Department of Education, National Center of Education Statistics.

Hereth, J., Kaba, M., Meiners, E., & Wallace, L. (2012). Restorative justice is not enough: School-based interventions in the carceral state. In S. Bahena, N. Cooc, R. Currie-Rubin, P. Kuttner & M. Ng (Eds.), *Disrupting the School to Prison Pipeline* (pp. 240–264). Cambridge: Harvard Educational Review.

Hibbard, L. (2011). Michael Davis, 5-year-old student, forcibly had legs and feet bound, arrested at school (VIDEO). *Huffington Post*. Retrieved from http://www.huffingtonpost.com/2011/11/29/michael-davis-5-year-old-_n_1118963.html

Holding, R. (2006, November 1). Why can't felons vote? *Time*. Retrieved on February 1, 2015 from http://content.time.com/time/nation/article/0,8599,1553510,00.html

Hull, J. (2012). *The principal perspective: Full report*. Alexandria, VA: Center for Public Education.

Human Rights Watch. (2009, April). *US: Prison numbers hit new high*. Retrieved from http://www.hrw.org/en/reports/2008/05/04/targeting-blacks

Jordan, J., & Bulent, A. (2009). Race, gender, school discipline, and human capital effects. *Journal of Agricultural and Applied Economics, 41*(2), 419–429.

Karp, D., & Breslin, B. (2001). Restorative justice in school communities. *Youth and Society, 33*(2), 249–272.

Kass, J. (2009). *Columbine: A True Crime Story*. Denver, CO: Ghost Road.

Keen, C. (2006). *Schools suspend poor students to raise test scores, study shows*. University of Florida News.

Knoff, H. (2005). *The stop and think social skills program: Exploring its research base and rationale.* Project ACHIEVE Press.

Ladson-Billings, G. (1996). Silences as weapons: Challenges of a black professor teaching white students. *Theory into Practice, 35*(2), 79–85.

Ladson-Billings, G. (2001). America still eats her young. In W. Ayers, B. Dohrn & R. Ayers (Eds.), *Zero tolerance: Resisting the drive for punishment in our schools* (pp. 77–88). New York: The New Press.

Laskshmi, A. (2011). The classroom to prison pipeline. *Rethinking Schools, 26*(2). Retrieved on January 1, 2014 from http://www.rethinkingschools.org/cmshandler.asp?archive/26_02/26_02_lakshmi2.shtml

Lawrence-Lightfoot, S. (1983). *The good high school: Portraits of character and culture.* New York: Basic Books.

Lawrence-Lightfoot, S., & Davis, J.H. (1997). *The art and science of portraiture* (1st ed.). San Francisco: Jossey-Bass.

Lewis, S. (2009). *Improving school climate: Findings from schools implementing restorative practices.* Bethlehem, PA: IIRP Graduate School: International Institute for Restorative Practices.

Loury, G.C. (2008). *Race, incarceration, and American values.* Cambridge, MA: MIT Press.

Lukas, J.A. (1986). *Common ground: A turbulent decade in the lives of three American families.* New York: Vintage Books.

Macready, T. (2009). Learning social responsibility in schools: A restorative practice. *Educational Psychology in Practice, 25*(3), 211–220.

Martinez, S. (2009). A system gone berserk: How are zero tolerance policies really affecting schools? *Preventing School Failure, 53*(3), 153–156.

Marxsen, P. (2003). *Exploring the healing paradigm: A conversation with Robin Casarjian and Judith Thompson.* Message posted to http://www.ikedacenter.org/thinkers-themes/thinkers/interviews/casarjian-thompson

Massachusetts Appleseed Center for Law and Justice. (2012). *Keep kids in class: New approaches to school discipline.* http://www.massappleseed.org/pdfs/kkic_newapproaches.pdf

Massachusetts Department of Elementary and Secondary Education. (2008). School district profiles. Retrieved January 1, 2010 from http://profiles.doe.mass.edu/

Massey, D.S., & Denton, N.A. (1993). *American apartheid: Segregation and the making of the underclass.* Cambridge, MA: Harvard University Press.

Maxwell, J.A. (2005). *Qualitative research design: An interactive approach* (2nd ed.). Thousand Oaks, CA: Sage.

Maykut, P., & Morehouse, R. (1994). *Beginning qualitative research.* London: Routledge.

McCluskey, G., Lloyd, G., Kane, J., Riddell, S., Stead, J., & Weedon, E. (2008). Can restorative practices in schools make a difference? *Educational Review, 60*(4), 405–417.

McCold, P. (2004). What is the role of community in restorative justice and practice? In H. Zehr and B. Toews (Eds.), *Critical issues in restorative justice* (pp. 155–172). Monsey, NY: Criminal Justice Press.

Meiners, E.R. (2007). *Right to be hostile: Schools, prisons, and the making of public enemies.* New York: Routledge.

Morrison, B. (2005). Restorative justice in schools. In E. Elliott and R. M. Gordon (Eds.), *New directions in restorative justice: Issues, practice, evaluation* (pp. 26–52). Cullompton, UK: Willan Publishing.

Morrison, B., Blood, P., & Thorsborne, M. (2006). Practicing restorative justice in school communities: The challenge of culture change. *Public Organization Review: A Global Journal, 5*(4), 335.

National Association of School Psychologists. (2010). *Zero tolerance alternative strategies: A fact sheet for educators and policymakers.* Retrieved from http://www.nasponline.org/resources/factsheets/zt_fs.aspx

National Center for Education Statistics. (2008). *Status and trends in the education of racial and ethnic groups.* Washington, DC: U.S. Department of Education.

National Economic & Social Rights Initiative. (2012). *Students, parents & teachers say changes in NYC's draft school discipline code don't go far enough to fix broken system.* Retrieved from http://www.nesri.org/news/2012/05/doe-releases-new-draft-discipline-code-students-parents-teachers-say-changes-dont-go-far-enough-to-fix-broken-syste

National Institute of Justice. (2012). *Victim—offender mediation.* Retrieved from http://www.nij.gov/topics/courts/restorative-justice/promising-practices/victim-offender-mediation.htm

Netzel, D. M., & Eber, L. (2003). Shifting from reactive to proactive discipline in an urban school district: A change of focus through PBIS implementation. *Journal of Positive Behavior Interventions, 5*(2), 71.

Northeastern University School of Law. (2012). *Legal skills in social context.* Retrieved from http://www.northeastern.edu/law/academics/curriculum/lssc/index.html

O'Brien, S., & Bazemore, G. (2006). Introduction to the symposium: Communities, organizations, and restorative justice reform. *Public Organization Review, 5,* 279–285.

OCR. U.S. Department of Education Office for Civil Rights 23. Civil Rights Data Collection: Data Snapshot (School Discipline). March 21, 2014.

Ogden, S. (2005). The prison industrial complex in indigenous California. In J. Sudbury (Ed.), *Global lockdown: Gender, race, and the rise of the prison industrial complex* (pp. 57). New York: Routledge.

Orfield, G., & Lee, C. (2007). *Historic reversals, accelerating resegregation, and the need for new intervention strategies.* UCLA: The Civil Rights Project.

Palazzo, D., & Hosea, B. (2004, Winter). *Restorative justice in schools: A review of history and current practices.* Columbus, GA: Association for Conflict Resolution.

Parnell, T. (2008). *An evaluation of the nine essential skills for love and logic.* PhD, Seattle Pacific University, Washington.

Payne, A., & Welch, K. (2013). Restorative justice in schools: The influence of race on restorative discipline. *Youth and Society, 20*(2), 1–26.

PBIS. (2015a). *Student training resources.* Retrieved from http://www.pbis.org/training/student.aspx

PBIS. (2015b). *Primary level.* Retrieved from https://www.pbis.org/school/primary-level

Perry, B., & Morris, E. (2014). Suspending progress: Collateral consequences of exclusionary punishment in public schools. *American Sociological Review, 79*(6), 1067–1087.

Peterson, R. (2005). *Alternatives to suspension and expulsion.* Midwest Symposium for Leadership in Behavior Disorders, Kansas City, MO.

Plocek, K. (2008). *Warehousing minority kids in Atlanta and Houston.* Houston Press. Retrieved from http://blogs.houstonpress.com/hairballs/2008/03/warehousing_minority_kids_in_a.php

Pollock, M. (2004). *Colormute: Race talk dilemmas in an American school.* Princeton, NJ: Princeton University press.

Pollock, M. (2008). *Everyday antiracism: Getting real about race in school.* New York: New Press.

Pranis, K. (2005). *The little book of circle processes: A new/old approach to peacemaking.* Intercourse, PA: Good Books.

Regoli, R., & Hewitt, J. (2007). *Exploring criminal justice* (2nd ed.). Boston: Jones and Bartlett.

Reyes, A. H. (2006). *Discipline, achievement, and race: Is zero tolerance the answer?* Lanham, MD: Rowman & Littlefield Education.

Roca, I. (2013). *Who we are.* Retrieved from http://rocainc.org/

Saltman, K. J., & Gabbard, D. (2003). *Education as enforcement: The militarization and corporatization of schools.* New York: Routledge Falmer.

Sandler, S., Wong, F., Morales, E., & Patel, V. (2000). *Turning "to" each other not "on" each other: How school communities prevent racial bias in school discipline. A preliminary report.* San Francisco: Justice Matters Institute.

Schenk, B. (2008). *Restoring community in a disconnected world.* Eleventh world conference of the international institute for restorative practices, Toronto, Ontario, Canada.

Schoonover, B. J. (2009). *Zero tolerance discipline policies: The history, implementation and controversy of zero tolerance policies in student codes of conduct.* Bloomington, IN: iUniverse.

Shaw, G. (2007, Fall). Restorative practices in Australian schools: Changing relationships, changing culture. *Conflict Resolution Quarterly, 25*(1), 127–135.

Skiba, R., & Peterson, R. (1999). The dark side of zero tolerance: Can punishment lead to safe schools? *Phi Delta Kappan, 80*(5), 372–382.

Skiba, R. (2000). *Zero tolerance, zero evidence: An analysis of school disciplinary practice* (No. SRS2). Bloomington: Indiana Education Policy Center.

Skiba, R. (2001). When is disproportionality discrimination? The overrepresentation of black students in school suspension. In W. Ayers, B. Dohrn, & R. Ayers (Eds.), *Zero tolerance: Resisting the drive for punishment in our schools* (pp. 165–175). New York: New Press.

Skiba, R. J., Horner, R. H., Chung, C. G., Karega Rausch, M., May, S. L., & Tobin, T. (2011). Race is not neutral: A national investigation of African American and Latino disproportionality in school discipline. *School Psychology Review, 40*(1), 85.

Smith, A. (2007). Soul wound: The legacy of Native American schools. *Amnesty International Magazine.* Retrieved on February 1, 2015 from http://www. amnestyusa.org/node/87342

Stampp, K. M. (1989). *The peculiar institution: Slavery in the ante-bellum south* (Vintage Books ed.). New York: Vintage Books.

Strauss, A., & Corbin, J. (1998). *Basics of qualitative research: Techniques and procedures for developing grounded theory* (2nd ed.). Thousand Oaks, CA: Sage.

Sugai, G., & Simonsen, B. (2012). *Positive behavioral interventions and supports: History, defining features, and misconceptions.* Storrs, CT: Center for PBIS & Center for Positive Behavioral Interventions and Supports, University of Connecticut.

Umbreit, S., Coates, R., & Vos, B. (2007). Restorative justice dialogue: A multidimensional, evidence-based practice. *Contemporary Justice Review, 10*(1), 23–41.

U.S. Constitution, XIII. (1865).

Vaandering, D. (2011). A faithful compass: Rethinking the term restorative justice to find clarity. *Contemporary Justice Review, 14*(3), 307.

Varnham, S. (2005). Seeing things differently: Restorative justice and school discipline. *Education and the Law, 17*(3), 87–104.

Vicini, J. (2006). US has the most prisoners in the world. *Common Dreams.* Retrieved from http://www.commondreams.org/headlines06/1209–01.htm

Wachtel, T. (1997). *Real justice: How we can revolutionize our response to wrongdoing.* Pipersville, PA: The Piper's Press.

Wacquant, L. (2000). The new 'peculiar' institution: On the prison as surrogate ghetto. *Theoretical Criminology, 4*(3), 377.

Wacquant, L. (2008). *Race, incarceration and American values* (pp. 57, Glenn Loury, ed.). Cambridge, MA: MIT Press.

Wald, J., & Losen, D. (2003, May 16–17). Defining and redirecting a school-to-prison pipeline. Framing paper for the *school-to-prison pipeline* Research conference, Northeastern University's Institute on Race and Justice, Boston, MA.

Warren, M. (2001). *Dry bones rattling: Community building to revitalize American democracy.* Princeton, NJ: Princeton University Press.

Wearmouth, J., Glynn, P., & Berryman, M. (2009). *Perspectives on student behaviours in schools: Exploring theory and developing practice.* New York: Routledge.

Wearmouth, J., McKinney, R., & Glynn, T. (2007). Restorative justice: Two examples from New Zealand schools. *British Journal of Special Education, 34*(4), 196–203.

Willis, C. (2012, March 26). *School officials 'reassess' students' punishment for nasal spray.* Retrieved February 3, 2015, from http://www.wsbtv.com/news/news/local-education/5th-grade-students-suspended-over-nasal-spray/nLckS/

Wilson, W. J. (1987). *The truly disadvantaged.* Chicago, IL: University of Chicago Press.

WOIW. (2014, October 31). *Local student suspended from school for what appears to be a harmless mistake.* Retrieved February 2, 2015, from http://www.19actionnews.com/story/27177026/local-student-suspended-from-school-for-was-appears-to-be-a-harmless-mistake

Woolford, A. (2009). *The politics of restorative justice: A critical introduction.* Halifax, N.S.: Fernwood.

Wu, S., Pink, W. T., Crain, R. L., & Moles, O. (1982). Student suspension: A critical reappraisal. *The Urban Review, 14*, 245–303.

Yin, R. K. (2009). *Case study research: Design and methods* (4th ed.). Los Angeles: Sage.

Zehr, H. (1990). *Changing lenses: A new focus for crime and justice.* Scottdale, PA: Herald Press.

Zehr, H. (2002). *The little book of restorative justice.* Intercourse, PA: Good Books.

Zellerer, E. (2011). *Security with care, in memory of Dr. Liz Elliott.* Retrieved December 28, 2011, from http://www.peaceofthecircle.com/security-with-care-in-memory-of-dr-liz-elliott/

Index